An Amateur Laborer

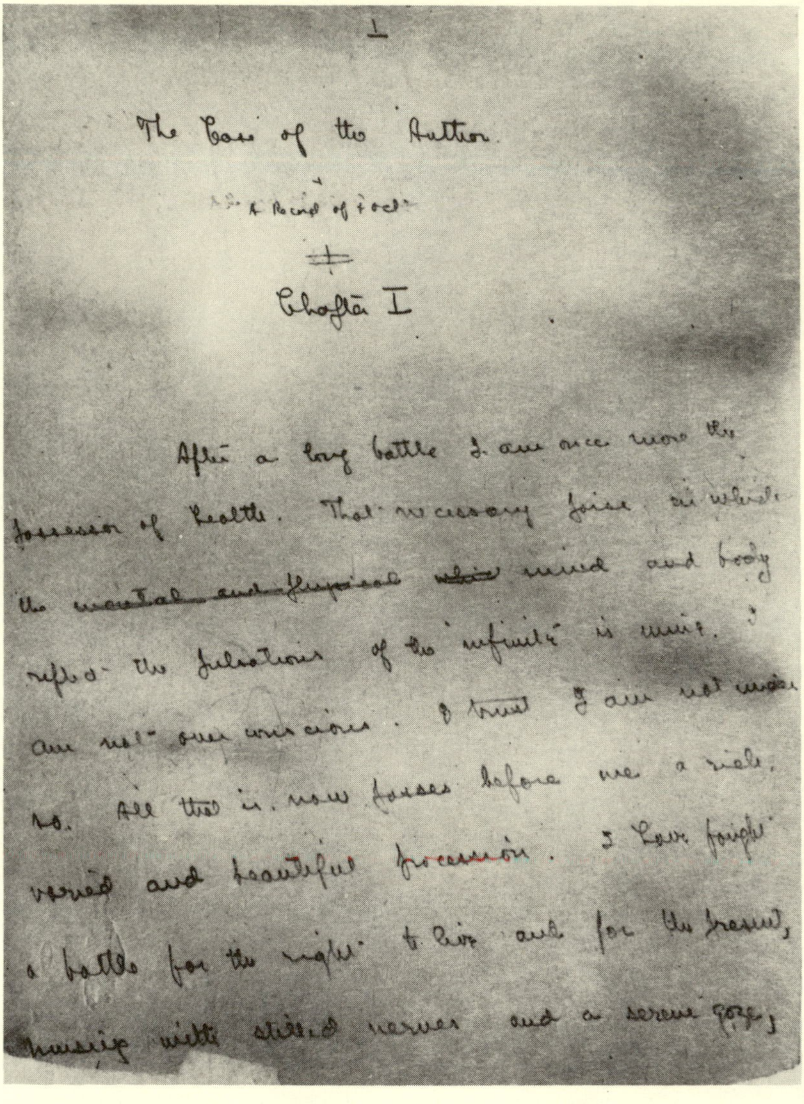
1

The Case of the Author

A Record of Fact

Chapter I

After a long battle I am once more the possession of health. That necessary poise in which the ~~mental and physical~~ ~~which~~ mind and body reflect the pulsations of the 'infinite' is mine. I am not over conscious. I trust I am not more so. All that is now passes before me a single, varied and beautiful procession. I have fought a battle for the right to live and for the present, musing with stilled nerves and a serene gaze,

First manuscript page from *An Amateur Laborer*

THEODORE DREISER

An Amateur Laborer

Edited, with an Introduction, by
Richard W. Dowell

James L. W. West III, Textual Editor

Neda M. Westlake, General Editor

University of Pennsylvania Press
PHILADELPHIA   1983

The preparation of this volume was made possible in part by a grant from the Program for Editions of the National Endowment for the Humanities, an independent federal agency.

Library of Congress Cataloging in Publication Data

Dreiser, Theodore, 1871-1945.
 An amateur laborer.

 1. Dreiser, Theodore, 1871-1945—Biography.
2. Novelists—American—20th century—Biography.
I. Dowell, Richard W. II. Title.
PS3507.R55A462   1984   813'. 52   83-3616
ISBN 0-8122-7890-9

Printed in the United States of America

Contents

Preface

Composed in 1904, *An Amateur Laborer* is the account of Dreiser's experience after he returned to New York from Philadelphia in February 1903—despondent, emotionally and physically exhausted, with only a few dollars between him and starvation. The dreary weeks in Brooklyn and his desperate and humiliating efforts to find any sort of job culminated in his rescue by his brother Paul and his stay in William Muldoon's sanitarium near Purchase, New York. His physical and mental rehabilitation was largely effected by Muldoon's treatment and by his work as a day laborer on the New York Central Railroad, until his return to New York in December 1903 and the gradual recovery of his editorial and creative capacities.

Dreiser made several attempts to put the harrowing experience on paper and only partially succeeded. The original manuscript remained as here presented: some finished parts of the text, together with fragments which illuminate his account or repetitive sections which suggest his efforts to bring the work to a satisfactory conclusion.

One might assume that the bitter episodes left such emotional scars that he could not cope with recalling the details of his illness, his abortive attempts to find work, or his mortification at Muldoon's sanitarium. However, Dreiser did not hesitate to make use of several other traumatic occurrences in his life that were woven into *Sister Carrie* in 1900 and that would figure in *Jennie Gerhardt* in 1911. In *The "Genius,"* published in 1915, Dreiser would make use of his work on the railroad, even to reproducing verbatim some of the dialogue appearing here in *An Amateur Laborer*. But it is apparent that, at the time of writing this document, he could not resolve his conflicting reactions to poverty and wealth, to the hypothetical superiority of the laborer with the mundane reality of daily toil. How could he reconcile his contempt and envy of the wealthy patients at Muldoon's "repair shop" with their boastful commercialism and tawdry ambitions? How could he harmonize his admiration for the railroad workmen, whose physical skills far surpassed his own, with his scorn for their banal responses to their environment, which were on a par with the motivations of Muldoon's guests? In both situations, Dreiser was the observant outsider, an amateur at gaining wealth and prestige, an amateur at physical endurance and dexterity. In 1904 he was too close to his material to reach a coherent solution to the questions which the experience had raised. However, he was sufficiently the artist to recognize that the supposed accomplishments of either set of his companions produced the same result: a failure to see the essential tragedy in the human condition.

When Dreiser was recording these tormenting months, he was still unknown, the author of one unsuccessful novel, a literary hack desperately trying to find himself, at thirty-three no nearer his goal of artistic accomplishment than ever. This text is vital to our understanding of Dreiser's later search for the strings that manipulate the human puppet. In spite of the flounderings of this amateur laborer, his instinctive grasp of comedy within human tragedy is revealed in his depiction of the unconscious humor and pathos of the tedious routine of daily life.

Richard W. Dowell, as editor, ordered and transcribed the manuscript, wrote the introductory essay, and supplied the annotations and identifications. James L. W. West III, as textual editor, devised the editorial principles, emended the text, and compiled the apparatus. Neda M. Westlake, as general editor, coordinated these efforts and served as liaison with the publisher. West and Westlake shared equally in verifying the transcription of the manuscript.

NEDA M. WESTLAKE

Acknowledgments

The editors wish to thank the University of Pennsylvania for access to the manuscript of this book and to supporting correspondence and photographs from the Theodore Dreiser Collection; the Museum of the City of New York for the photograph of the Mills Hotel; and J. B. Lippincott Company for permission to use the two Muldoon photographs, reproduced from Edward Van Every's *Muldoon, the Solid Man of Sport*, New York: Frederick A. Stokes, 1929.

The editors appreciate the concern of Robert H. Elias in his early transcriptions of the text and his helpful replies to inquiries. We are grateful to Dr. Vera Dreiser for her contribution of family information, which has been of inestimable value.

Dr. West wishes to thank the National Humanities Center and the National Endowment for the Humanities, both of which supported his work.

Introduction

After a long battle I am once more the possessor of health. That necessary poise in which the mind and body reflect the pulsations of the infinite is mine. I am not overconscious. I trust I am not under so. All that is, now passes before me a rich, varied and beautiful procession. I have fought a battle for the right to live and for the present, musing with stilled nerves and a serene gaze, I seem the victor.

With these words, probably written in early 1904, Dreiser began *An Amateur Laborer*, a project that was destined to remain uncompleted. Many of the incidents from the manuscript did find their way into print, however, for the *Laborer* and the desperate struggle with neurasthenia that it dramatized ultimately served as the basis of various semi-autobiographical essays, sketches, and episodes of *The "Genius."* Later in his career Dreiser often spoke of resurrecting the unfinished manuscript and including it, or the events it chronicled, in a projected third autobiographical volume, tentatively titled *A Literary Apprenticeship*. Writing to H. L. Mencken in 1943, Dreiser recalled with considerable embroidery an incident from the *Laborer* and then concluded, "But I will have to write *A Literary Apprenticeship* before you can learn all about that. Incidentally, that is why I said to you that *A Literary Apprenticeship* would be a scream."[1]

This light-hearted tone was doubtless a pose, for even after forty years Dreiser could hardly have found anything humorous about the events of 1903. Certainly he did not in 1904, when he first attempted to narrate this period of physical suffering, despair, and poverty that all but ended his promising career as an author. Though Dreiser had always been something of an insomniac and as early as the winter of 1899 was under a doctor's care for a tension-related illness, the neurasthenic condition that debilitated him grew in part out of the trauma and disappointment associated with Doubleday, Page and Company's reluctant publication of *Sister*

---

1. Dreiser to Mencken, 27 March 1943, *Letters of Theodore Dreiser*, ed. Robert H. Elias (Philadelphia: University of Pennsylvania Press, 1959), 3:981. Subsequent references to this source will appear in the text as *Letters*.

Carrie.[2] Dreiser weathered the turmoil preceding the novel's publication without overt despair, but its subsequent commercial failure was another matter. Then the death of his seventy-nine-year-old father on Christmas Day, 1900, contributed to his despondency, and soon he found himself in the throes of what he later described as a "black storm of combined ill-health and morbid depression."[3] Friends like Richard Duffy, noting Dreiser's dour mood, tried to rally his spirits. "You must school yourself to a habit of cheerful thinking, especially now that the encouraging reception of 'Sister Carrie' impels you to write another novel," Duffy wrote on 30 December. "I am happy to know . . . that you have been receiving complimentary letters from readers. Such comment is worth columns of hackneyed criticism from book-weary reviewers."[4] This sanguine evaluation fell on deaf ears. Magazine editors began to find Dreiser's temperament peevish and his work careless. When they complained or rejected his material, he began to feel that opposition to his novel had developed into a conspiracy, and these suspicions were not allayed by his futile attempts during most of 1901 to place *Sister Carrie* with another firm. The publisher at Century Company, Dreiser later recalled with bitterness and perhaps some exaggeration, hid in his office to avoid discussing the novel; a reader at A. S. Barnes and Company threw his copy in the fireplace when asked for an evaluation; and the "chief literary adviser" at McClure-Phillips Company called *Sister Carrie* "vulgar and impossible—a poor novel" and warned Dreiser that he was becoming "a social pariah."[5] The J. F. Taylor Company was more receptive and in October 1901 did purchase the plates and remaining stock of the novel from Doubleday, Page for $500; however, both Taylor and his editor, Rutger B. Jewett, advised against a

2. On 3 January 1899, Dr. W. Seman Bainbridge gave Dreiser a prescription for Panopepton, a medicine containing the digestive enzyme pepsin to soothe a nervous stomach, one of Dreiser's early symptoms of neurasthenia (Dreiser Collection, Lilly Library, Indiana University). Later in his career, Dreiser claimed that a "malignant appendix" and a spot on his lung also contributed to his decline during this period. See "The Irish Section Foreman Who Taught Me How to Live," *Hearst's International* 46 (August 1924):20; also Dreiser to William C. Lengel, 6 March 1924, *Letters*, 2:423. For the most comprehensive discussion of Dreiser's problems and negotiations with Doubleday, Page and Company, see the Pennsylvania Edition of *Sister Carrie* (Philadelphia: University of Pennsylvania Press, 1981), pp. 523–29.

3. TS titled "Down Hill and Up," pt. 1, p. 1, Dreiser Collection, University of Pennsylvania Library. A severely edited version of this TS became "The Irish Section Foreman Who Taught Me How to Live."

4. Duffy to Dreiser, 30 December 1900, Dreiser Collection, University of Pennsylvania Library. Subsequent quotations from unpublished correspondence are, unless otherwise indicated, from the Dreiser Collection.

5. "Down Hill and Up," pt. 1, pp. 8–9.

reissue in the near future, particularly with the original title. "Doubleday sprinkled enough of the book around the country to leave a few copies on many shelves," Jewett argued. "They still remain on these shelves, and when our salesmen tried to talk *Sister Carrie* to those who had bought the book, they said—'Well, we gave it a trial, and still have the books we ordered. Show us something new'" (30 December 1901).

A source of greater trauma was Dreiser's growing inability to write effectively. "The Rake," a projected novel presumably started in a state of euphoria following Walter Hines Page's agreement to publish *Sister Carrie*, was abandoned after only ten or twelve chapters, perhaps as a result of the Doubleday furor.[6] If Dreiser was daunted by this failure to make progress on a second novel, however, he did not show it openly when he wrote Page on 6 August 1900 to insist that his future as a novelist did not rest on *Sister Carrie*. "Even if this book should fail," Dreiser asserted with considerable aplomb, "I can either write another important enough in its nature to make its own conditions and be approved of for itself alone, or I can write something unimportant and fail, as the author of a triviality deserves to fail" (*Letters*, 1:61). For reasons that remain conjectural, Dreiser did not persist with "The Rake" following the publication of *Sister Carrie* but instead turned his attention immediately to *Jennie Gerhardt* and made a promising start. He began the composition on 6 January 1901 and had completed nine chapters by 2 February.[7] When he offered the novel to Macmillan Company on 16 April, the chapter count had risen to more than forty, but problems had begun to develop. To George P. Brett, an editor at Macmillan's, Dreiser wrote that with financial assistance he could finish the manuscript by "midsummer," but he admitted that he needed to revise most of what he had done. "I have already written more than forty chapters," he informed Brett, "but an error in character analysis makes me wish to throw aside everything from my fifteenth chapter on and rewrite it with a view to making it more truthful and appealing."[8] The self-doubt and indecision that were to plague Dreiser for the next two-and-a-half years had set in.

Brett offered Dreiser neither an advance nor a contract, so finding himself without a publisher and feeling the need to rethink his novel,

6. Thomas P. Riggio, Introd., *American Diaries, 1902–1926* (Philadelphia: University of Pennsylvania Press, 1982), p. 8; Dorothy Dudley, *Forgotten Frontiers: Dreiser and the Land of the Free* (New York: Smith and Haas, 1932), p. 196; and Dreiser to Fremont Older, 27 November 1923, *Letters*, 2:418.

7. For an analysis of Dreiser's progress on *Jennie Gerhardt*, see Donald Pizer, *The Novels of Theodore Dreiser: A Critical Study* (Minneapolis: University of Minnesota Press, 1976), pp. 96–105.

8. Macmillan Collection, New York Public Library.

Dreiser, along with his wife, accepted an invitation from Arthur Henry and his paramour, Anna Mallon, to spend a few weeks in June at Miss Mallon's cabin on Dumpling Island, near Noank, Connecticut. During the writing of Sister Carrie, Henry had given Dreiser the counsel and encouragement needed to keep him going and might have served a similar function with Jennie Gerhardt, but by June Dreiser was so moody that he was not particularly receptive. He complained about the cabin's primitive conditions, was jealous of Henry's attention to Anna, and bickered with everyone. Ultimately the tension became so oppressive that the Dreisers cut short their stay and returned to New York. When Henry published An Island Cabin the following year, he did not hide his annoyance at Dreiser's despondency and petulance.[9]

The return to New York was not a triumphant one. Financial straits during the negotiations with Doubleday, Page had forced the Dreisers to give up their comfortable apartment near Central Park and move to a depressing location on East End Avenue overlooking the East River and Blackwell's Island, where the ill, criminal, and insane were institutionalized. Here the gloomy environment, mounting debts, and belief that he had been blacklisted by the conservative literary establishment combined to stymie all progress on Jennie Gerhardt. There were triumphs that Dreiser might have taken heart over, particularly the critical and commercial success of the Heinemann edition of Sister Carrie, but he refused to be consoled. Recalling this period on East End Avenue, Dreiser later wrote:

Life took on a darker look for me than it had ever worn before. I seemed destined to defeat in the one field that seemed worth while to me—the one realm that spelled escape from monotony and humdrum. I began to brood. This coupled with a physical condition which was never sound up to that time quite did for me. I became morbid and in attempting to continue my writing, regardless of market conditions, I suddenly found myself too nervous to concentrate. Days and weeks even went by and I accomplished nothing. Instead I walked the streets, wondering how I was to manage in the face of a situation which seemed to preclude my writing in any form.[10]

The 1902 New York City Directory lists Dreiser's occupation as "clerk," perhaps a sardonic joke on his part that reflects his plummeting self-esteem.

When this directory appeared, however, Dreiser was no longer trapped amid such dreary surroundings. His escape had been made possible

9. Henry, An Island Cabin (New York: McClure, Phillips, 1902), pp. 159–236. Though identified in the book as "Tom," Dreiser recognized himself and resented the criticism.

10. "Down Hill and Up," pt. 1, p. 9.

by advances on *Jennie* from J. F. Taylor and Company. "I believe in you and in your work," Rutger B. Jewett had informed Dreiser on 30 September 1901, "and intend to make it possible for you to finish that second book by advancing enough for you to live on while you do it." The arrangements ultimately worked out were that Dreiser would receive one hundred dollars a month "on account" to complete the novel for a September publication.[11] On 6 November he received his first installment, closed his New York apartment shortly thereafter and set out for Bedford City, Virginia, where he felt he could live economically and work effectively. Amid the beauty and tranquillity of the Virginia mountains, his "malarial feelings were certain to quickly leave" (*Letters*, 1:66). He began the task of revising *Jennie* with renewed vigor and on 25 November notified Taylor that he had regained his "full interest in the idea" (*Letters*, 1:69). Soon, however, his spirits began to flag, and by mid-December he had abandoned Virginia to spend Christmas with his wife's parents in Missouri. His nervous condition was by now apparent to all. Early in 1902, Dreiser and his wife were again on the move, traveling first to the Gulf Coast and then settling briefly in Hinton, West Virginia. On 10 February, the ebullient Duffy wrote, "How does the one-night-stand regime agree with Mrs. Dreiser and with you? I think you are living a bully kind of life now; and that you ought to be pretty near easy in mind. This wander impulse of the literary man seems very natural."

Dreiser remained in Hinton for seven weeks but made virtually no progress on the novel. By 17 March, Jewett, who was still awaiting the first chapters, was becoming impatient. "You are simply hopeless," he wrote Dreiser in a bantering tone, then added a more somber warning: "The last time I saw you I told you that if you did not learn how to laugh some times just for the sake of relief, you would go crazy, or die of grief." This letter had hardly arrived before Dreiser was on the road again, this time leaving his wife behind as he journeyed to Lynchburg, Virginia. When she followed a few days later, he was already enroute to Charlottesville. At this point, faced with a husband whose frayed nerves and fear of failure made him totally incompatible, she returned to Missouri. Clearly the "one-night-stand regime" did not agree with Mrs. Dreiser. Dreiser himself made another stop in Charlottesville, remaining through April and May. On 12 April, Jewett wrote to say that if Dreiser expected to finish the novel by June he should submit a few pages for a publisher's

---

11. Dreiser received seven checks from J. F. Taylor and Company, the first on 6 November 1901 and the last on 3 June 1902, when it became obvious that he could not meet the deadline for a September publication of *Jennie Gerhardt*. On 7 July 1905, J. F. Taylor wrote Dreiser: "The arrangement which you propose making for settling your debt of $750 with interest is satisfactory."

dummy. Dreiser sent the requested pages, but by the end of April he had only ten chapters to submit. Throughout May, Jewett continued to urge him on, praising the revision, admonishing Dreiser for sloppy manuscript copy, expressing a "strong sense of eagerness for chapter 11," and signing his letters "Yours in great haste." Eager Jewett would remain, for by June Dreiser had again surrendered to restlessness and begun a trip northward on foot that would ultimately take him over three hundred miles through Virginia, Maryland, and Delaware to Philadelphia in mid-July.

By this time Jewett had abandoned hope of bringing *Jennie Gerhardt* out in September and on 27 June wrote to suggest February as a more realistic target month. "Do not get discouraged," he added almost perfunctorily. Yet there was little to dispel Dreiser's growing despair. Although his wife returned to care for him once he settled in Philadelphia, and friends from New York periodically came to visit, Dreiser's health continued to deteriorate, and his attempts to write brought only frustration. On 20 August, the tolerant Jewett complained that July's installment of *Jennie*, the last he would receive, was labored and rambling. "You elaborate certain parts of a narrative to excess," Jewett cautioned; "the reader becomes confused and wearied. When Dreiser tried to supplement his income by selling articles to periodicals, the results were equally depressing. His friendship with Joseph Horner Coates, editor of *Era*, and Seymour Eaton of *Booklover's Magazine* did result in the sale of some material, but Dreiser chose to dwell on the rejections. "A Samaritan of the Backwoods," for example, was refused in rapid succession by *Harper's Monthly*, *McClure's*, *Cosmopolitan*, and the *Atlantic*. For the brooding Dreiser, his four periodical contributions accepted for 1903 must have seemed an ominous contrast to the forty-eight he had published in 1899, the year before he had seriously begun to think of himself as a novelist.

On 22 October, Dreiser finally surrendered to the inevitable and placed himself in the care of an eminent Philadelphia dermatologist, Dr. Louis Adolphus Duhring, who diagnosed his condition as nervous exhaustion. Duhring also gave him the first of several prescriptions and suggested that he begin a journal which could serve as a reference during future visits.[12] Over the four months that Dreiser maintained this journal, he recorded a myriad of symptoms: headaches, muscular pains, constipation, dizziness, skin irritation and itching, loss of appetite, indigestion, feverishness, and pain in his urinary organs. The overriding concern, however, was insomnia and the attendant emotional instability: listlessness, depression, irritability, and an incapacity to sustain mental activities. In particu-

12. See "Philadelphia, 1902–03," *American Diaries*, pp. 53–113.

lar, he noted that his imagination had abandoned him and that his power to reason was greatly diminished.

Despite nine visits to Dr. Duhring and a variety of medication, Dreiser's condition worsened. By mid-December he had decided that further work on *Jennie* was futile. Thus, in the throes of sleepless nights, an upset stomach, and deep despondency, Dreiser wrote Jewett that he was abandoning the novel and would someday repay the advances. Probably with some sense of relief, Jewett responded on 19 December to reaffirm his faith in Dreiser and the novel's ultimate success but also to recommend a period of rest. "Until you are in a better condition than at present," he concluded, "you cannot do good work."

Any hope of profiting from *Jennie Gerhardt* now gone, Dreiser was forced to simplify his already-Spartan existence. His wife had proved a loyal nurse/editorial assitant, reading him to sleep, bathing his forehead, rubbing his chest with grease, correcting manuscript copy, and occasionally serving as his amanuensis, but she also complicated his desperate financial situation and tempted him to indulge in sexual activities that he had come to regard as physically harmful. As a result, on 26 January, he borrowed money from Coates to send her back to Missouri, then braced himself to face the crisis alone. His mood at this time is reflected in the 3 February diary entry:

> Today like so many others spent in the idleness which I despise and deplore. I have no money, or very little left. I am alone. I am homesick. All the courage I have seems to have gone out of me and I sit in my chair brooding. . . . All the desire of my heart is centered on getting well, on getting my wife back, on having a home and yet, but why go on. All I can do apparently is wait, but oh the weariness of it.[13]

By mid-February Dreiser could not pay for his room and board; his last visit to Dr. Duhring had been made on credit; and an eye infection had forced him to accept the charity care of the University of Pennsylvania's Free Dispensary. On 15 February, he spent his last six cents for stamps. Clearly there was nothing to hold him in Philadelphia; he dunned Coates for a small unpaid balance and set out for New York, where he would make a last stand on familiar ground.

When he returned to New York to begin the struggle later narrated in *An Amateur Laborer*, Dreiser had no illusions. He knew that the worst was yet to come and thus tried to conserve what little money he had by taking a $2.50-a-week room in a rundown section of Brooklyn, at 113 Ross

13. Ibid., p. 92.

Street, where he would remain for two depressing months. At first he persisted in his determination to support himself as a writer, contacting among others Jewett and Ripley Hitchcock, who had recently moved to the A. S. Barnes Company and was known to be interested in *Jennie*. To Hitchcock, Dreiser confessed that "nervous prostration" had compelled him to abandon his plans for the novel and forced him to subsist on "special work" (*Letters*, 1:71). Dreiser also enlisted the help of Arthur Henry, who inquired at the *Outlook* and *Nation*. These contacts yielded some assignments, but as in Philadelphia his attempts to write were unproductive and increased his anxiety. "Day after day," he recalled in *An Amateur Laborer*, "I rose to a futile effort to produce some literary article which I might sell and night after night I lay down to a sleepless couch, the ravages of worry and brooding keeping me wide awake" (p. 11). Ironically, the only successful attempt that has been traced to this period is a pollyannaish essay titled "On Being Poor," ultimately published in *The Color of a Great City*.[14] In this piece, Dreiser contended that the "most dreadful and inhibiting and destroying of all forms of poverty" was spiritual poverty that blinded one to the pleasures of museums, books and natural wonders. These joys, he argued, made his own life meaningful:

. . . I have never felt poor, or that I have been cheated of much that life might give. . . . A distant, graceful tower from which a flock of pigeons soar. The tortuous, tideful rivers that twist among great forests of masts and under graceful bridges. The crowding, surging ways of seeking men. These cost me nothing, and I weary of them never. And sunsets. And sunrises. And moonsets. And moonrises. These are not things to which those materially deficient would in the main turn for solace, but to me they are substances of solace, the major portion of all my wealth or possible wealth, in exchange for which I would not take a miser's hoard.[15]

But sunsets would not pay the rent, so within a few weeks Dreiser was forced to seek employment outside the literary world. He toured sugar refineries, transit companies, coal packets, canal boats, and a wholesale bakery. Surely the scenes he had created two years before in *Sister Carrie* must have haunted him as, Hurstwood-like, he walked the streets of Brooklyn and Manhattan, tormented by memories of his former prominence and paralyzed by an aversion to the menial positions for which he was now applying. Most unmanning was the fear that he would encounter friends of better days and be asked questions about his situation or have to

14. Elias dates "On Being Poor" from the Brooklyn period, and internal evidence supports this dating. See *Theodore Dreiser: Apostle of Nature* (New York: Knopf, 1949; emended ed., Ithaca and London: Cornell University Press, 1970), p. 126.

15. "On Being Poor," *The Color of a Great City* (New York: Boni and Liveright, 1923), pp. 77–80.

endure their pity. He was painfully aware that his clothing, if a bit threadbare, belied his need and that his bearing made him seem superior to the work he sought. It was excruciating to appeal, hat in hand, to common clerks or to endure brusque dismissals by minor functionaries. Equally unnerving were the stares of other unemployed men. Seeing their young, strong bodies and believing that they saw him as an interloper, Dreiser would hover about the periphery for a time and then move on, pretending that he had come on other business. "Dozens upon dozens of times," he recalled, "have I stood outside of all sorts of institutions wondering, debating, saying that I was unsuited to it or the business was unsuited to me and in the end turning back disconsolately to my room, there to brood and worry over my fate. . . . Sickness had apparently made a coward of me" (p. 17).

This inability to find work, even the most menial, resulted in a steady drain on his meager finances and forced him to curtail his expenses dramatically by moving into a dreary cell-like hall bedroom that rented for $1.25 a week. He also limited his meals to milk and bread, occasionally supplemented by an apple or a potato which had fallen from a cart in Wallabout Market. This lifestyle, later described as "the lowest states of life, this side of suicide or death" (p. 23), inevitably led to further physical deterioration. His weight dropped rapidly; the insomnia became more extreme; and he began to have terrifying dreams and hallucinations. Blisters formed on the tips of his fingers and toes, and everything appeared to be out of alignment. He was trapped in a paradoxical situation: as his desperate financial need drove him to apply for all possible positions, his physical condition rendered him increasingly unemployable.

On 6 April, Dreiser received a letter from Wilson Potter, a New York architect who had heard of his plight. Potter offered him a position as farmhand at his summer home near Forestville, Connecticut. "There would be regular farm and garden work," Potter wrote, "taking care of chickens, ducks, cows, etc.; also drawing water from the well, and occasionally some beating of rugs and possibly washing windows; in short someone to be generally useful. . . . There is of course plenty of rougher and harder work on the place for one who is able to do it." Dreiser replied immediately, expressing an interest in the offer. The fates, however, continued to be unkind. By the time Dreiser's letter arrived, Potter had left his office for a few days. When he returned and wrote to make the final arrangements, Dreiser had exhausted his money and left Brooklyn.

Dreiser's Brooklyn residence ended on Saturday, 18 April. With his rent due and less than a dollar in his pocket, he set out on foot for Manhattan, carrying only letters from publishers and a half-eaten loaf of bread. Once there, he wandered aimlessly, eventually arriving at the

United Charities Building, where he hoped to secure a night's lodging and aid in finding work. Only a few days before, he had sought the help of another charitable organization, but upon admitting that he had relatives in New York, Dreiser had been given only a letter of introduction which his pride compelled him to tear up and throw in the gutter. On this second attempt, he was once again paralyzed by the thought of accepting charity, and as he procrastinated at the door, weighing the options, the building closed at noon for the weekend. Then the idea of appealing to the New York Central and Hudson River Railroad came to him. Five years earlier he had interviewed the company's president, Chauncey Depew, and found him quite cordial.[16] Dreiser had also heard that the General Passenger Agent, George H. Daniels, took an interest in writers. As it turned out, he saw neither Depew nor Daniels, but he did get the promise of a job by presenting himself as a neurasthenic writer who needed the therapy of physical labor. The nature of the work was to be determined the following Monday. To survive until then and pay possible transportation expenses to the site of his new job, Dreiser pawned his watch for twenty-five dollars.

At this point Dreiser's plans were altered considerably by a chance meeting with his song-writing brother, Paul Dresser. Paul, at the zenith of his career, had composed numerous popular songs and owned a third interest in Howley, Haviland & Company, a music-publishing firm. From 1895 to 1897, Dreiser had been employed by Paul's firm to edit a trade journal called Ev'ry Month. Eventually Dreiser's literary ambitions for the periodical clashed with the firm's view of it as primarily an advertising vehicle. Dreiser resigned, filled with resentment at Paul's pedestrian tastes and attitudes. Because of this estrangement, Dreiser was loath to accept any help from Paul and parried all questions about his obvious physical deterioration. In the end, however, Paul succeeded in forcing him to accept seventy-five dollars and gained his promise to return to Paul's hotel the following Monday. In the meantime Dreiser took a room at the Mills Hotel, a philanthropic institution built to provide unemployed and transient men inexpensive food and shelter. In this depressing environment, surrounded by "such a company of wretched patrons as might have served to stock the almshouse of almost any community" (p. 56), Dreiser must have been acutely sensitive to the turn his career had taken. In "A Wayplace of the Fallen," written some months later, he recalled "the ne'er-do-wells, and bums even, panhandlers, street fiddle and horn players, street singers, street cripples and beggars of one kind and another.

16. See "Life Stories of Successful Men—No. 11, Chauncey Mitchell Depew," Success 1 (November 1898):3–4.

Some of them I had even encountered in the streets in my more prosperous days and had given them dimes, and here I encountered them again."[17] Once more Hurstwood might well have come to Dreiser's mind, for he noted that the "great provision against would be suicides here was the open condition of the rooms, the wall or partitions of each only reaching high enough and low enough to conceal the main operations of ones toilet. The rest of the distance was protected against entry by an open wire netting. There was no chance to turn on the gas here because there was none" (p. 136).

When he saw Paul on Monday, Dreiser discovered that all plans had been changed, for Paul had arranged to send him to William Muldoon's sanitarium, the Olympia, located three miles north of White Plains near Purchase, New York. Muldoon, a former champion wrestler and trainer of prize fighters, was not a complete stranger to Dreiser, at least by reputation. To Dreiser's brother Al, Muldoon had been a boyhood idol, and when three of the Dreiser brothers, Paul, Theodore, and Edward, lived together briefly at the Hotel Martinique in 1895, Muldoon had been one of the celebrities Paul entertained.[18] Since 1900, Muldoon had operated a sanitarium for the wealthy, many of whom were seeking treatment for alcoholism. Among his clientele had been Austin Brennan, Dreiser's brother-in-law, and Patrick Howley, Paul's partner. On Tuesday, 21 April, Dreiser entered this "repair shop" to begin a regimen that included regular hours, balanced meals, abstinence from tobacco and liquor, vigorous exercise, and savage attacks by Muldoon on weakness, self-pity, and slovenly habits. Four days later Brennan wrote Paul, who he thought was also a patient:

I hear you are at Muldoon's—with Dorsh—drop me a line. If you can stand the treatment I have no doubt of good results. Are you riding a horse or mule—I might say in a state of convulsion that I would like to be remembered to the Professor. He seemed to take an interest in me possibly that I did or could not appreciate—I think I endured more pain during the three weeks I spent there than at any like period of my life—probably on account of my old bones having been enfeebled by the excesses of youth but at all events it was a sort of premonition Dante's Inferno. I hope the stars & stripes that unfurl themselves over the grounds will at least cause you to think that you are not in Siberia.[19]

Perhaps the best evidence that Dreiser prospered physically and emotionally in this Spartan environment is the fact that by May he had

17. "A Wayplace of the Fallen," The Color of a Great City, pp. 172–73.
18. See Vera Dreiser, My Uncle Theodore (New York: Nash Publishing Co., 1976), p. 74.
19. "Dorsh" in the first line of the quotation is family nickname for Dreiser.

reopened negotiations with publishers to reissue *Sister Carrie.*[20] Also, during the first month of his stay, he wrote and sold an article about the sanitarium. "Scared Back to Nature" appeared in *Harper's Weekly* on 16 May 1903, while Dreiser was still a patient. Writing as one who had completed his treatment, Dreiser described Muldoon as a tyrant bullying and humiliating his socially prominent clientele. "There was . . . an all-pervading atmosphere of good-fellowship," Dreiser wrote, "except for a marked strain of autocracy on the part of the host and a certain helpless servility on that of the guests, none of whom seemed able to rise above it."[21] The bulk of the article consisted of examples of Muldoon's intimidating his victims and concluded with the ex-champion's rationale: "It is a part of a theory I have—this rough manner; a method of wresting a man's mental control from him in order to increase his mental energy. If his will has nothing to do with the arrangement of his day, his mind is much more likely to contemplate nature and to rest."[22]·

In the chapter, "Culhane, The Solid Man," in *Twelve Men* (1919), Dreiser provided a further sketch of Muldoon, his sanitarium, and his therapeutic regimen. The biography of William Muldoon (1845–1933) takes exception to Dreiser's treatment of the former champion and promoter, calling it a vivid but inaccurate account of Muldoon's background and behavior, resented by Muldoon's friends. In his biography, Muldoon is quoted concerning Dreiser's stay at the Olympia Sanitarium: "I was very fond of Paul Dresser, a half-brother of Theodore's. I have always resented the way in which he was made out as a weak and rather loose-living character by Dreiser in his story entitled 'My Brother Paul' [another chapter in *Twelve Men*]. . . . Paul spoke to me about his half-brother, Theodore, and how the latter might have in him the makings of a genius. Paul asked me to take his brother up to my place and I agreed. The morning after his arrival Theodore Dreiser came to me and secured permission to return to New York for the purpose of bringing back some additional clothing. He never came back. Just one night was all he could stand." Obviously irked by the picture of him in *Twelve Men*, Muldoon states that Dreiser "deliberately sets out to give the reader the impression that he has endured all of the hardships (such as they are) of my course through its entire six weeks. Personal friends have explained the nature of his article to me and pointed out its untruths and errors, so I have never bothered to read it."[23]

20. Responding to inquiries from Dreiser, both J. F. Taylor (1 May 1903) and Rutger Jewett (8 May 1903) agreed to allow Ripley Hitchcock of A. S. Barnes Company to reissue *Sister Carrie.*
21. "Scared Back to Nature," *Harper's Weekly* 47 (16 May 1903):816.
22. Ibid.

During his first days at Muldoon's, Dreiser thought of accepting the light work at Wilson Potter's farm once his treatment was completed. On 3 May he wrote Potter that he might come in June. As his strength returned, however, Dreiser was once more drawn to the strenuous work offered by the New York Central Railroad. Late in May he contacted Paul to ask for the address of A.T. Hardin, the engineer of maintenance of way, who had earlier promised him a position. By 2 June, after six weeks at the Olympia, Dreiser had gained some weight and recovered enough emotional stability to leave. His bill, which totaled $256.75, was sent to Paul.

After three days of leisure in New York and a brief visit with Peter McCord in Newark, Dreiser contacted Hardin, who assigned him to the chief engineer at Waverly. On 5 June, bearing Hardin's letter, he reported to the chief engineer and was immediately passed on down the administrative ladder to the supervisor of buildings, R. P. Mills, for a congenial assignment. After considering Dreiser's physical limitations and lack of experience, Mills offered him the choice of working in a carpentry shop at Spuyten Duyvil or being the timekeeper of a section gang.[24] When Dreiser chose the former, Mills drafted a letter to the shop forman, F. A. Strang, asking that the bearer be "put to work doing general labor around the shop and outside" (p. 99). His pay was to be fifteen cents an hour. The shop to which Dreiser was assigned made depot and office furniture and employed about one hundred men, including carpenters, millwrights, tinsmiths, blacksmiths, painters, and unskilled laborers. Its most impressive feature was the picturesque location on a penisula at the juncture of the Hudson and Harlem Rivers, across from the Palisades. Dreiser was immediately pleased by the beauty of the spot.

After determining the location of the shop, Dreiser began to look for living accommodations in the vicinity. At first the search proved frustrating, for most of the neighboring cottages were summer dwellings of wealthy families, who wanted no renters. Eventually, however, he found a comfortable room in nearby Kingsbridge. The head of the household was a widow, Mrs. Hardenbrooks, who shared her home with a widowed daughter, a nephew, and a cousin. Her cottage, as Dreiser described it, had "a most summery appearence. The awnings were nearly always down and the various red and yellow and blue jardinieres flourished with plants and vines upon the porch. Inside all was airy and clean" (p. 138). Except for

23. Edward Van Every, *Muldoon, The Solid Man of Sport* (New York: Frederick A. Stokes, 1929), pp. 25–26, 265–66.

24. The *Laborer* manuscript indicates that A. T. Hardin selected the carpentry shop at Spuyten Duyvil as the most suitable place for Dreiser to work; however, a draft of a letter from Dreiser to R. P. Mills (31 July 1903) reveals that the assignment was made by Mills.

the cousin, whom Dreiser found cold and insincere, the Hardenbrooks family was a congenial group. Mrs. Hardenbrooks was a forceful woman, well informed on many subjects. She was also a storehouse of diverting local gossip. The daughter, who had seen her share of tragedy, appealed to Dreiser's philosophical nature, and the nephew was a light-hearted, humorous fellow. They were all interested in Dreiser and his dilemma, offering him much-needed support during his first weeks in Kingsbridge.

At 7:10 A.M. on Monday, 8 June, Dreiser entered the world of manual labor. He was greeted by an acting foreman, who immediately assigned him the task of carrying bark-covered ash posts, eight feet long by six inches in diameter, up to the second floor of the shop—a feat which proved so physically demanding that Dreiser feared he would not survive the first day. His next assignment, mercifully, was easier. He became a "shaving boy," charged with cleaning the floor of all debris created by sawing and planing. Armed with a bushel basket and a long-handled scoop, he removed sawdust and shavings, often crawling under benches and between the legs of workmen to perform his duties. The latter part of his first day was spent stacking lumber in railroad cars. He was apparently never asked to carry ash posts again, and the roles of shaving boy and lumber stacker occupied the rest of his first week with the New York Central.

This physically taxing ten-hour routine brought nights of sound sleep and encouraged Dreiser to believe that he was making progress. During his rounds as a shaving boy, he also found some amiable companions with whom he exchanged pleasantries and even engaged in the maritime fantasy later narrated in "The Cruise of the *Idlewild.*" On the whole, however, his time in the carpentry shop was depressing. Most of the men proved dull, sullen, and suspicious, creating an atmosphere of fear and subterfuge. They spied on each other or developed tactics whereby they appeared to be working harder than they actually were. Soon Dreiser realized that he was the cause of a minor power struggle between workmen who vied for his services, not because they liked him personally but because they wanted to transfer some of their own work. "I did not like many of the men working here," Dreiser later observed. "They struck me in the main as a barren lot, narrow in ideas, small in mental calibre, well fitted to bother with the infinitely common things with which they were laboring. The only people I saw there whom I really truly liked, were the Smith and his helper little Ike, old John the Engineer, Henry the night watchman, Joseph the assistant to the millwright in whose room I was working, and old John Caffy the carpenter" (p. 173).

The appearance of the regular foreman, Fred A. Strang, on Dreiser's third day at the shop increased his apprehension. Strang immediately struck him as a weak, tyrannical man. "He had a cruel leer and a shifty, uncertain glance, which struck you [as] treacherous," Dreiser recorded. "On our first meeting I took an innate dislike to him. . . . When I handed him my letter he took it in an uncertain, gingery way and read it without a word. Then he shoved it in his pocket and walked away. This reception troubled me a little at first. I saw that he did not like me, or at least did not know how to take me, and I felt that he might make it very disagreeable for me if he chose. With that foolish self-consciousness of the neurasthenic I ran ahead looking for trouble and wondered how I should come out" (p. 146).

Finally the work itself proved dispiriting. Though occasionally diverting, his role as shaving boy just as often dramatized his fallen state. To be forced to scoot about the floor gathering stray blocks of wood for fifteen cents an hour was humiliating, particularly when the windows of the shop looked out on the Hudson River and the yachts of the wealthy. He felt the shame of being tutored by mental inferiors to perform menial tasks and then having them witness his ineptness. His lack of strength and agility was a constant source of embarrassment, for he imagined that everyone in the shop viewed him as an interloper, perhaps a spy. "I learned," he confessed, "that there was no gulf like that which separates the layman from the man who toils, and I saw that I was as unfitted to be a hewer of wood as I was to be president of a railroad. These people, the least of them, had served their apprenticeship and knew their business. All I could do was to stand and look on, or to do in a half cringing half blundering way what they did with ease and grace" (p. 160).

Later, when narrating this phase of his career as a laborer, Dreiser referred to his time in the carpentry shop in terms of months, but facts indicate that he stayed only a week. During that week he contacted the supervisor of buildings, R. P. Mills, asking for a new assignment. On Saturday, 13 June, Mills wrote Strang and ordered the transfer: "You will arrange to release Theodore Dreiser from work at Spuyten Duyvil Shop going into effect Monday morning until further notice." On the bottom of that letter, which was transmitted to Dreiser, Mills had added the following instructions:

As per conversation with you to-day you may arrange to go to Tarrytown Monday morning so as to act as inspector while piles are being driven for Tarrytown freight house.

You should watch and see that the contractors drive the piles where the stakes are set.

See that they are driven full length and keep the usual record as to the weight of hammer, average length of drop, number of blows struck, distance piles are driven into the ground, length of the pile and distance that pile is driven for each of the last three or four blows.

You had best keep track of this in the manner shown you in my office.

You can confer with my foreman Mr. Richards on the ground at Tarrytown for any other information you may require.

The following day, 16 June, Dreiser wrote A. T. Hardin to complain about his wages. Hardin responded immediately: "Our Division officers will keep in touch with you, and do the best they can in the matter of salary."

Hearing of this new assignment, Paul wrote on 22 June to admonish Dreiser to stop brooding. "Remember," Paul bantered, "the future of the great N.Y. Central system must not weaken. . . . I hope to hear of your advancement as general all around Supt. of the tie lifting gang of Gorillas." On that same day, Dreiser again heard from Mills, this time informing him that his salary had been increased to seventeen-and-a-half cents. This outdoors work with a section gang was apparently more to Dreiser's liking, for shortly after beginning the Tarrytown assignment he wrote optimistic letters to Jewett and J. E. Bowler, a Negro pants-presser whom Dreiser had met in Bedford City. As usual, Jewett had words of encouragement. "Good for you!" he replied on 19 June. "Health is bound to come to you through some strenuous channel. Keep a stiff upper lip, and you will come out all right." Ten days later Bowler wrote: "Indeed I was overjoyed to hear from you and to learn you are well."

Little is known about Dreiser's activities from the middle of June until September. The manuscript of *An Amateur Laborer* breaks off prior to that time, and other literary uses of the railroad experience ignore that period. The best evidence suggests that he was eventually returned to Spuyten Duyvil, probably as a member of a section gang, for on 31 July Paul wrote joshingly to encourage Dreiser to drive the spikes so deep that they would cause wonder in the ages to come. On that same day, Dreiser wrote Mills to ask for yet another change in assignment: "If my services are not especially required at Spuyten Duyvil and the Plumber's staff is to be increased by the addition of a helper, I would esteem it a favor if you would transfer me to that position for the remainder of my stay. I was given to understand by Mr. Hardin that a change could be had if I desired and I now think one would be beneficial to me." Dreiser had also altered his living arrangements and was now receiving his mail in care of Mrs. Hughes, Kingsbridge Avenue. The sense of restlessness had not yet subsided.

Perhaps by this time Mills was feeling beleaguered by his neurasthenic charge, for on 3 August he wrote to ask Dreiser to see him

personally about the latest request for reassignment. The immediate outcome of that meeting is unknown, but four weeks later the arrangements
sending him to Mike Burke's masonry crew had been made. On 31
August, Mills informed Burke of the transfer: "Mr. T. Dreiser, at present
in Mr. Washburn's gang at Spuyten Duyvil, will report to you on September 1st. You may arrange to engage him as mason's helper, carrying him at
the rate of $.17½ per hour." The following day Burke dispatched a terse
memorandum to Dreiser: "Come to Wms Bridge Station today, gang is
working there."

By this time, after a separation of seven months, Mrs. Dreiser had
returned, necessitating still another change in living arrangements. To
accomplish this, Paul, at Dreiser's request, sent a check for fifty dollars on
2 September, and the following day the Dreisers reclaimed their furniture
from the Standard Storage Warehouse, where it had been for thirty-one
months. Thereafter they received their mail in care of Mr. Schill, Natha-
lie Avenue, Kingsbridge, Dreiser's third address in three months. Thus
began his most stable period in Kingsbridge, as he remained at that address
and with Burke's crew for the final four months of his employment with
the railroad.

Dreiser later referred to himself as a "kind of assistant foreman"
under Burke, and in an essay titled "The Toil of the Laborer," he
indicated that ultimately he was made foreman.[25] The best evidence,
however, suggests that his role on the masonry crew was primarily clerical,
keeping track of materials used and needed, filling out requisitions, doing
monthly reports and assuming the responsibility for other paper work that
Burke found odious and frustrating. In "The Mighty Burke," Dreiser
recalled that his first task was to go to Mills' office to straighten out an
administrative snarl involving the acquisition of a keg of bolts. This
episode demonstrated Burke's clerical and diplomatic ineptitude and revealed to Dreiser a function he could usefully perform in his physically
debilitated state. When he returned from Mills' office, Dreiser recalled, he
decided "that it would be better to take the clerical work into my own
hands—to find out what was wanted in this line and to do it. I knew that I
could not very well work with a pick and shovel, and this was about all
that was left outside of that."[26] Memoranda from Mills' office to Burke
substantiate this description of Dreiser's work. They refer to "your man
Dreiser" and ask that he be sent "in regard to reporting material received"
(16 September 1903).

25. See "The Irish Section Foreman," p. 121; "The Toil of the Laborer,"
New York *Call*, 13 July 1913, p. 11.
26. "The Mighty Burke," *McClure's* 37 (May 1911):44.

Dreiser's later accounts suggest that his time with Burke was a period of considerable rehabilitation, and his correspondence immediately after the transfer was apparently filled with optimism.[27] On 10 September, Rutger Jewett replied to a recent Dreiser letter: "I am glad that you are feeling better, and hope that you will be able to get back into the old line of work again." Nine days later, after a hiatus of seven months, Dreiser resumed his correspondence with Joseph Horner Coates. "As you see we are living in Kingsbridge at present," he wrote. "I am working on the New York Central as a mason's helper for my health. It is out of door work and very interesting. I went completely to pieces with neurasthenia after I left Philadelphia." The periods of depression, however, were not at an end. On 18 October, for example, Paul responded to a distress signal by assuring Dreiser that he thought no less of him and inviting him to come downtown to "look over the winter suit & overcoat." A week later, J. E. Bowler wrote to commiserate with Dreiser: "Allow me to express my sincere sympathy for you in your illness. And am glad to see from your letter you are bearing it so patiently & philosophically, which is what few of us do." On 9 November, S. J. Griffin, an admiring reader distressed by Dreiser's depressed state, suggested that he turn to God and read Charles C. Haskell's *Perfect Health.* In the meantime, obviously at Dreiser's urging, Paul was trying to secure him a position on the New York *Daily News,* where Robert H. Davis, Paul's collaborator on the play *Boomerang,* was managing editor. On 23 December, Davis contacted Paul: "Am trying to arrange things for Theodore along about the 1st and think something can be done to keep the gentleman busy." In turn, Paul informed the clearly eager Dreiser that Davis could probably do something for him after the beginning of the new year. "But up to the 1st nothing can be done," Paul added. The generally accepted date of Dreiser's resignation from the railroad, Christmas Eve, 1903, is probably accurate, as Christmas fell at the end of a work week.

Davis kept his word, and by early January Dreiser was at work as an assistant feature editor for the Sunday edition of the New York *Daily News.* He had also moved to 399 Mott Avenue in the Bronx. Obviously impoverished when he left the railroad, Dreiser now turned for assistance to a brother-in-law, F. V. White of Montgomery, Missouri. On 5 January, White responded by lending the Dreisers money and returning some editorials that he had typed and proofed for submission to periodicals. In an accompanying letter to Mrs. Dreiser, White praised Dreiser's editorials,

27. See "The Mighty Burke," p. 47; "The Mighty Rourke," *Twelve Men* (New York: Boni and Liveright, 1919), pp. 309–10; "The Irish Section Foreman," pp. 120–21.

expressed the hope that they would be accepted and admonished her to turn to him rather than let "Theo put up his watch."

Immediately upon his return to the literary world, Dreiser began to try to turn his laboring experiences into salable articles. By 16 January, "The Toil of the Laborer" was making the rounds, only to be rejected by John S. Phillips of McClure's, who informed Dreiser that readers were more interested in facts than philosophical conclusions. Phillips might well have said "gloomy philosophical conclusions," for there is nothing in this three-part essay to suggest that Dreiser found his experiences with manual labor anything but agonizing. "The toil of the laboring man is artless," he began the first section. "There is in it neither form nor color nor tone. For months I have been working as only workingmen work, and in the dreary round of the hours, it has come to me that the thing which was wearisome and disheartening about it was [that it was] utterly devoid of art. In the construction of a building whereat we labored for three long months, I discovered that with every day's labor I was in contact only with that which was formless and colorless and toneless."[28] The use of the present perfect progressive, "I have been working," and the nature of the work described would suggest that Dreiser began this piece before he left Burke's crew, or immediately thereafter. In this first section, Dreiser did not mention his personal role in the construction process; rather, he emphasized the average laborer's inability to find beauty or satisfaction in his tasks. "These mixers of mortar and carriers of brick," Dreiser lamented, "toiled in the grime and dust without seeming to realize that it was a wretched condition—hard, grim and, so far as the sum of their individual lives was concerned, but meagerly profitable."

For the second section, Dreiser drew upon his experiences as a shaving boy in the carpentry shop. The tone remained somber, as Dreiser focused on the degrading nature of the work and the indifference of his superiors, particularly the "strange, egotistic, vainglorious" foreman. "The slow, unchanging, imperative nature of the work," wrote Dreiser, exaggerating the time of his personal involvement, "the fact that it went forward whether one man came or another one stayed away, the dreary persistence with which it was necessary to repeat the same motion day after day, week after week, month after month and year after year, was to the thinking and restless mind maddening."

In these first two sections, Dreiser remained relatively true to the known facts of his labor experiences. In the third section, however, he altered the circumstances of the narrative considerably to fit his thesis:

28. "The Toil of the Laborer," p. 11. Quotations from the essay in the paragraphs that follow are from this same page.

"The toil of the laborer is without mercy. Its grim insistent durance unrequited by anything save the meager wages with which it is paid." To support this grim contention, Dreiser returned to his experience with Burke's masonry crew and pictured the Irish foreman as a tyrant whose loyalty to management induced him to drive his men relentlessly.

> We were under a foreman whose conception of life was that it meant toil, and who was perfectly equipped physically to meet it. He did not stop to parley or to temper the necessities with tenderness, but shouted his commands, the fulfilling of which was as much a burden on his mind as upon our bodies. . . . I pondered over this, wondering at the fierceness of the temper of the foreman, the persistence of his frown, the manner in which, when anything was delayed, or the work went wrong, he visited the blame upon the heads of those who were the carriers and serfs of his commands.

The men became sullen and rebellious in the face of such tyranny, until one day, Dreiser wrote, indulging in some obvious fiction, "I was made foreman." Dreiser then told how by degrees the pressures to meet the demands of superiors and the occasional indolence of the laborers eroded his idealism and made him as insensitive as his predecessor. At length he was rebuked by one of the men he too was driving tyrannously. Shocked at what he had become and realizing that he could not alter the exploitation, Dreiser felt compelled to tender his resignation. "Not to drive where I could not release," he concluded, "not to exact where I could not repay, not to be a tool in the hands of those who were tools themselves, only that they were closer to the owners who did not think, was something, even though by quitting I could not relieve the situation of its pain."

"The Toil of the Laborer" reflects the negative mood with which Dreiser left the labor force. Prior to his illness, he had admired variety and accepted inequities as part of Nature's law. Strength and weakness, wealth and poverty were contrasts which gave life its charm and drama. But having experienced weakness and poverty, having cringed before strength and viewed luxury from a distance, he now found himself outraged by the indifference and brutality of his immediate superiors and keenly sensitized to the unjust economic gap between capital and labor. Thus in "The Toil of the Laborer," he cried out for greater equity: "That none should suffer, that none should want! This after all seemed the worthiest thought that sprang at the sight of a toil-weary man." On the other hand, though he sympathized with the plight of his co-workers, he could not totally identify with them: the dullness and lack of imagination which kept them under-lings seemed appalling, even disgusting. A tone of ambivalence and isolation pervaded this first attempt to write of his labor experiences, giving the essay an unrelieved bitterness and despair that would not be duplicated in future efforts.

This dark view of the labor world proved unmarketable. Within five months, *Scribner's*, *Harper's Monthly*, *Harper's Weekly*, *Leslie's* and *Pearson's* followed *McClure's* lead and rejected "The Toil of the Laborer." Ultimately, the essay languished until 1913, when it appeared in the New York *Call*. In 1920 a revised version was included in *Hey Rub-a-Dub-Dub*. The burden of these revisions was a return to a survival-of-the-fittest philosophy by removing the most passionate pleas for equity and replacing them with passages asking whether it was possible or even desirable. "I wondered [at the possibility of life without contrasts], and still do," Dreiser wrote in revision, "for in spite of endless personal inconvenience I have never been able to believe that an unbreakable dead level of equality should maintain."[29] The laborer's plight, which in 1904 had seemed to dramatize the failure of our economic system, could now be viewed as a demonstration of Nature's law that the strong must prosper by exploiting the weak. Though he could express sympathy for the downtrodden, Dreiser by 1920 had come to see their condition as part of the inevitable process. "Nature," he asserted in a passage added to the *Hey Rub-a-Dub-Dub* version, "had established these inequalities, the smallness of mind in some, the strength and vision in others. Who was I to set about establishing exact justice or equation, where I had not created? . . . Nature apparently went on the theory of great reward for those who could or would originate and conduct in a large way, little for those who could not: and these at the bottom did not and apparently could not originate. Their reasoning powers were not as yet sufficiently developed for that. They were, by reason of their mental equipment, hewers of wood and drawers of water."[30] Over the intervening sixteen years, the bitterness and humiliation Dreiser felt as a laborer had faded significantly.

The manuscript of *An Amateur Laborer* was probably written during the early months of 1904. Throughout his illness, Dreiser had been intrigued by the autobiographical possibilities of his struggle to regain his health and resume his career. As early as 13 February 1903, when he was down to his last dime in Philadelphia and had just walked five miles to save a nickel carfare, Dreiser had noted in his journal that he was "thinking how I would write all this. What a peculiar story my life would make if all were told."[31] Perhaps the suggestion by the editor of *McClure's* that readers preferred facts to philosophical conclusions renewed Dreiser's interest in autobiography. At any rate, in early February, when he lunched with novelists Hamlin Garland, Henry Blake Fuller, and Irving Bacheller,

29. "The Toil of the Laborer," *Hey Rub-a-Dub-Dub* (New York: Boni and Liveright, 1920), p. 98.

30. Ibid., pp. 101–3.

31. *American Diaries*, p. 108.

Dreiser was so preoccupied with his railroad days that Garland came away thinking he was still on the section gang. Garland recorded in his journal:

Bacheller and Theodore Dreiser lunched with us. Fuller was also present. Dreiser turned out to be a tall, thin, ugly and very uncouth fellow of serious not to say rebellious turn of mind. He was bitter over his treatment by Doubleday and disposed to take the world hardly. . . . Dreiser stayed on and on, telling of his struggles. He became a bit tiresome at last and we were glad when he went back to his work as boss of a gang of excavators.[32]

The assumption that Dreiser was involved with *An Amateur Laborer* between late January and early May is further supported by the fact that, other than his feature articles for the New York *Daily News,* he submitted no new material for publication during that period.[33]

Also, correspondence with Joseph H. Coates during March and April indicates that Dreiser had turned much of his attention to writing based on his experiences as "an amateur laborer." On 20 April, Coates wrote encouragingly, "I think you would do strong work on the laboring man's side of life, and it is a good subject." By May, however, Dreiser's plans for the material had apparently changed. After bringing what he had originally conceived to be a book-length narrative through twenty-four completed chapters, to the point where he had finished his first day at Spuyten Duyvil, Dreiser began to raid the manuscript for shorter, more immediately publishable pieces. His motives might well have been economic, for the Sunday edition of the *Daily News* was suspended in early April, so Dreiser was again unemployed. There is also evidence that he was having difficulty sustaining the narrative: fragments of at least three drafts of various chapters accompany the truncated manuscript.

The first short piece submitted for publication was "The Mighty Burke," rejected by *McClure's* on 16 June. In striking contrast to the bitterness and sense of injustice of "The Toil of the Laborer," "The Mighty Burke" is a humorous, sentimentalized sketch of a man Dreiser clearly admired. Perhaps his failure to market the grimmer side of his labor experiences had prompted Dreiser to turn to the more positive episodes. Certainly there was no attempt to dwell on his neurasthenia or his poverty and humiliation, all of which are dismissed with a single sentence: "I was

32. *Hamlin Garland's Diaries,* ed. Donald Pizer (San Marino, Cal.: Huntington Library, 1968), p. 123.

33. Dreiser preserved nearly all correspondence pertaining to his submission of manuscripts, but there are no letters in the Dreiser Collection from editors between 16 January and 26 May 1904, except rejections of "The Toil of the Laborer." For additional evidence that Dreiser was working on the *Laborer* manuscript in the early months of 1904, see the discussion of the manuscript evidence, pp. li-lii of this edition.

working on the road for my health, at fifteen cents an hour."[34] He then focused almost exclusively on Mike Burke, who now emerged as a blustery, contentious, tender-hearted foreman.

At their first meeting, as Dreiser recast the characterization, Burke seemed the swearing, slave-driving tyrant described in "The Toil of the Laborer"; however, Dreiser was quick to point out that this gruff, dictatorial demeanor masked a warm, fatherly concern for his men. The "victims" of his menacing outbursts seemed neither fearful nor particularly aware of the constant harangue. Recognizing the amusing incongruity and wishing to escape his capricious foreman at Spuyten Duyvil, Dreiser asked to join the masonry crew and was accepted by Burke, who desperately needed a clerical assistant. To Dreiser, Burke proved the ideal antidote for the cynicism engendered by his previous experiences. Intensely loyal to the company, the sturdy Irishman believed in a day's work for a day's pay, as meager as it might be. "'They're not payin' me wages fer lyin' in bed,'" he parried Dreiser's complaints. "'If ye were to get up that way [4:00 A.M.] every day fer a year, it would make a man of ye.'"[35]

As Dreiser learned over the next few months, Burke was a craftsman who worked uncomplainingly, taking pride and pleasure in his job. In regard to his men, he was a model of humane concern. Though their errors and indolence drove him to frenzied tirades, Burke was ultimately forgiving and supportive, thereby earning the love and respect of his "Eyetalians." Burke's gang, as Dreiser now described it, was a close-knit family, constantly bickering but affectionately loyal. All in all, "The Mighty Burke" is a portrait of the laborer at his best. It is also a portrait for which Dreiser took considerable liberty with the facts, particularly in his sentimentalized conclusion. Though Burke was obviously alive and well when Dreiser left his crew, the sketch ends with the foreman's accidental injury and death, which brings into final focus his courage and the devotion of his men.[36]

If Dreiser expected magazine editors to find this idealized view of labor more appealing, he was destined to be disappointed. Following its rejection by *McClure's*, "The Mighty Burke" was returned by *Harper's Weekly*, *Scribner's*, *Saturday Evening Post*, *Everybody's Magazine*, and *Tom Watson's Magazine*. Finally, in 1911, the sketch was published where it had first been submitted, at *McClure's*. Dreiser then placed the detached

34. "The Might Burke," p. 42.
35. Ibid.
36. On 8 January 1904, Robert H. Davis, managing editor of the New York *Daily News*, wrote Dreiser that Burke refused to have his picture taken by the *Daily News* photographer. Davis asked Dreiser to "induce him," but Dreiser was unable to do so.

magazine pages with the *Laborer* manuscript, writing across the front: "To be included in volume entitled *An Amateur Laborer*." As it turned out, however, "The Mighty Burke" was included eight years later in *Twelve Men*, this time as "The Mighty Rourke." For the *Twelve Men* publication, Dreiser made numerous revisions. In addition to giving the protagonist a fictitious name, he reworked the dialect for greater consistency, cut some technical jargon, increased the descriptive detail and dialogue and added one lengthy farcical episode in which Rourke's Prince Albert coat was torn up the back when he came from mass to fire a drunken workman on Sunday. Overall Dreiser was working to increase the drama and humor without altering the character of his protagonist. What had changed, however, was his presentation of himself. In "The Mighty Burke," Dreiser had kept himself in the observer's role, but in "The Mighty Rourke," he used his own physical and emotional debility to dramatize Rourke's strength and self-sufficiency. Even exaggerating his pitiable state somewhat, Dreiser revised his hourly wage downward to twelve cents an hour and made specific references to his depression, his laughably spare frame, his bony chest and his acute awareness that the Italians were his physical superiors—all of which made him dependent on and envious of "so wonderful a lamp of health" as Rourke.[37] Apparently during the intervening fifteen years, Dreiser's painful memories had dimmed to the extent that he could now use himself as a foil.

The second sketch to be carved out of the *Laborer* manuscript was "The Cruise of the *Idlewild*," which was crossing editors' desks by early August. It was based on an incident Dreiser had narrated briefly in a rough draft describing his friendship with an engineer at the carpentry shop identified as John Peters:

Between us we got up a little fiction about the shop being a boat, and the engine room the Captains cabin, and then I called him Captain and he called me Mate, and together we went sailing over a fictional main with as reckless a crew as ever hoisted a Jolly Roger. We made the Smith the bosun and Ike, his helper, the bosun's-mate, and we induced Joe, of the front room to take the position of day watch, seeing that he commanded the view from what we considered the prow of necessity. There was all sorts of foolishness about "heaving ho", and "blasting our top-lights", and shivering our timbers, and finally we fell to disputing as to who was the true orginator and what the rights of the mate and captain really were. I think there was a mere touch of feeling in this matter on Johns part, for the honor of being a captain even of a fictional ship was something and he was hurt when I suppressed him and called him Stoker. Finally we agreed to scuttle the old Idlewild as we named it and start a new boat which we called the Harmony, and to the day

37. "The Mighty Rourke," p. 310.

that I departed we were still sailing that goodly craft and John was Captain and I
was Mate. [p. 151]

The characters alluded to—John, Ike, Joseph, and the Smith—as well as
some of the incidents used to flesh out "The Cruise of the *Idlewild*" were all
described in discarded sections of *An Amateur Laborer,* often in passages
repeated verbatim in the sketch. When Dreiser wrote "The Cruise of the
Idlewild," he obviously had the *Laborer* manuscript close at hand and at
times copied from it.

In "The Cruise" Dreiser described how the imaginary *Idlewild* had
grown from the envy generated by yachts of the wealthy cruising the
Hudson, just outside the shop window. The fantasy was then given
impetus by the tedium of their jobs, the dullness of their co-workers and
their frustration at being underlings. Yet Dreiser did not dwell on the
negative implications. Even the tyrannical shop foreman was indicted
only for his lack of imagination. As with "The Mighty Burke," Dreiser's
concern was with the positive features of the episode: the whimsicality of
the concept, the humorous situations it spawned and the greater harmony
ultimately forged among the participants. The sketch ends on a note of
sentimentality as Dreiser and John realize that their positions of authority
have made then tyrannous. They therefore go to the object of their
persecution, little Ike, to beg his forgiveness and persuade him to rejoin
the crew of the newly created *Harmony.*

"The Cruise of the *Idlewild*" was also to have a long wait before
publication. In quick succession it was refused by *McClure's, Harper's
Weekly, Saturday Evening Post, Everybody's Magazine,* and *Tom Watson's
Magazine.* Henry Mills Alden, the editor of *Harper's Weekly,* thought the
sketch "rather light by itself." Finally in 1909 Dreiser took charge of
the editorial policy of the *Bohemian* and published "The Cruise" in the first
issue under his supervision. As he had determined to make the *Bohemian*
"the most genial little publication in the field" (*Letters,* 1:93), the light-
ness of tone was well suited to his purpose. Following the sketch's publication, Dreiser placed a copy with the *Laborer* manuscript and labeled it: "To
be included in 'An Amateur Laborer.'"

As with "The Mighty Burke," however, "The Cruise of the *Idlewild*"
was instead resurrected in revised form for another volume, *Free and Other
Stories* (1918). By the time Dreiser got around to reworking the sketch, he
was apparently in agreement with *Harper's* editor, for his additions and
changes darken the tone and develop the grim sociological implications.[38]

38. See D. B. Graham, "'The Cruise of the "Idlewild"': Dreiser's Revision
of a 'Rather Light' Story," *American Literary Realism 1870-1910,* 8 (Winter
1975):1-10.

In numerous passages Dreiser emphasized the tedium and hopelessness of the laborers' lives, making the fantasy more a psychological escape than a whimsical invention. For example, Joseph, a character described in the original sketch in less than a sentence, was fleshed out in the following manner:

Amiable Joe! I can see him yet, tall, ungainly, stoop-shouldered, a slight cast in one eye, his head bobbing like a duck's as he walked—a most agreeable and pathetic person. His dreams were so simple, his wants so few. He lived with his sister somewhere in Eleventh Avenue downtown in a tenement, and carried home bundles of firewood to her at night all this great distance, to help out. He received (not earned—he did much more than that) seventeen and a half cents an hour, and dreamed of what? I could never quite make out. Marriage? A little cheap flat somewhere? Life is so pathetic at times.[39]

Against this background, Joseph's eagerness to gain the dignity and enjoy the diversion of being "day watch" takes on a pathos not achieved in the earlier version.

Dreiser also gave greater emphasis to the tyranny and exploitation that come with power. Little Ike's persecution was more fully developed, and one lengthy incident was added to show Ike driven into exile by the captain and mate. The outcome of this harassment, humorous in the original, became pathetic in the revised sketch:

All we could do now was to watch him as he idled by himself at odd free moments down by the waterside in an odd corner of the point, a lonely figure, his trousers and coat too large, his hands and feet too big, his yellow teeth protruding. No one of the other workingmen ever seemed to be very enthusiastic over Ike, he was so small, so queer; no one, really, but the captain and the mate, and now they had deserted him.

It was tough.[40]

As in the first version, the captain and the mate came to recognize the pain they had caused and restored Ike to his former status, this time on the *Harmony*. The euphoria of this conclusion was lessened, however, by Dreiser's insistence on the desperate human needs that made the escape into fantasy a necessity. If "The Cruise of the *Idlewild*" was initially "rather light," by 1918 it had developed a somber undercurrent.

Dreiser's final attempt in 1904 to rework some of the *Laborer* material was a sketch of the Mills Hotel, rejected by *Cosmopolitan* in August and not published until 1923 in *The Color of a Great City*. This sketch, titled "A Wayplace of the Fallen," was based on the three-night stay at the

39. "The Cruise of the *Idlewild*," *Free and Other Stories* (New York: Boni and Liveright, 1918), pp. 308–9.
40. Ibid., p. 318.

Mills Hotel described in *An Amateur Laborer;* however, the two approaches to that experience were quite different. Dreiser's stay at the Mills Hotel, as described in the *Laborer,* occurred immediately after he had been promised a job on the New York Central and had encountered Paul. The period of despair and extreme poverty in Brooklyn was at an end, and the Mills Hotel, though dreary, was a way station to improved circumstances. As a result, Dreiser experienced some ambivalence. He recoiled at the depressing environment—the cell-like rooms, the nauseating odors, the sounds of anguish, the utter lack of privacy, and the hopelessness of many patrons—but he did not have to live there beyond the weekend. He was an interloper, a man with new hope and a revitalized interest in life's color and drama. As such, Dreiser found the Mills Hotel a fascinating spectacle. He was intrigued by the ruses used by some to conceal their poverty and by the seeming indifference, even sense of comfort, others displayed. Constantly he speculated about the earlier conditions of the vagrants and the circumstances that had reduced them to this level. "I cannot describe now just what effect this had on me at the time," he wrote in *An Amateur Laborer.* "It was depressing to me, I'll admit, and yet it had the element of charm which comes to one who is interested in the spectacles which his fellow man presents. During the three days, or nights rather, that I was compelled to stay there I was never weary of looking at this tremendous throng" (p. 57).

Since "A Wayplace of the Fallen" exists only in the 1923 version, it is impossible to determine how much it differs from the text that was circulating in 1904; however, the later sketch is clearly more negative than the *Laborer* version. By 1923, the Mills Hotel had become for Dreiser a symbol of America's failure and an appalling demonstration of the vast economic gap "that was not supposed to exist in a republic devoted to human brotherhood and the equality of man."[41] In "A Wayplace," Dreiser obscured the ameliorating circumstances of his stay at the Mills Hotel and instead identified himself as one driven there by illness, poverty, and isolation from family and friends. The Mills Hotel was supposedly a philanthropy founded to give the downtrodden some relief, but, as Dreiser pointed out, its patrons in reality consisted of only the defeated and impoverished, the drug-addicted and criminal. For them there was no hope. The hotel instead was a kind of prison, with its tiers of cells, endless rules and restrictions, and total denial of human dignity. Unlike the *Laborer* account, "A Wayplace of the Fallen" does not focus on the color and drama of the Mills Hotel; rather, the institution is presented as a social experiment that had failed, a last stop for society's dregs. "Men such

41. "A Wayplace of the Fallen," p. 171.

as these," Dreiser concluded the sketch, "are not absolutely worthless, but they have reached the lowest rung of the ladder, are going down, not up, and beyond them is the Bowery, the hospital, and the river—the last, I think, the most merciful of all."[42]

Dreiser became an assistant editor at Street and Smith's in mid-August and apparently discontinued work on the *Laborer* material. He did not, however, cease to make plans for its eventual use. In September he wrote Coates that he was planning a book based on his recent experiences, possibly a novel. In his response on 28 September, Coates tried to dissuade Dreiser from fictionalizing the material:

> What you say about a book of personal experiences interests me, and naturally I think of your work on the New York Central Railroad among those who toil with their hands. . . . If your personal experiences are in similar fields to those that Jacob Riis has browsed in, I fancy they might do quite as well in the shape you have first cast them as to put them into fiction. Human documents have as forceful appeal just now as they have ever had I think. Indeed if they are put forth in sober fact, that would not bar the later fiction; perhaps it would help it.
>
> People like true things, and the truer even fiction is the better; even the mere semblance of truth goes a long way. I do not believe there has ever been a greater desire for truth than there is today. So you see that a "true story" told as you can tell it, with all your keen insight and power and sympathy ought to have a good chance of its value being recognized. Bear in mind.[43]

As it turned out, Dreiser did not again make active use of the *Laborer* material until late in 1910, when he began the first draft of his most autobiographical novel, *The "Genius,"* devoting chapters nine through thirty of Book Two, "Struggle," to his battle with neurasthenia.[44] However, Dreiser did not plunge his protagonist, Eugene Witla, into the physical and emotional depths that he had endured. Perhaps after a period of success as editor-in-chief of the Butterick publications, Dreiser did not wish to dwell on the poverty and emotional instability of his earlier years, or perhaps the darker episodes of his struggle did not seem germane to the philosophical purposes of the novel. Whatever the reasons, when he

42. Ibid., p. 181.

43. Jacob Riis, whom Coates mentions in the first paragraph of this quotation, was a Danish-born reformer, journalist, and author whose exposés of the New York tenement and slum conditions brought about numerous reforms. His books include *How the Other Half Lives* (1890), *Children of the Poor* (1892), *The Battle with the Slum* (1902), *Children of the Tenements* (1903), and his autobiography, *The Making of an American* (1901).

44. According to Donald Pizer, Dreiser wrote the first draft of *The "Genius"* between late December 1910 and late April 1911 (*The Novels of Theodore Dreiser*, p. 133).

returned to the *Laborer* experiences, Dreiser was most selective and often changed the emphasis and interpretation of those incidents he did use.

In *The "Genius,"* Eugene's neurasthenic condition was consistent with the early symptoms Dreiser recorded in the Philadelphia diary and the *Laborer* manuscript—sour stomach, nervousness, irritability, and indecisiveness about his work. This inability to work effectively led to greater apprehension and morbidity, sleeplessness, and loss of weight. Unlike Dreiser, however, Eugene was struck down after the critical and financial success of his first painting exhibition. His collapse was brought on by overwork and overindulgence in sex—something Dreiser had feared in his own case—but it was not complicated by the sense of failure that haunted Dreiser after the *Sister Carrie* debacle. Like Dreiser, Eugene first spent some time on his in-laws' farm in the Midwest and then sought a tranquil atmosphere in various towns in the South. The itinerary and time consumed in this quest differed considerably from Dreiser's own, however. The desperate Philadelphia months were not included in *The "Genius."* Instead, Eugene sent his wife back to her parents from Biloxi, Mississippi, and went directly to New York to make his stand alone. Eugene's return was far less grim than Dreiser's had been. According to the *Laborer*, Dreiser arrived in New York with less than forty dollars; Eugene returned with one hundred seventy five, which was periodically supplemented by the sale of a picture. Never did his savings drop below one hundred dollars. Also, Dreiser chose not to subject his protagonist to the dark days in Brooklyn and instead located him on West 24th Street in a "semi-respectable neighborhood" where the people were "poor but fairly intellectual."[45] Eugene's first months in New York, similar to Dreiser's own, were consumed by futile attempts to find work on a magazine or newspaper and then at sugar refineries, railroad freight offices, and streetcar companies. Like Dreiser, Eugene was ashamed to apply for menial positions and was abashed when unemployed men stared at him with hostility. Unlike Dreiser, however, he was not driven by destitution.

For Eugene's decision to turn to the railroad for employment, Dreiser introduced a variant he would thereafter use whenever he retold his own story. In the *Laborer*, Dreiser's quest had begun with the general passenger agent. As Dreiser initially recalled the incident, "I thought of the General Passenger Agent, a man who made himself known to literary people by reason of his interest in literary matters, and decided that my appeal should be made to him. He liked writers and boasted of his acquaintance with some of them. I would go to him if I could get in to see him and state how I was situated" (p. 46). In *The "Genius,"* however,

45. *The "Genius"* (New York: John Lane Company, 1915), p. 299.

Eugene recalled the story of a nervously debilitated writer who sought out the president of a railroad and was given an opportunity to work. Eugene therefore appealed directly to the president of one of the "great railroads that entered New York," just as Dreiser thereafter would insist that his decision to try the New York Central grew out of his acquaintance with Chauncey Depew. Otherwise the details of Eugene's initial employment followed the *Laborer* closely enough to suggest that the manuscript was at his elbow as he wrote.

At this point, however, there was another major change in the narrative. Eugene spent no time in a sanitarium; rather, he was hired immediately, assigned to the carpentry shop, and two days later arrived at Spike, called Speonk in the novel. Like Dreiser, Eugene found a room in an adjacent community by appealing to a minister who directed him to the Hibberdell cottage, a residence much like the one where Dreiser first stayed in Kingsbridge, though here again Dreiser made some significant changes in detail. The Wollestencraft household (a fictitious name Dreiser used in the *Laborer*) was made up of a widow, her nephew, a cousin, and a widowed daughter. In creating the Hibberdells for *The "Genius,"* Dreiser remained faithful to the *Laborer* description of the widow and her nephew, but he eliminated the cousin, whom he had not liked. The widowed daughter was transformed into Carlotta Wilson, a woman with whom Eugene was destined to have an extended affair. In the *Laborer*, the twenty-five-year-old woman was described as being "a weary-looking lady, rather pale" (p. 107). Her mood was philosophical and melancholy, which appealed to Dreiser in his depressed state, but though he found her pleasant, tolerant, and knowledgeable, there was no suggestion in the *Laborer* that their relationship went beyond diverting evening chats. Carlotta Wilson, on the other hand, was anything but weary or melancholy. She was the fast-living, free-loving wife of a gambler, from whom she was temporarily estranged and in search of a lover. Her initial meeting with Eugene paralleled Dreiser's first encounter with the widowed daughter, but his description of Carlotta on that occasion was quite different in emphasis. "Her shapely figure, beautifully proportioned to her height, was set in a smooth, close fitting corset. Her hair, laid in great braids at the back, was caught in a brown spangled net. She carried herself with thoughtfulness and simplicity, seeming naturally indifferent" (*"Genius,"* p. 336). Unlike the contemplative widowed daughter of the *Laborer*, the thirty-two-year-old Carlotta was flirtatious, daring, and totally hedonistic. She was sexually attracted by Eugene's handsome appearance, intellectual nature, and "certain swift force that filled the room" (*"Genius,"* p. 337). Challenged by his apparent detachment, she launched a Circe-like campaign to lure him into a clandestine affair. Lonely and varietistic by nature, Eugene quickly responded, thereby involving himself in the sexual intrigue that dominated Book Two.

Eugene's work in the carpentry shop followed Dreiser's own experiences in outline but not in detail. Dreiser remained relatively faithful to the events of his first day at Spike, and most of the workers described in the *Laborer* were recreated in *The "Genius,"* usually with name changes. Otherwise Eugene's stay in the shop bore little specific resemblance to Dreiser's own. Eugene did not suffer the frequent periods of self-doubt, humiliation, and despair that Dreiser confessed in the *Laborer,* nor did he lose confidence in his ultimate recovery. He was painfully aware of the valuable time being wasted, but his spirits remained high. As Dreiser described him, "Eugene himself . . . was a curiosity to the others, even more so than they to him. He did not look like a workingman and could not be made to do so. His spirit was too high, his eye too flashing and incisive. He smiled at himself carrying basketful after basketful of shavings" (*"Genius,"* p. 324). Eugene's superiority and talent were soon recognized by his fellow workmen, who elevated him to celebrity status. He in turn was amused by their picturesqueness and responded with a kind of noblesse oblige rather than the compassion and camaraderie Dreiser demonstrated in the *Laborer* and "The Cruise of the *Idlewild.*" Even the foreman, whose tyrannical attitude had intimidated Dreiser, was awed by Eugene and quickly became solicitous. All in all, Eugene "made for himself an atmosphere which was almost entirely agreeable to him" (*"Genius,"* p. 319).

Dreiser also drew upon his time with Mike Burke, called Deegan in *The "Genius."* In fact, some description and a considerable amount of dialogue were taken verbatim from "The Mighty Burke," but the sympathy and admiration for Burke and his men in that earlier sketch now gave way to an emphasis on Eugene's superiority. To Eugene, the work quickly grew monotonous and depressingly unaesthetic; Deegan's comments on Eugene's physical weakness caused resentment; and Deegan himself was an unimaginative, insensitive man. Eugene soon became disenchanted: "His work with Deegan had given him a sharp impression of what hard, earnest labor meant. Deegan was nothing but a worker. There was no romance in him" (*"Genius,"* p. 394). Ultimately, Eugene's desire to escape Deegan and his men prompted him to seek a position in the art department of a newspaper, a first step toward the resumption of his career. In contrast to "The Mighty Burke" and later "The Irish Section Foreman Who Taught Me How to Live," where Burke's influence gave Dreiser the courage and stability to return to the literary world, the Deegan episode in *The "Genius"* was the grimmest phase of Eugene's experiences as a laborer.

A study of Dreiser's use of the *Laborer* materials in *The "Genius"* leads to the inevitable conclusion that the term "autobiographical" is indeed tenuous when applied to that section of the novel. By eliminating the most desperate episodes and emphasizing Eugene Witla's intellectual and aesthetic superiority, Dreiser turned the most tragic and dramatic period of his own life into little more than an annoying hiatus in the career of his protagonist.

Perhaps Dreiser's return to the material while writing The "Genius" and the belated publication of three sketches based on his railroad experiences stimulated him to reconsider the book possibilities of An Amateur Laborer, for in November 1912, shortly after completing The Financier, Dreiser sent Mencken a list of viable projects to oversee "in the case of a sudden demise." On that list was "over half of a book on my labor experiences" (Letters, 1:50). Then in December of the following year, Dreiser apparently offered the Laborer to the Century Company in an effort to secure an advance on A Traveler at Forty. Douglas Z. Doty, a Century editor, responded with interest on 6 December: "If you could let me have the script of "The Amateur Laborer" I think I could quickly size up its possible commercial value and immediately determine how far I thought the house was justified in going in the matter of further advances." Either Dreiser did not feel that the manuscript could be submitted at that time or Doty was unimpressed by its incomplete state, for on 9 January he wrote Dreiser a brief note denying the advances and making no mention of the Laborer.

Over the next five years Dreiser pursued other interests. Then in April 1919 he published Twelve Men, containing two previously unpublished sketches which drew upon the Laborer material—"My Brother Paul" and "Culhane, the Solid Man."[46] As previously noted, a revised version of "The Mighty Burke," retitled "The Mighty Rourke," also appeared in this volume.

In "My Brother Paul," Dreiser recalled the time Paul had rescued him from poverty on the streets of New York and had sent him to Muldoon's; however, there is no evidence that he depended on the Laborer manuscript for the telling. The details, major and minor, were

46. Elias speculates that "My Brother Paul" was written around 1909, and while there seems to be no concrete evidence to support this dating, it is evident that the sketch was obviously not among the ones Dreiser carved out of the Laborer in 1904, for Paul did not die until 1906. See Theodore Dreiser: Apostle of Nature, p. 146. "Culhane, the Solid Man" is on occasion erroneously considered a revision of "Scared Back to Nature" (see Ellen Moers, Two Dreisers [New York: Viking Press, 1969], p. 342). Though based on the same incidents, the two pieces are clearly independent compositions. Internal evidence suggests that Dreiser attempted this more ambitious sketch of Muldoon around 1906.

altered so extensively in "My Brother Paul" that it must be assumed Dreiser was calling on a faulty memory or reshaping the incidents intentionally. For example, in this later sketch Dreiser said nothing about applying for work on the New York Central or about pawning his watch. Instead he recalled that he was enroute to see a publisher when he encountered Paul. Dreiser also eliminated the complication that Paul was leaving town for the weekend and thus gave him money for the interim, money which Dreiser guarded by spending three dreary nights at the Mills Hotel. As Dreiser recast this incident, Paul was able to give him no money at their initial meeting but did succeed in learning Dreiser's Brooklyn address.[47] The next day Paul visited him there and, seeing the shabby dwelling, pled with Dreiser to accept help. When Dreiser resisted, Paul reminded him that half the royalties to the commercially successful "On the Banks of the Wabash" were by rights Dreiser's, since he had contributed the idea, first verse, and chorus.[48] At that point Dreiser acquiesced and allowed Paul to set him up in a posh hotel room, buy him a new wardrobe, and pay for his stay at Muldoon's. This reshaping not only resulted in a tighter narrative but also shifted the emphasis from Dreiser's grim struggle to Paul's brotherly compassion. The revision also salved Dreiser's pride by making the financial aid more or less payment of a long-overdue debt, not outright charity.

For "Culhane, the Solid Man," Dreiser again drew on the *Laborer* manuscript for descriptive passages and occasional incidents. The two presentations of Dreiser's stay at the "body shop," however, differ radically in focus. In the *Laborer*, Dreiser had been primarily introspective, dwelling on his ambivalent attitude toward the other "guests" and Muldoon himself. Clearly the materialism, arrogance, and vacuity of Muldoon's other patients disgusted Dreiser and convinced him of life's injustice. "In these days," he wrote in the *Laborer*, "I think I took about the bitterest view of humanity that I have ever had. It was not that I had not felt and observed the cruelty of life before—I had, but here the spirit of criticism was roused in me by what I deemed the materiality of these men" (p. 87). By contrast, the fates of the people he had met in Brooklyn and the Mills Hotel, indeed his own fate, seemed cruel and unjust, and he insulted the indolent rich at every opportunity. Yet, facing an uncertain future and realizing that he was living on the charity of his brother made Dreiser

47. In what may have been a lapse of memory, Dreiser recorded his Philadelphia house number, 130, instead of his Brooklyn number, 113.

48. For a discussion of Dreiser's contribution to "On the Banks of the Wabash," see Richard W. Dowell, "'On the Banks of the Wabash': A Musical Whodunit," *Indiana Magazine of History* 66 (June 1970):95-109.

envy their security and self-confidence. These wastrels, "with all their fine things excited my envy," he admitted. "I was sick of poverty, or worse yet want, and would have gladly exchanged my end of the bargain for theirs, or for at least a competence. As for the pleasures in which they indulged I am quite sure I could have dispensed with most of them" (p. 92).

Dreiser's attitude toward Muldoon in the *Laborer* was equally ambivalent. Terrified by tales of the sanitarium's strenuous regimen and fully aware of his own physical and mental debilitation, Dreiser found Muldoon's aloofness, his obvious disdain for weakness, and his tendency to mock and browbeat his patients to be daily sources of irritation, particularly when the harangues were directed at him. The ex-champion, to Dreiser's mind, was an egotistical, sadistic brute. On one occasion, Dreiser tried to convince Muldoon that his strength was not of his own making but a product of inheritance. This gift, Dreiser argued, should inspire tenderness, not intolerance. Muldoon, of course, scoffed at this deterministic assumption and considered Dreiser a "long-legged ignoramus" (p. 82).

In his more objective moments, however, Dreiser admitted the justice of Muldoon's intolerant outbursts: "I was selfish, and I had thought that I was somewhat of a philosopher. It might be true that I was an ignoramus after all for who can tell. Anyhow my mind was riveted on myself and I was having a hard time getting it off. Besides he was big and strong and trying to cure me and could have cracked a dozen such men as me together and broken our heads" (p. 82). Also, the benefits of Muldoon's treatment were undeniable: Dreiser gained weight, slept better, and got relief from other neurasthenic conditions. As a result, he left the sanitarium with some misgivings. For all its annoyances and intimidation, the institution had offered a security and identity that seemed suddenly desirable compared to his uncertain future. In leaving, Dreiser acknowledged his debt to Muldoon: "'You may not think you do good, but some of us cannot help but be better for having known you. I know I shall be'" (p. 95).

This tough humanitarianism Dreiser chose to emphasize in "Culhane, the Solid Man," an amalgam of scenes from the *Laborer* and "Scared Back to Nature" mingled with new episodes recalled or invented to emphasize Culhane's disdain for weakness. Dreiser's own participation was reduced largely to the role of observer. At the beginning of the sketch, he briefly described the circumstances that brought him to the sanitarium: "I met him [Culhane] in connection with a psychic depression which only partially reflected itself in my physical condition. I might almost say that I was sick spiritually. . . . I myself was introduced or foisted upon him by my dear brother. . . . I was taken to him in a very somber and depressed mood and left."[49] Dreiser made no other references to his particular difficulties at the time—his poverty, his inability to write, his sense of life's injustice, his intention to become a manual laborer, or his ambivalence toward Culhane and the wealthy patrons. In fact, Dreiser implied that he too was affluent, stating at one point: "I had paid my six hundred."[50] His earlier bitterness toward the idle rich was replaced by a bemused tolerance. The job of castigating them and exposing their vanity and self-indulgence was given almost exclusively to Culhane. Dreiser also eliminated most of his own former annoyance with the ex-wrestler. Though he occasionally included himself among a group that felt the sting of Culhane's sarcasm, Dreiser cut the one-to-one confrontations dramatized in the *Laborer* or else substituted another guest as the victim. The effect of this shift in emphasis was to minimize the personal trauma of his stay at The Olympia and focus the reader's attention on Culhane, now described by Dreiser as "really one of the most remarkable men I had ever known."[51] Whereas the Muldoon section of the *Laborer* is essentially a narrative of despair, "Culhane, the Solid Man" is a tribute to strength and to the belief that human dignity grows out of discipline and cleanliness.

Twelve Men sold poorly, but the reviews were generally favorable. Several critics singled out "My Brother Paul" and "Culhane" for special praise.[52] Mencken was impressed and wrote Dreiser: "You missed a fine chance when you didn't write a whole book about your brother" (*Letters*, 1:288). Having completed the manuscripts of *Dawn* and *A Book About Myself*, and encouraged by the critical reception of *Twelve Men*, Dreiser responded that the third volume of his autobiography, including the Dresser material, was underway. "I do a small bit—now and then. Ah, the opportunity that lies there, my good brother—the nobles of the nineties & nineteen tens" (*Letters*, 1:289). From this point on, the *Laborer* materials were consistently thought of as part of this larger work, a four or five volume "History of Myself."

Although Dreiser continued to discuss this project with Mencken and to negotiate with prospective publishers, work on it was halted in favor of *An American Tragedy*. Dreiser had to support himself while he wrote this massive novel, however, so he began to flood magazine editors with suggestions for articles, many of them based on episodes from the

49. "Culhane, the Solid Man," *Twelve Men*, pp. 134–35.
50. Ibid., p. 142. This statement is inaccurate on two counts: Paul paid the bill, and it was only $256.75.
51. Ibid., p. 161.
52. See Jack Salzman, ed., *Theodore Dreiser: The Critical Reception* (New York: David Lewis, 1972), pp. 319–44.

unpublished autobiographies. One such editor was William C. Lengel, Dreiser's longtime friend who was then managing editor of *Hearst's International.* When Lengel expressed interest in an article on Dreiser's battle with neurasthenia, Dreiser responded on 6 March 1924 with a somewhat altered synopsis of the events narrated in the *Laborer.* This synopsis was then followed by a sloppily prepared seventy-three-page typescript titled "Down Hill and Up." Ultimately this typescript was cut by almost half and published in August 1924 as "The Irish Section Foreman Who Taught Me How to Live."

In composing "Down Hill and Up," Dreiser made no apparent use of the *Laborer* manuscript, nor did he bother to check the accuracy of his memory. There were many obvious errors, inventions, and omissions in the retelling. Dreiser, for example, chose to ignore Paul's involvement completely, saying instead that he refused throughout the ordeal to be beholden to his relatives. As he now recast the circumstances, "I had relatives in New York, two sisters and a brother, to whom for reasons of my own I did not wish to appeal. I had felt them to be, if not ungenerous, at least unfriendly at the time. . . . In my days of modest achievement here and there I had not troubled to consider them to any extent. Now in my poverty, why should I expect them to look after me. It seemed petty and cowardly and I refused to do it."[53] This reluctance to acknowledge Paul's assistance also necessitated dropping all mention of Muldoon's. Dreiser now insisted that he had gone to work on the railroad immediately after his struggle in Brooklyn. Thus the chronology of events and some of the detail in "Down Hill and Up" were closer to Dreiser's recasting of *The "Genius"* than to *An Amateur Laborer.*

Perhaps the most dramatic departure from the *Laborer* was Dreiser's introduction of his suicidal mood toward the close of the Brooklyn period. This flirtation with suicide has become a staple of Dreiser biography, but it actually did not become a part of the narrative until "Down Hill and Up." In the *Laborer,* Dreiser had instead emphasized his refusal to surrender. "It is curious," he wrote, "to what stretches a human being will sink and not give up. Low as my condition was physically, mentally and financially I never once truly yielded. People rejected me and I thought I was like to die but I would not give in" (p. 28). Remembering his last night in Brooklyn, the night typically identified as the time of his contemplated suicide, Dreiser noted: "In spite of me I felt rather a feeling of relief as if the worst were over. A storm like this could not last forever. I was not dead and I was not going to die tomorrow. I would leave my trunk and grip here and

53. "Down Hill and Up," pt. 1, p. 13. Although Dreiser here indicated that he had only "one brother" in New York, Paul and Edward were both in the city at the time.

go to New York, where I would look around and get something to do. Something would turn up" (p. 43).

In "Down Hill and Up," however, Dreiser stressed his death wish. "Mentally and physically," he began that essay, "[neurasthenia] reduced me until at last, at one time, I was thinking of ending it all in some way which would be neither painful nor too disagreeable" (pt. 1, p. 1). Dreiser now indicated that this near surrender came when his funds had been reduced to a quarter and he faced eviction from his wretched room. Desperate, he wandered down to the East River. The ease with which he could find peace was indeed tempting. "The sight of the icy cold and splashing waters actually appealed to me," Dreiser now recalled. "It would be so easy to drop in. The cold would soon numb me—a few gulps and all would be over. All that was necessary was to slip down into this gulf and rest. No one would know. I would be completely forgotten" (pt. 1, pp. 14–15). Thus one of the most familiar episodes in Dreiser biography was born.

In Part Two of "Down Hill and Up," Dreiser exaggerated the dreariness of his early days with the railroad. Instead of revealing his comfortable living arrangements with the Hardenbrooks family, he now claimed that he had been compelled to live in a "poor section" of the community in "an old hotel and saloon combined." There he had occupied "a cheerless, barren room. . . . dirty and almost unfurnished—a chair, creaky iron bed and a wobbly, unsanitary washstand with a bowl and pitcher" (pt. 2, p. 5).

In describing the carpentry shop, Dreiser said little of his own duties, indicating only that his primary task was to carry lumber, manufactured furniture, and other items to and from a loading platform. What he did stress was the hopelessness of the laborer, who was tyrannized and exploited by management. The familiar cast of carpentry-shop characters was reassembled and given the names they bore in The "Genius." Their function was to exemplify the intellectual sterility and pitiful lack of imagination that characterized the world of labor. Like Eugene Witla, Dreiser longed to escape, as he saw his "golden youth by degrees slipping away" (pt. 2, p. 19).

This desperation set the stage once more for the Irish foreman, Mike Burke (again called Rourke). The description of Dreiser's first meeting with Rourke and his clerical duties upon joining the crew was taken almost verbatim from "The Mighty Rourke," but at that point Dreiser departed significantly from the earlier portrait. Instead of depicting Rourke's exasperated paternalism and concluding with the sentimentalized account of his injury and death, Dreiser stressed the foreman's zest for life. This hardy enthusiasm, so refreshing after the fear and sullen resignation of the carpentry shop, proved infectious. "I found after a time," Dreiser noted, "the spirit of the wild, yet genial Rourke, his love of work, his puzzled and inexplicable, and yet convincing love of life had entered into me, and I was wild to be as vigorous, as dynamic, as enthusiastic and yet as contented with things as they were, as was he" (pt. 2, p. 30).

As Dreiser now reconstructed the experience, he was inspired and began to work alongside the crew members. "I preferred to work at whatever the 'guineas' or 'wops', or as he always called them 'the nagurs' were compelled to work at, and do it gladly. . . . Also, single-handed, or with two Italians to help me, I would unload a half carload of bricks somewhere or an entire car of stone. . . . And with a dozen of them to aid me, I personally took up all the cobblestones in the square facing the depot at White Plains, and on my knees with the rest of them afterwards, found actual delight in proving that I could lay as good a road of vitrified brick as the next" (pt. 2, p. 29). The self-deprecation that had characterized Dreiser's earlier descriptions of himself as a laborer had been replaced by a certain pride in his accomplishments.

Though Rourke, ever the realist, reminded Dreiser that he was still an amateur when it came to hard physical labor, the exercise had salutary effects. He slept well, ate heartily, and found his self-confidence returning. Dreiser even wrote and submittted a poem for publication.[54] When it was accepted, he decided to return to his rightful place, the world of literature, now buoyed by courage and determination he had gained from Rourke. Ending his tenure as an amateur laborer, Dreiser vowed: "'This is the attitude and this is the man—and his policy and his viewpoint are mine from this day forth. I will not whine and I will not tremble, anymore, come what may'" (pt. 2, p. 43).

Hackwork though it was, "The Irish Section Foreman" added several new and contradictory episodes to Dreiser's career as a laborer. It was also the last published material based on his struggle with neurasthenia. Over the years he continued to discuss with friends and publishers a projected third and possibly fourth volume of his autobiography, variously titled *Literary Experiences* and *A Literary Apprenticeship*, but those books were to remain in the planning stage. As late as 8 March 1943, Dreiser expressed to Mencken his ambition to complete *A Literary Apprenticeship*. "I dream of doing it," he wrote. "It is a scream! Yet it only goes up to *Sister Carrie* (1900) and her fate" (*Letters*, 3:979). Apparently Dreiser had

---

54. Dreiser identified "They Have Nourished as Abundant Rain" as the poem he wrote and had accepted just prior to his leaving the railroad; however, Pizer found no evidence of the poem's being published before its inclusion in *Moods: Cadenced and Declaimed* (New York: Boni and Liveright, 1926). See *Theodore Dreiser: A Primary and Secondary Bibliography* (Boston: G. K. Hall & Company, 1975), p. 40.

forgotten the chronology of events or had reconsidered the scope of the third volume, for he again wrote Mencken on 27 March about his plans for the autobiography, this time including the *Laborer* experiences and elaborating on his near suicide.

I, myself, in my day have *cursed Life* and gone down to the East River from a $1.50 a week room in Brooklyn to a canal dock to quit. My pride and my anger would not let me continue, as I thought. And yet a lunatic canal boatman ferrying potatoes from Tonawanda to the Wallabout Market in Brooklyn did. Wanting me as a companion to accompany him on his return trip to Tonawanda, he stated as his excuse for his liberality or charity that he "thought maybe I was trying to run away from my wife." And my wife was in the west living on her parents while I struggled and starved on alone. To a guy with a total of 15 cents left and a $1.50 a week room to return to, this brought an ironic laugh and, in consequence, a change of mood that saved me from going to Tonawanda and instead—the next day—moved me to cross over to Manhattan Island with a new idea. But I will have to write *A Literary Apprenticeship* before you can learn all about that. [*Letters*, 3:980–81]

During the last two years of Dreiser's life he repeated the story of the Tonawanda boatman to biographer Robert H. Elias, thereby adding yet another episode to the *Laborer* accounts.[55] Aside from Dreiser's letter to Mencken, however, this episode never found its way into print. Only *An Amateur Laborer* was left to chronicle that period of his life.

An Amateur Laborer is a particularly valuable addition to the Dreiser canon, for it describes with uncompromising and verifiable truth the most tragic and humiliating period of his life. Never again throughout a long, turbulent career would he struggle so desperately to save his art, his self-esteem, possibly his life. As a story of courage and perseverance, *An Amateur Laborer* is in its own right a compelling narrative. More importantly, these experiences provided Dreiser with colorful and dramatic material that he drew upon throughout his creative life. As the years passed, his attitude toward his physical and emotional collapse changed, and his exact memory of the events faded. Also, the narrative demands of each derivative piece necessitated deletions or changes in detail, and the storyteller in Dreiser often yielded to the temptation to heighten the drama by embroidering or inventing episodes. For all of these reasons, Dreiser repeatedly stretched a fabric of fiction over a framework of truth. Many of these semiautobiographical pieces, however, have been accepted by Dreiser biographers, and thus numerous errors and inconsistencies mar accounts of this period in his life. *An Amateur Laborer* is clearly the most reliable account; its availability should do much to separate fact from fiction.

RICHARD W. DOWELL

55. *Theodore Dreiser: Apostle of Nature*, pp. 128–29.

Editorial Principles

An *Amateur Laborer* survives only in Dreiser's holograph manuscript at the University of Pennsylvania Library. This manuscript, which serves as copy-text for the present edition, came to the library in 1949 as part of a group of materials acquired from Helen Dreiser. The leaves were later laminated, and the manuscript was bound in loose signatures and laid into five fall-down-back boxes. The leaves were foliated and bound in the order in which Dreiser had left them. The *Laborer* manuscript is typical of Dreiser's holographs from the late 1890s and early 1900s. Much of it resembles the manuscript of *Sister Carrie*. The first 138 leaves are inscribed in black pencil on sheets of pulp paper measuring approximately 200 × 271 mm. The remaining 945 leaves are also inscribed in black lead, but on half-sheets of the same stock measuring approximately 142 × 223 mm. All writing is on the rectos.

It is possible to date precisely the inscription of some of the early leaves. They are apparently fair copies of earlier drafts and were prepared by Dreiser in the offices of the New York *Daily News*, where he worked as assistant feature editor of the Sunday edition from early January until early April of 1904. To give himself a smooth writing surface, Dreiser took a newspaper fresh from the press and used it as a backing pad. The ink was still wet, and mirror images of several headlines and columns of type were "offset" onto the versos of some of the early leaves. Two headlines are discernible: "STIRRUP CUP TO | SAMUEL GOMPERS" and "CHARLES FROHMAN | AS DOG RAISER." A search of the *Daily News* files reveals that these headlines and their accompanying stories appeared on page 3 of the issue for Saturday, 13 February 1904. The manuscript leaves were certainly inscribed on this date, while the printing ink was still wet. The earlier rough drafts were presumably composed a short time before. It would therefore appear that Dreiser began writing the *Laborer* in late January, or certainly no later than 13 February—only six weeks after leaving his job on the railroad. This deduction is important because with Dreiser, as with many writers, the farther he moved in time from an event, the more "imaginative" his account of it was apt to be. The dating of these leaves shows that Dreiser's experiences were still fresh in his mind when he began the *Laborer*. His memory was undoubtedly more accurate than it would be in later re-creations, fictional and autobiographical, of this period of his life.[1]

The first chapter contains a section, written in black ink, which Dreiser appears to have added to the manuscript at a later date, perhaps in 1913 when he showed the *Laborer* to the Century Company. This passage, a short digression on the nature of neurasthenia, may represent a later reflection by Dreiser on his illness. It seems to differ slightly in tone from the remainder of the chapter, and it may spring from a different set of creative impulses. One might argue that the passage not be included in the text of this edition, but the date of its inscription is uncertain, and there is no hard evidence necessitating its exclusion. The editors have decided to include the passage—an interesting and revealing one—but the reader should know that it may not have been part of the original draft of the first chapter. The passage appears in this edition from "Let me animadvert" at page 5, line 23, to "circumstances can guess." at page 7, line 27.

The most important textual decision facing the editors of *An Amateur Laborer* was whether to treat the surviving document as "public" or "private." "Public" documents, in current editorial usage, are those created by authors for public view and, usually, commercial sale—novels, poems, short fiction, autobiography, essays, journalism, and occasional writings. Such documents are usually presented in public dress: grammatical errors and misspellings in the drafts are rectified; misused words are corrected; reasonably consistent punctuation is supplied. The editor aims to present a reading text accessible to a relatively wide audience.

"Private" documents, on the other hand, are those that authors create with no intention of publication or sale. The journals, diaries, correspondence, and other personal papers of most authors are obvious examples; modern scholarly editors normally publish them with as little emendation as possible. Grammatical errors, misspellings, misused words, and slips of the pen are preserved in an effort to retain the private, unfinished character of the texts. Trial drafts and *ur*-texts are also sometimes treated as "private" documents and are published virtually without emendation, especially if they reveal information about the author's working methods or show him in process of creating later, finished, "public" texts.[2]

1. See James L. W. West III, "Mirrors and Microfilm: The Dating of Dreiser's *An Amateur Laborer*," *Manuscripts*, 35 (Winter 1983):5–11. See also the illustrations on pp. 198–99 of this edition.

2. Within the Pennsylvania Dreiser Edition, for example, *Sister Carrie* (1981) has been edited as a public document, the *American Diaries, 1902–1926* (1982) as private documents.

The surviving manuscript of *An Amateur Laborer* is composed of both "public" and "private" texts. Dreiser was writing the book for publication. There are twenty-four finished chapters totalling approximately 47,000 words; Dreiser wrote these chapters as a continuous narrative, and they follow one another logically, with obvious transitions from chapter to chapter. These chapters are "public" texts. They were apparently ready for the typist; Dreiser might have polished them a bit more before having them typed, but in the main they are fair copies of finished work. The remaining parts of the *Laborer* manuscript, however, are "private" texts. There are twelve identifiable chapter beginnings; a few of these chapters are nearly complete but most of them are brief false starts. And there is a great body of loose fragmentary material, most of it discarded work from the first twenty-four chapters or notes and trial drafts from which some of the later chapters would probably have been drawn. The incomplete chapters and the fragments together total some 36,000 words. These parts of the manuscript are working papers; they were not ready for typing, and Dreiser would have had to rewrite and recopy them before including them with his twenty-four finished chapters. They are also in much rougher shape verbally and syntactically than the completed chapters.

The editors of the Pennsylvania edition of *An Amateur Laborer* have decided to present the finished chapters as "public" texts. Orthographic errors are rectified and misused words corrected. Dreiser was very casual about punctuating, even in fair copies; often he simply omitted routine punctuation, assuming that his typist would supply it. In the main he seems to have preferred a free, open system of pointing; we have therefore added only such punctuation as is necessary for correctness or reader comprehension. A very few substantive emendations have been made for sense. These are recorded in the apparatus of this volume along with those emendations in punctuation that have an effect, however slight, on meaning. Other editorial emendations in punctuation are routine: commas and quotation marks are introduced in dialogue, periods are added to the ends of sentences, apostrophes are supplied in contractions, and so forth. A complete record of emendation is available for examination in the Rare Book Room of the University of Pennsylvania Library.

The fragments, on the other hand, are treated as "private" documents and are published here without emendation. To present them in emended form would be to misrepresent their character; they are not finished thinking or writing and should not be read or judged as such.

The fragments present other problems. As a body they are quite lengthy: some individual fragments are sizeable, others are of medium length, still others are only scraps. The fragments frequently repeat or echo material in the finished chapters, and sometimes they repeat one another. Part of the material in the fragments is of great interest, but much of it is not. In the best of possible worlds, financial and practical, one might include all of the fragments in an edition of An Amateur Laborer, but it has not been feasible to do so in this edition. We have also kept the user of this edition in mind: many of the fragments are so scrappy and reveal so little about the composition of An Amateur Laborer that they are almost beneath interest. We have therefore made a generous selection from these fragments totalling some 15,000 words and including all of the lengthy and significant passages that Dreiser preserved. All fragments are given in their entirety, even when such a practice produces repetitions.

There is no sure way to establish the order in which Dreiser inscribed these fragments. We have therefore arranged them by subject matter into five sections: the first deals with Dreiser's illness, the second with the Mills Hotel, the third (a nearly complete chapter) with his stay at Kingsbridge, the fourth with the workers at Spuyten Duyvil, and the fifth with his thoughts on labor. This ordering reflects the sequence in which these events occurred in Dreiser's life. Within each section the fragments appear in the order Dreiser left them, as nearly as that can be determined. Fragmentary sentences are introduced or ended with three ellipsis points. Fragments are separated one from another by heavy rules, and inclusive folio numbers for each passage are given within parentheses. This foliation is not Dreiser's; it was added at the University of Pennsylvania Library when the manuscript was catalogued, laminated, and bound. The foliation is given by box and leaf number: "I:118, 120" refers to leaves 118 and 120 in box I; "IV:16–21" refers to leaves 16 through 21 of box IV. Dreiser left most of these fragments in rough order at the end of the Laborer manuscript. A few scrambled sections were also included with the materials in box I. Dr. Dowell has reordered photocopies of the leaves and has transcribed all surviving texts. His verified transcriptions, which contain the passages omitted from this edition, are on deposit at the University of Pennsylvania Library.

One short but significant chapter, numbered "XXV" by Dreiser, is among the fragments at the end of the Laborer manuscript. This chapter is brief, and Dreiser probably did not think of it as finished. Yet evidently it was written to follow Chapter XXIV, which is complete, and it provides an appropriate ending, both in subject matter and tone, for Dreiser's account of his laboring experiences. For the purposes of this edition, the editors have decided to move the chapter from among the fragments to the end of the finished narrative and to present its text in public dress. The reader should be aware, however, that Chapter XXV was not finished enough, in Dreiser's mind, to be placed with the twenty-four completed chapters.

By presenting the finished chapters as public texts and the remaining materials as private texts, this edition reflects the state of the surviving manuscript. One can see Dreiser in the process of writing the first two dozen chapters of his book, attempting to continue, losing his focus and impetus, and finally stalling entirely. Such a presentation of materials, we believe, is faithful to the surviving document. *An Amateur Laborer* is unfinished work; we have not attempted to make it seem other than what it is—a regrettably incomplete but nonetheless fascinating document from the darkest period of Theodore Dreiser's life.

JAMES L. W. WEST III

An Amateur Laborer

The Case of the Author
A Record of Fact

CHAPTER I

Aꜰᴛᴇʀ a long battle I am once more the possessor of health. That necessary poise in which the mind and body reflect the pulsations of the infinite is mine. I am not overconscious. I trust I am not under so. All that is, now passes before me a rich, varied and beautiful procession. I have fought a battle for the right to live and for the present, musing with stilled nerves and a serene gaze, I seem the victor.

For three years preceding the writing of this statement I was a victim of neurasthenia. For that period I endured all the pains, all dreads, all the agonies of one whose mind is under a cloud. From me, as I beheld it then, and as I know it to be now, a world or given order was passing. I was about to lose consciousness of these things that collectively we call life. Thought failed me, reason failed me. I could not follow out a given chain of ideas if my life had depended on it. For days and weeks and months and years I seemed absolutely alone with a vast sea that urged and persuaded without explaining. I was to change but I could not see why. The wonder of it, the indifference of it, the inexplicableness of it, seized me as with an icy hand. I was afraid. I did not want to die.

The terror of this was augmented by the keenness with which I had previously lived. Up to this time I had enjoyed a vigorous physical and mental life. Youth was mine. Aspiration also. Such joys as the world had to offer were worth struggling for. I had grieved, of course, as all men do. I had railed at fate. Through it all 3

I had maintained a freshness and interest which bid fair to realize for me some of my desire. Then came ill health.

Those who have never experienced that misfortune cannot conceive what miseries may exist in it. I was a writer, but now my power to write was taken away from me. I could not think of anything to say or if I did I could not say it. Suddenly, as if by a stroke, I found myself bereft of the power of earning a living with my mind and was compelled to turn to my hands. These had never been trained in any labor.

In this crisis I paused and procrastinated, a thing which I sometimes think is the dominant note in my character. It could not be that I was really losing my power to express myself. That was a slight physical indisposition, a mental weariness. It would soon pass.

In this state I lingered nearly three years struggling against insurmountable conditions, planning, brooding, dreaming to return to the contest. During this time I traveled through Virginia, West Virginia and Delaware and finally went to Philadelphia where I lingered for six months, and until my money was almost entirely gone. Then driven by the absolute need of doing something whether I was ill or well, I came to New York.

I should say here that the metropolis had been and was now my only home. Here I had come, just ten years before, and had toiled and struggled for that personal recognition which I deemed so important. The streets and avenues were as familiar to me as those of my native village. I was as familiar with the sights and the sounds which I had once so ardently craved to share as if they were personally arranged by me—all the energy, all the wealth, all the beauty and power I knew, and the knowledge of it and of the fact that I might someday hold a position of power and fame in it, had been the thought that had urged me on and sustained me in many a weary hour.

Now however I found that I held a different attitude toward it. Where once the ability to struggle and in a small way to gain had been a delightful thing to me, now I was indifferent. What did it all amount to, I asked myself. What was the difference whether I rose or fell? In so vast a sea where generation after generation broke upon the horizon of the world, like the long inrolling waves of an endless and restless sea, what was I? A waif, a stray, a bit of straw, a breath of air. And if I succeeded, what of it? Supposing that I rose. Supposing out of this endless restlessness I was raised for one short moment on the crest of affluence, seen by the world as a doer of something, envied by some as the possessor of something—was it not as the preacher had long ago written, a vanity and a travail of the flesh? Truly I thought so.

And moreover I was weary. Insomnia had reduced me to the state where I was in actual physical torture. Introspection and lonely brooding had reduced me to the verge of despair. Sick, thin, illy equipped with clothing and still less the necessary comforts which aid one to struggle in sickness, I looked about me wondering what I should do, which way I should turn and in so doing, instead of realizing that it was change I needed, something to divert my mind from its old course, a new form of labor such as manual toil, I decided that I must do a little literary work—anything editorial, reportorial or special—to keep me alive and then wait. Meanwhile I hoped that my indisposition would pass and that without further damage I should be as well and sane as ever.

Let me animadvert here to some of the curiosities of neurasthenia, psychothenia and plain everyday commonplace insomnia. I remember one of the learned specialists whom I sought—a hard, self-centered, arrogant, active man who somehow in his alertness of manner and sharpness of eye reminded me of a crow or jack-daw, referring solemnly to my "psychic stretch," whatever that is, and indicating that there were periods in every life—at ten, at twenty, at thirty and so on—when something, an intangible rope of nerve force perhaps, like a tight wire, sagged and the result was this heavy nervous depression. Up in the stratum of nervous force, where by right of good health I belonged, all was serene, gay, unconscious—a buoyant, unreasoning tittilation and activity. Down here in a region where the universal force was just as valid no doubt, I was out of a place, being crossfired by antipathetic waves of some kind which gave me this sense of fear and the imminence of destruction. Be that as it may. It cost me fifteen dollars.

Another eminent specialist who by the way held the chair of nervous disease in a large university not so far from New York looked at me with a heavy, deprecatory gaze. He was a tall, bony, pale, whiskered man with a bluish-agate eye and rich black hair and beard.

"Yes, yes," he commented, his hands folded over his chest, his body comfortably ensconced in a faintly squeaky, black-leather-upholstered swivel chair. "I see. I see. The usual symptoms. The problems involved in connection with the central nervous system are very elusive—very. Now you have come to me just now complaining of pains in your finger tips and occasionally in your heart. Previous to this you say you imagined your hair was beginning to come out. No doubt it was. No doubt it was. I have a theory of my own, based on twenty years of study, that a condition such as yours can be reached by medication. Most specialists in nervous diseases would not agree with me and I would not try it in your case except with a full understanding on your part that I was undertaking a system of medication novel with myself. You say your appetite is abnormally large. That is a sure sign of nervous shock and under-average condition. You find yourself preternaturally exalted at times and then at others in the depths of despair. Try to overcome that as best you can by seeking amusing and companionable society (fancy me in my state, eagerly evaded by most) and go to the theatre as much as you can. Don't be alone. (But I was alone, due to the absence of friends, strangeness in a great city, lack of means to connect up socially and the like.) Exercise some and come and see me. Now I will give you this prescription which you should have filled," etc., etc. The opening fee in this case was ten dollars.

There were still other doctors. But neither their medicine nor their advice helped one whit.

Reader, did you ever suffer from insomnia? It is an interesting experience if carried to sufficient lengths. No merely temporary or undergraduate service in this respect will do. Your "psychic stretch" wants to be duly disarranged, and you want to be poor and eager and your means of subsistence invalidated by your sleeplessness. Then you will understand. Mine, which resulted in neurasthenia and which the doctors examining me for causes insisted must be due to shock—some secret excess of some kind which I would not reveal—was due to no such thing. For the physically powerful—inherently so—there is rarely any such thing as shock—unless one might call being hit by a locomotive a slight derangement of some kind. Mine was not due to shock unless the fact that I could not get along in New York as a newspaper man after I had done fairly well in New York as an author could be called shock. I was trying to write short stories and finding that I couldn't write them. I was trying to write verse and finding the muse was elusive. I was trying to earn even so much as fifteen dollars a week regularly and that was escaping me. I had no friends to speak of and no pull. I was comparatively young.

I sought in this crisis a little room in Brooklyn which came within my means. In the chill glow of a dying February day I crossed the ferry that runs from 23rd Street on the East River to Broadway in Brooklyn, and wandered about in the neighborhood which adjoins Fifth Avenue and the Wallabout wondering where I should find a room. Poverty was the guiding motive in this for I had but thirty-two dollars in my pocket and did not know how soon I should have more. I instinctively felt that I was doomed to weather a worse storm of want and suffering than I had yet experienced. How sadly I faced the prospect, only those who have faced poverty under similar circumstances can guess.

The neighborhood into which I had wandered was dreary enough. It was composed for the most part of old-fashioned three- and four-story brick dwellings formerly occupied by people of afflu-ence who had evidently led a comfortable existence here, but who had departed and left it to families who found it impossible to keep up the original dignity of the builders. There were old houses so large and dignified that one wondered at the wealth which had formerly maintained them. There were quiet, unassuming-faced residences which bespoke a comfort entirely beside the mark of show. For blocks westward there was a ruck of old tenements, stables, manufactories and docks filled with all sorts of hardworking, drinking, ignorant and dirty people as served to give the section a sombre and even depressed look. I remember one old home in particular, a large, square, brownstone affair with large, modestly ornamented windows and a distinguished flight of steps leading to the front door, which was the scene of nightly revelries—dances, parties, musicals and the like, entirely incongruous with its appearance. It had once been the residence of an exorbitantly wealthy sugar manufacturer who having wearied of the neighborhood had moved away. Now churches, social clubs and various society sets which did not have a suitable entertainment hall of their own rented this exquisite old mansion for their functions and filled it with a kind of gaudy clamor. It was a sad old neighborhood, redolent of the changes that men and neighborhoods and cities are subject to—the shifting, aging, wearying and decaying hand of time.

The room which I was able to engage in this neighborhood was a poor one. It was only found after much wandering and that in a spirit so desolate that I marvel now that I did not weep at every step. It was in a plain red-brick dwelling built, like most New York residences, upon a twenty-five-foot front of ground and rising to a height of four stories. It was upon the fourth floor, looking out through two small windows upon the street below and the adjacent corner, with its crossfire of traffic. There was a great angle of wallpaper hanging down from one corner of it, where the roof above had leaked, and from the door one could see that the floor visibly sloped. It had an old-fashioned, high-backed, round-topped wooden bed, a homely, round, folding-leaved table covered with a rough red cloth, a time-worn bookcase of black walnut, filled with a curious collection of religious and reference literature, and a single rocking chair that squeaked with every move. One small gas jet lighted the room from a side wall and a mantle of an unequipped and never-intended-to-be-used fireplace held the only ornaments of which the room was possessed.

I confess that it did not impress me favorably. Too keen a

judge of life and of nature not to realize the makeshift and decline which it all represented, I looked at it only with a melancholy eye. "To be compelled to come to this," I thought. "To be forced to dwell in a neighborhood despoiled by the filching hand of time." Here was a woman robbed by fortune of everything that was worth having, who was still dividing the sum total of her meagre living with all and sundry who should come and pay her a suitable pittance for it. She was tall and bony with a dark head of hair, a sallow, bony face, and keen, piercing black eyes. The first day I saw her she had on a solemn black dress over which was fastened a white apron, and she explained to me the points and merits of the room with a cautious, somewhat exacting and at the same time religious demeanor which denoted long contact with difficulty and roomers. Somehow she reminded me of a cat in her quiet undemonstrative way and I thought, "Well anyhow she looks as if she would not bother me, and the room is clean." At that I took it, for two dollars and fifty cents per week.

CHAPTER II

THE installation of my effects was a matter of small labor. They consisted of a trunk, a dress-suit case, containing much of everything but a dress suit, a hat box and a wooden soap-box containing books—which latter did not arrive however until a week or two later having been lost in transit from Philadelphia. After paying for my room I made a long trip by ferry to Roosevelt Street and secured my dress-suit case from the Liberty Ferry Station where I had left it. Then I journeyed back and having put it in place and secured a key sallied forth to find a place to dine. It was my idea to get some place where I could get two or three meals a day, preferably two for four or four-and-a-half dollars a week so that I would be free to take my lunches where I pleased. In doing this I had the hope that I would be able to get some literary work to do, and that, despite my sickness, by taking my leisure I might be able to do it. I was foolishly continuing my faith that without any change I might regain my mental strength. Failing that, and before my thirty dollars should give out I hoped to find some manual work which would pay my board. If I did not—but I dreaded to think what should befall me when my money was gone.

The boarding house which I did secure offered me an opportunity to continue adjacent to one of the handsome old churches which still adorned this neighborhood, a boarding house which I believe laid claim to being the best in that vicinity. It was a fine old brownstone residence, still in good condition and sublet, in rooms, to a dozen persons of more or less local standing—a doctor for one, a preacher for another, a musician, a superintendent of schools and several business men, as I found in my two or three weeks' observation. There were women also, a number of curious, to me seemingly self-deluded, thoughtful souls—the kind who talk music, literature and art in a soulful, insistently conventional way—and one or two really pretty girls who were charmingly self-conscious and human. Together with the landlady—a fair, fat and forty widow possessed of a crafty laugh, they made a curious combination never wholly uninteresting to look upon.

This boarding house offered me admission at the rate of four dollars and fifty cents a week for two meals, or five dollars for three—the meal which they considered being worth only fifty cents if you did or did not take it, being the lunch. I figured that I could better afford to take the two meals as I did not know where I would be during the day, and that for the lunch I could sometimes do without it if my cash ran short. Two meals would sustain me. For the rest, if I were exceedingly hungry I could buy a sandwich and a cup of coffee somewhere for a dime—a fact which I thought over carefully, for money was exceedingly important to me. Having secured these things I settled down to what I considered a grim but not a hopeless struggle to regain my lost health and prestige, which owing to my long illness I deemed to be pretty well dimmed.

The effort I made in this respect I now consider to be one of the most foolish and hopeless of my career. As I have indicated before I was in no mental condition to do it and could not accomplish any saleable results. All I could do was to sit there and try, which was the most wasteful disposition of mind that I could make. However I was in no mood to see this. I had always made my living that way before. Previous to my nervous breakdown I had been able to earn at the lowest thirty and at the highest two hundred dollars for an article from my pen. It had not been quite two years since I had left New York, high in the favor of a small circle of those who might honestly have been called my literary admirers. I had successfully finished one novel and had begun another and my literary standing with a few editors who had purchased my material was of the best. That after two years of traveling and supposed successful literary composition I should now find myself unable to write a line or to earn a living by my pen seemed ridiculous. I thought that it really could not be and hence decided to try again.

The period of my trying covered just fifty-six days in all. During that time I tested every misery to which want can compel. Day after day I rose to a futile effort to produce some literary article which I might sell and night after night I lay down to a sleepless couch, the ravages of worry and brooding keeping me wide awake. During the time that I was not trying to write or trying to sleep I walked the streets brooding over my lot, the difficulty of my situation combined with my great physical weakness causing me to develop the form of cowering fear which I have described—the fear of contempt, of pity and of heaven knows what all upon the part of my friends, my acquaintances and the world in general.

The attitude which I bore toward the world during this trying period now strikes me as interesting. Having no money except what was barely sufficient to pay my individual expenses, and very meagre ones at that, and no clothes except such as had become more or less threadbare during a long period of enforced idleness, I was compelled to wander gloomily about, the end of my sufferings being a perpetual problem with me. How I should obtain anything to do which would sustain me, once my little cash in hand had been used. What form of work I should look to. How I should be able to manage once I did secure it—all these were interesting problems.

During this time I reflected on the curious problem of my existence in this world which some of us do not trouble about and few are but rarely forced to consider. I did not hesitate now to look the facts in the face, to canvass my own weaknesses and inefficiency and to trace out the steps by which I myself had been part contributor to the misfortunes which now seemed to have overwhelmed me. Why had I not been more economical, I asked myself. Why not more conservative and careful? I had had money. I had had health. Yet here I was poor, friendless, practically helpless and in so wretched a state of health, mentally and physically, that I was bordering on insanity. My fault, my fault, I echoed to myself repeatedly—and then I would begin to catalog the facts by which I could either resist or admit this conclusion.

The nature of my arguing in this instance had a curious touch of inconsistency about it. While admitting that I myself was really wretchedly to blame for all misfortunes, which now assailed, and while constantly condemning myself as a person wholly unfit to ask favors of either Providence or society, I yet deemed, indeed felt perfectly sure that there was an element of fatality about my troubles, that they were foreordained—worked up by invisible and adverse powers and that I would simply have to submit and wait patiently for a turn of the tide, or battle on and obtain nothing for my efforts until the adverse powers did choose to cease annoying me.

The curiosity of this reasoning or rather feeling, for I could not base it upon anything reasonable in the catalog of facts at my command, was that it was involved with a still larger conception or idea and that was that all life—animal and vegetable—was bound up, so far as their individual conditions were concerned, in a great overruling Providence—fate, power or star, under which they were born, by which they were protected, with which they were compelled to suffer or prosper accordingly as this particular force, Providence or star was successful in the larger universe of which it was a part. Whenever it was unsuccessful, worried or harassed, by other large forces, powers or stars, of which it was but one in many, they were unsuccessful, worried or harassed. Whenever it was prosperous they were so. An integral, though, of course, infinitesimal part of it, I conceived myself to be—involved as any microscopic portion of our own body is involved with it, and suffering because it was suffering, and for my particular deity the times were out of joint.

This form of reasoning or feeling had a very peculiar effect on me. It caused me to accept my situation rather philosophically at times and to feel that any attempt I might make to do anything at all, outside of a mere effort to keep body and soul together, would be fruitless. At the same time it gave me a somewhat wavering faith that my misfortunes would right themselves and that I would eventually come out whole and unharmed. That it would not serve to gratify my immediate wants or to save me from the approaching calamity of homelessness and hunger I was in great fear and for this reason I did not choose to trust to it entirely nor to diminish efforts in the search of something to do, by which I could sustain myself until the tide should turn.

My efforts in this line were of a wavering and uncertain character at first. Although I was really anxious to find something to do and perfectly willing to do anything which I could, the fear which I had of becoming the mark of someone else's humor was a powerful deterrent. What would people think, was the question that I asked myself over and over. What would the average clerk who did the perfunctory run-and-write work of an office think of me, if he should suddenly see me appearing in the office of his superior hat in hand, a tall, dignified and rather thoughtful person as I conceived myself to be, asking for work? And what would the other persons who command in the world of labor and who have such a sneering contempt for indigent intelligence think? I should be looked upon as a freak by intelligent underlings, a failure by self-sufficient older ones—a poor broken-down author who was more to be pitied than blamed, but a rather inconsequent and useless person at that.

And if I went to the shops for something to do, those great

black factories whose walls I had often surveyed with a melancholy and poetic interest over the wide reaches of the city, how would I be received? Would they, the real workers and toilers of the world, find a place in their midst for me? What could I do that would be valuable in a shop? Run a machine? I had never had any experience in that line. Drive a wagon? I did not know how to handle a horse. Lift and bend and carry? Yes, but would my slight strength be of any value in a shop or yard where as a rule strong men were required? How ridiculous, I thought. And what a waste of time. They would not have me. People were expected to keep their places in this world. Once they had made their bed they were expected to lie on it. I had made mine. All my life I cultivated my art as a writer and now behold I could not do anything. I was like a fish drawn out of its native water to die in the air. Untoward conditions—things different from those to which I had been accustomed—would prove my undoing.

How well I reasoned in this situation I will not say, but well or ill I found myself confronted with the necessity of doing something. My literary labors were not progressing any, and my aimless wanderings were not bringing me any food. Shortly after my arrival in Brooklyn I went over to New York and consulted with the different editors, some of whom approved of different ideas I had, but nothing came of that, as I could not write. Then I went to the different newspapers in New York and Brooklyn but the majority of the editors would not even see me. I did get in to the editors of the *Evening Sun* and *World*, but they had nothing. The editor of the *Standard-Union* of Brooklyn told me frankly that he would not hire me because I was too bright—besides I was too good for the position. One of the editors of the Brooklyn *Eagle* came very near giving me a place as a correspondent out on Long Island, at fifteen dollars a week, only he didn't. Everywhere in my own field I met with the most disturbing setbacks which I felt to be due partially to my own sense of failure and partially to that ruling fate which was making me suffer. I did not seem to be able to surmount it and daily crept back to my room haunted by the most dreadful sense of impending disaster.

My condition at this time struck me as truly pathetic. I used to come back from my breakfast in the morning, where I saw myself eating away my little substance, and look out the window wondering what I should do next. I had no friends to go to or none that I felt that I could go to, for I was exceedingly proud. A brother of mine was a publisher in New York. Another was an actor. I had a sister who had a comfortable home in Washington Square and another who had a pretty flat in Brooklyn. Nevertheless I felt that I could not turn to them. What would they say, I asked myself, knowing me as a fairly successful writer and one who had never done them any favors, should I come knocking at their doors and saying that I was in want? Impossible. I felt that I should rather die first and I confess that I faced that alternative with considerable equanimity.

Concerning my literary friends and acquaintances I did not feel so sensitive. I had never needed to borrow money in my life and never wished to do so but now I felt that I would be willing to gamble on my future if I could, to the extent of obtaining advance royalties or payment for work that I should do when I regained my health. I made a special trip one day to one of the great publishing houses but the manager, who knew me as a successful special writer in the past, looked upon me with anything but favor, and I myself saw the wretchedness of my proposition after I had made it. I walked all the way back from New York to Brooklyn, a distance of seven miles, that day to save my nickel and decided that I had not learned the lesson too dearly.

CHAPTER III

THE approach of actual want was such an insidious thing that I really did not perceive how far I was getting into the depths before I was fairly caught and unable to extricate myself. I had always been accustomed in the past to make some arrangement with a magazine or publishing house to do some work which would pay me fairly well and this hope was now all the time acting like a will-o'-the-wisp leading me thoughtlessly over the meadows of idleness and meditation to the slough of despond. Day after day I would get up and sit at my desk a little while feeling that this morning surely some ray of inspiration would arrive, but finding that it did not I would get up and go out, wandering around and saying to myself that if I could but rest a bit it would all come back to me. I was not really sick in the sense that anyone is prostrate in bed. I could walk and run and laugh and read, but I could not write, and worst of all I could not sleep. This latter difficulty was gradually undermining me though it did not seem as bad at first as it did later. I used to go down to the water's edge of the East River, which was only a few blocks below me, and there in the neighborhood of the Brooklyn Navy Yard and the Wallabout Bay sit and enjoy the wonderful panorama which the river invariably presented. It seemed to me that when I came within the vicinity of these great warehouses and factories, with their tall black stacks that gave the water's edge so varied and picturesque an aspect, I could lounge and dream forever. Not to worry, not to haste, not to be caught in the great turmoil of the city beyond from whose distant shore came subdued echoes of the clangor and strife that was always there— that seemed heaven to me. I sat and looked into the soft green waters gurgling and sipping about the docks and the stanchions below me and listened to the crying of the boats, until my heart was full to overflowing with it, but alas my purse was empty. And that was where the love of beauty undid me.

The approach of actual want was such a terrible thing how-ever that whenever I thought of it distinctly I would get up and return to my room, or would hurry out into the streets almost in a cold sweat, saying, "I must do something." Frequently I would start out and after walking the streets trying to think of some business that would likely offer me a means of making a living I would fix my eye on some distant shop and say to myself that when I came to it I would go in there. I would walk toward it, my feeling about life and labor wonderfully heightened for the moment, but as I drew near a cold fear of inability would lay hold of me. What would they think, I would begin to ask myself. What could I do in there? Sometimes I would see someone looking at me from one of the windows, a man or girl, or from the houses about and I would say to myself, "Pshaw, they see me coming. They think I am someone who is above that kind of work. They will not believe that I need it and turn me away. And how will I look to them anyhow?" And I would turn away carrying myself as if the thought of that sort of labor was the farthest thing from me imaginable. Or I would stand about and parley with myself, weighing the pros and cons until I had harrowed myself into the belief that I would not be acceptable. Always I would think of my own work, and hard as it was, would contrast my appropriateness to that with my inappropriateness to this and then I would weaken and hurry away. Dozens upon dozens of times have I stood outside of all sorts of institutions wondering, debating, saying that I was unsuited to it or the business was unsuited to me and in the end turning back disconsolately to my room, there to brood and worry over my fate.

The remembrance of this weakness has proved a great wonder to me since. I am not naturally afraid to face people and these sentiments do not as a rule rule me, but I was so rundown nervously that I did not have my usual feeling about things. Sickness had apparently made a coward of me.

As these reflections did not relieve my situation any I would after a night of sleepless tossing usually pull myself together again and make another effort. Once in these early days I went to a great sugar refinery far down on the water's edge where many a day I had stood looking at the wagons and the men and the evidence of industry inside and wondering at the complicatedness of it all. (What a mystery the life we lead is. How strangely we divide this problem of sustenance, how narrowly some of us work in small dark corners all our days and never think or at least never attain to the heights of our thinking.) On this day however my mind did not busy itself with this larger spectacle. I was anxious to get something to do there and I was wondering how I could persuade the foreman or the management to accept me. Once I had read a long account of the labor struggles of another writer who had dressed himself to look the part of a laborer and I had always wondered how he would have fared if he had gone in his own natural garb. Now I was determined or rather compelled to find out for myself and I had no heart for it. I realized instinctively that there was a far cry between doing anything in disguise and as an experiment and doing it as a grim necessity.

However I went in after hanging about for some time and asked for the manager. As I expected he was busy but a clerk who came over to me wished to know what my business was. I told him I wanted work. He looked at me in a quizzical way as much as to say, "You?"

"What kind of work is it you wish to do?" he asked.

I tried to explain as quickly as I could that I wished to do any kind of work, manual or mental, but he did not seem to understand me. "You couldn't do the physical work here," he said. "All our clerical positions are filled. We don't change very often."

"Is there something you could give me to do out there?" I said, motioning with my hand toward the great dark mass behind.

"Nothing at present," he said. "We are not taking on men at this time of year. I'm quite positive you couldn't do the work if you had it. It's very hard."

He turned with a brusque manner to his work again and I fell back abashed. His loud voice had attracted the attention of others, who looked at me curiously. I felt as if he might have been a little more quiet and a little more considerate, but I found here as everywhere what seemed to me the old indifference to the underdog. People do not see—I said—they have not the faculty to grasp what it means to be the other man. Otherwise they would never do such things.

My next effort was in search of a motorman's or conductor's position, a place I had long had in mind as I was sure it was something that I could do. It was not a thing that I could get quickly, for I knew that unless I had a "pull" or could bring some extraordinary pressure to bear I would have to go through the usual

formality of enrolling my name somewhere and then waiting patiently for my turn to be called. I had vivid dreams of forcing my
way into the office of the president, who I conceived to be a man
who could tell by my appearance that I was not exactly of the
ordinary run of men, and who on my putting the matter before him
would understand and give me something to do. I went down to the
section where this great railroad building was located but as usual
when I reached there my heart failed me. It was an hour before I
raked up courage enough to go in.

This building was a mass of little offices devoted to different
phases of the street railway and when I looked over the immense
directory painted on the wall I could scarcely tell which office it was
at which I wished to inquire. I saw the name of the president posted
as being in room one hundred and something, on the fourth floor,
but now my idea of going in and talking to him looked awfully
foolish and hopeless to me. The idea of intruding on a man with
endless affairs weighing on him and the financial end only of the
great company before his gaze struck me as exceedingly useless. He
would have nothing to do with me. All he would do would be to
refer me to the department which handled such cases as mine and
they would not dare to make an exception. It seemed impossible
and yet I went up.

In an ante-chamber I was met by a clerk. As I expected he
told me the president was busy and asked me my business. When I
explained to him, he looked at me curiously also and said the
president never attended to such details—that I would have to go
to the regular department, mentioning the number. I saw how
hopeless it was of making a boy see—an inexperienced youth who
knew nothing of the world, and went away. I could have written an
essay that morning on how nature meets want with inexperience
and pain with those who cannot see. Blind! Blind! Blind!

The office of the Superintendent of Something, who hired
men, was on the floor below and there I went. It was a small room
filled with motormen and conductors who were there being measured for new suits or answering to complaints of various kinds. All
of them looked at me with curious eyes as I came in, for I was still

comparatively well-dressed, and some of them stood aside in so deferential a way that I felt that I was sailing under false colors. I went up to the counter where the official was standing and stated my business. When I had come in he had looked at me with so much consideration that I felt he mistook me for someone who had important business with him. When I finally explained that I wished to know where applications for positions were made his face changed immediately and he told me in brusque tones where to go. I felt like an imposter slinking out for it seemed to me I had in some indefinable way misrepresented myself to him. I had not turned out to be what he took me for.

This phase of my reception discouraged me greatly but I went down to the little office on a side street near the East River, in a one-story red brick building, where I found a room containing a few old benches and an inner door marked "Applicants" but no persons. A sign hung up over a window informed me that those who wished to register should come between the hours of seven and nine A.M. on Tuesdays and Fridays, which I confess was a great relief to me. I had anticipated another such ordeal as I had just gone through and the mere fact that it was postponed was something. I turned on my heel, temporarily relieved from the ache that inquiring under such conditions gave me, and promised myself that I would come back on Tuesday. I then wandered about saying that I must look for something elsewhere but, being out and moving, I did nothing. It was the old story of the previous days. I could not find the heart to go in.

That such a quest would soon prove disastrous I was constantly seeing and yet I could not get anything. I went back to the newspapers—they had nothing. I came over to New York and thought to put an application in over there, but I did nothing but walk the streets. On Tuesday I returned to this little office again, desperately clinging to the fatuous belief that having managed to go so far, something would come of it. I had dressed myself carefully to make as good an impression as possible but when I got there, or rather in the vicinity of it, I was sorry that I had done so. At a distance of three blocks I saw quite a crowd standing around so early as seven o'clock and in the vicinity, at distances of from one to two blocks, other individual stragglers, who impressed me at once as people who like myself were anxious to register but were ashamed to go up. They were a little better dressed than those who were gathered about the door—not so strong-looking and not so coarse. They pretended to be doing anything but heading for this particular institution though one could see by their averted glances that that was just the thing they were trying to do. I encountered two or three of them three or four times in a radius of as many blocks and each time they exchanged that shamed look of understanding with me, which convicts one of ulterior designs. It was all very painful.

What interested me on this occasion was my own wretched attitude. For the life of me I could not summon up sufficient courage to join that crowd. Three or four times I went toward it, getting as close as the corner, but each time I would see some of those at the door looking up toward me and I would say to myself, "They see what I am coming for," and would turn off. Once I did go down absolutely determined to stop and take my place among them, but the keen conception of the difference between them and me which flared up in my mind as I approached drove me on by. They were so young, most of them, so raw and so inexperienced. They looked at me as though they thought I was some critical business man or other citizen merely passing on my way to my office. They had such sharp eyes which seemed to say, "Now let us see what he does," that I could not bring myself to stop.

For this feeling—vanity or weakness as it may seem to some, I have now no excuse to offer. I will say that the difference I felt was not based on a sense of superiority—far from it. I was only conscious that I was out of place and they knew it. It was more like the case of an old man who would like to play with children on their own basis, but who has lost the how of it.

My first visit to this registering room was a failure as was my second, but on the third time I managed to go in and put down my name, which brought me nothing. I left my address, the chain of which has never been broken, but I have never heard a word.

Meanwhile my money was getting lower and lower and I was

in danger of being shortly turned out in the street. To obviate this I began curtailing my expenses by giving up my four-and-a-half dollar boarding place and taking my meals anywhere I happened to be, a move by which I managed to save something like two dollars a week as I ate less and frequently went without lunch or dinner altogether. Then I changed my room having for some time had my eye on a little hall bedroom which adjoined mine and which when I came there was occupied by two young men—mechanics—how, I have never been able to conceive. It was certainly one of the smallest rooms I have ever been in, a mere cell, six by eight feet, which contained a small bed, a diminutive table, a vile smoky oil stove and a red and yellow chintz curtain fastened up on the wall at one side which was used as a wardrobe. Naturally it contained only one window and that a small one which looked out into the dreary street, and the dark hall on which it opened led back to a dingy closet of a room which was used by an old lady cripple, who lived, cooked and slept in the room adjoining. She was a pitiful creature, stout, gray and rather helpless, who used to go in and out once or twice a day and get her loaf of bread or her can of milk. She was always silent, and sometimes when her door was open slightly I would see her sitting in there, her hands folded on her lap and her mind evidently lost in thought. How she stood it I often wondered for it seemed the acme of desolation to me. No one ever seemed to call on her.

This little room as I say had been in my mind however for some time as the landlady had told me that the men who occupied it were going to move. I had thought that if things got much worse I could move into that temporarily though I confess I did not see how I could stand it. I once inquired in a roundabout way how much they paid her for it and she told me one dollar and a half. When my finances got so low I began to think that if I could get it for a dollar or a dollar and a quarter that I might find it advisable to take it.

This idea seemed to work its own fulfillment without my saying much about it. I had announced about three weeks before, when I thought that my money would soon be all gone, that I might have to move away in a short time and this set the cautious landlady to thinking. She came to me herself one day with the suggestion that if I were intending to go I should fix a date so that she might persuade the two young men to wait and accept my room. As I did not know that I had more than a week or two to remain, my cash was so low, I gave that time as my limit and then she suggested that I move into the little room and let her have the larger one. The thought of saving enough to continue my existence even here for a few weeks longer was so great that I readily accepted. I took my trunk and stored it in the dingy closet in the back part of the hall and hung my various necessary garments under the red and yellow chintz curtain. Then I put my papers and few books on the very little table and shut the door which closed me in the smallest room I have ever lived in in my life.

CHAPTER IV

THE period of my occupancy of this chamber proved unquestionably the dreariest of my life. It combined the various qualities of sickness, want, friendlessness and limitation which go to make up the lowest states of life, this side of suicide or death. I do not know that ever in my previous existence, even in my most despondent moods, I touched the level of permanent gloom which now characterized my daily life. It was as if a pall or grey cloud had settled down about me and obliterated all the traces of a surrounding life. To me as I viewed it then, the world seemed a great dark sombre sphere in which all life was being maintained by a sad and unutterably revolting struggle and whenever I looked into the eyes of men I saw only anger, unrest, selfishness, greed. What did it all stand for, I wondered. Why did the creative force will it? Why not preferably gas and elemental fluidity, static and indifferent, than this constant turmoil and worry in which so few could get food and clothing, let alone the flashing tinsels of joy that were forever being waved, Tantalus-wise, before the hungry eye. A spider weaving its net in a window ledge; a house fly caught in the toils of some untoward paste and slowly dragging out its life in a vain effort to obtain its freedom; a bug caught in the water or trampled to death on the floor—oh how I gazed at these spectacles of misery, feeding my cankered soul upon the heartlessness and brutality of it and asking myself over, and over and over—why?

And then the unfortunate ignorance of man as I deemed it. What a stupid and yet a stupendous thing. If nature were wise, if anywhere there eixsted that vast intelligence which makes for happiness, why conceal it? Why let man toil up through the long ages from protozoan simplicity to complicated manhood suffering all the agonies of war, pestilence, famine, fever, and yet conceal, conceal, conceal the better way? Who had it? Why did He not reveal it? What purpose was served by so vast, so grim, so merciless a strife? There was none. It was all a great cruel mystery—a vast, shapeless, interminable and horrible unrest and now at last it had me in its clutches, it would not let me go and I was to sink back—sick, weary, dissatisfied—in the gloom and mystery of it. What was I to do? Which way to turn to escape? As I looked, stared into the mist and rain, I often questioned whether I wished to or not.

And worst of all my insomnia seemed to be racking the soul out of me. I do not know when I ever suffered such tortures. Night after night I used to lie in my little uncomfortable bed thinking, thinking, thinking through the long stretches of silence, and wondering what was to become of me and how I was to get well. Sometimes I would rise and look out on the street where the night lamps were burning and wonder why I could not sleep. What was the art of it? I once slept. I could remember distinctly how as a child I used to lie down so tired that my eyes fairly drooped with weariness and I would sleep so restfully. Other people were sleeping. Through the partitions that divided this little room from my old one I could sometimes hear the heavy breathing of the men who were now occupying it, but I could not sleep. All I could do was to lie there or go through exercises which I had been told would produce sleep, and then lie down, intensely fatigued, only to get wide awake again. It seemed sometimes that if I did not get sleep pretty soon I would go mad. But I did not.

In addition to this a strange half-wakefulness seemed now to come over me, in which I was neither fully awake nor yet wholly asleep. All day long I used to go about wondering, dreaming, turning corners as if I did not know where I was and forgetting half the time what I was doing, and in this state I seemed to lose consciousness of that old, single individuality which was me and to become two persons. One of these was a tall, thin, greedy individual who had struggled and thought always for himself and how he should prosper, but was now in a corner and could not get out, and the other was a silent, philosophical soul who was standing by him watching him in his efforts and taking an indifferent interest in his failures.

Sometimes he seemed to be no part of me at all—a creature that had nothing to do with my wants and needs. I marveled at him, thinking this was truly the oversoul in me—this was the thing that would last and be extant when I in my corporeal form was no more.

That such constant brooding should have a serious effect on my physical appearance you cannot doubt. I had been losing flesh for some time, having come down in the past three years from a normal weight of 159 pounds to 140, but now I dropped still lower and was soon at the place where I weighed but 130. This for my height, six feet, was light weight indeed and I felt as if I had no strength at all.

Coupled with this my nervous system grew weaker and I was now subject to the most distressing hallucinations. I used to imagine, when I was lying in my room at night, that there was someone in it—a person perhaps or a spirit whose footfalls I would hear and whose slow approach frequently caused my hair to rise on end. Then a hand—I frequently felt a hand—would come softly reconnoitring my pillow, as if to see whether I was asleep, and I would jump up and look about me, terrified and cold with sweat. Then I would light my lamp and gaze out of the window or read. Sometimes I would leave the light burning and lie down again only to toss until it was nearly morning.

I experienced about this time also the most remarkable physical variations that I have ever known. My nerves, particularly those in the tips of my fingers and toes, began to burn me badly and I would have something like little fever blisters at the ends of them, when the irritation was long continued. Also I began to have the idea or hallucination that angles or lines of everything—houses, streets, wall pictures, newspaper columns and the like, were not straight and for the life of me I could not get them to look straight. I also had the strangest desire to turn around, as if I must go in a circle whether I would or no, which was nothing more nor less than pure insanity.

These things were of course a great distress to me. I knew they were unnatural and that I ought not to pay any attention to them, yet I could not help it. Always when I was sitting in a chair I would keep readjusting it—trying to bring myself into correct alignment with something, and at the same time would keep turning to the right until I would be quite turned around. At the same time if I were reading a newspaper I would keep turning it from angle to angle trying to get the columns to look straight, a thing which they never did. Always when I was walking I would look straight ahead, wondering at the obstruction which fixed objects like houses and trees offered to a direct progress and feeling an irresistible desire to be rid of them or to go right through them.

That anyone in this condition was in no fit state to look for work—to impress anyone who was looking for help with his capabilities as a servitor—must be apparent to all, and yet I continued to look. People do not hire other people out of charity and when they want anyone they want someone who can render effective service in some capacity. I knew that I could not, unless it were in the line of a conductor or motorman, brakeman or driver of some kind, and I tried for these positions. I finally in my desperation summed up courage to go in anywhere but it seemed too late.

People did not like my appearance. They seemed to take it for granted that I was physically unable to do anything and passed me by.

In this crisis I do not know what would have become of me if it had not been for the presence of the sane, conservative oversoul which I have mentioned, the other person who sat in judgement over all that I did and seemed to brood apart like another person, over my fate. This other person was a more courageous individual than I—cold, immovable, indifferent—for he did not trouble over my worries in the least. Always he was with me when I stood outside shop doors and hesitated to go in, when I waited at the ferry wondering whether I could afford the few pennies that it would take to carry me across, when I wandered from magazine room to magazine room trying to get a place, and when I returned to the bleak room, and he laughed at me as I stared hopelessly out the window. He was at my bedside during the long hours of the night when I tossed and tumbled and he rose with me in the morning only to dog me patiently through another day. He was not sorry for me. He was not ashamed of me. He seemed rather to look upon me as I looked upon those flies I had so often seen caught in the paste of a paper, or the moths that I watched turning about my lamp and burning their wings. He was not exactly cruel. He was not kind. He seemed to look upon me as some poor, disturbed and rather distraught creature who really did not deserve much to live and who did not really deserve to die. He was very wise and sane and I had great faith in him.

What the presence of this superior consciousness meant to me I can hardly say. It was my refuge and my salvation. He would not go crazy. In all probability he would bring me through. Something would happen.

In this room too I saw the worst stretch of my money troubles. Here it was that my last twenty dollars dwindled to fifteen and that to ten and that to five and yet I did not give up. Once when I was down to one dollar and I was thinking of storing my trunk with it and walking out empty-handed, a check for ten dollars, the fruits of an old poem that I had resurrected and sent to one of the magazines, arrived and I began to live again. Another time when I was down to three dollars the remembrance of a man who owed me ten dollars on a loan which I had made him four years before, and which I had long since canceled out of pure good nature, came into my mind and now I looked him up and demanded it. Then I began curtailing my food items even more than I had, eating one meal a day in a restaurant or none at all, and buying apples and bread and milk and living on them until I felt that I must have another cooked meal again. Finally I got down so low that my diet consisted of bread and milk, which I bought in a neighborhood store, and which I used to slip out in the evening to secure. There was a large and a famous market at the end of my street called the Wallabout where I used to wander and brood and where I managed to pick up a potatoe or an apple which had fallen from a wagon, with which I served to vary my diet. The apple of course I would eat on the spot but the potatoe I would take home and bake on my little oil stove, eating it, when cooked, with my bread and a little salt. Once in a while I used to buy an egg and boil it in a glass but they were dear and I could not afford to have many of them.

It is curious to what stretches a human being will sink and not give up. Low as my condition was physically, mentally and financially I never once truly yielded. People rejected me and I thought I was like to die but I would not give in. I had a faith that something would happen, that someday I would come out of it, and in this faith I lingered. I had a watch which though heavily engraved with my initials, I thought I might pawn, though watches so engraved are not wanted sometimes, but I would not do it, saying that I would be destroying my chances to do anything if I began to part with the things that made up my personal appearance. I had a hat box which cost me six dollars at one of the big stores but I would not think of selling that either. I had some books also, but I thought I would wait until the last penny of my resources was gone, before I would part with anything that I had and then no doubt storing them and walking out empty-handed. Perhaps I would not perish, perhaps someone would take me in—a farmer, or someone. I proposed to wait and see.

One of the most curious notions I had at this period was to see what the attitude of the representatives of organized society would be towards a person of my calibre and condition. Once when my first supply of money was about out and I thought I should not be able to get any more I decided to go and see what they would say. I waited until my money was nearly gone, all but three dollars, when I went down to the main offices of the society and presented myself as a candidate for assistance, taking my place in the ante-chamber of the principal assistant's office where a host of distressed-looking foreigners were sitting. I waited patiently until all had had their turn and then went in, only to receive that peculiar greeting which indicated that I was supposed to be coming for any other reason than poverty. However I sat down and laid my situation before the woman, who became decidedly interested. She was curious to know all about me and I concealed no details. She became very sympathetic and asked me what I wished to do and I told her that I wished to get something to do—preferably before my three dollars gave out. I told her that I had not eaten a cooked meal of any kind in two weeks and that I was decidedly hungry.

"This is too bad," she said, looking at me with wide, sympathetic eyes, and she got up and went into another room, from which she presently returned to say that the president wished to see me. I went into the latter's office and was greeted by a small, sallow, very shrewd-looking little man, who looked at me with dark, calculating and piercing little black eyes.

"Now just sit down and tell me who you are and all about yourself," he said. "What is it you want?"

I told him as I had told her that primarily I wanted work, but after that I might wish to make some arrangement by which I might draw enough money to live on, until I could draw my salary, though of course I was willing to give my watch and whatever else I had, as security. I explained also that I would do this now providing I got something to do right away, but that if I waited I would not even have those things to fall back on. I explained just how it was that I was in this position, and how well I had done previous to getting into the position.

"Why don't you go to the magazines and try to borrow some-thing on the future work you may do?" he asked.

"I did try that once," I said, "but I would not do it again and I wish now that I never had." I then related my experience.

"Have you tried the newspapers?"

"Yes."

"Why don't you go to the big stores?"

"I have been," I replied.

"Well, have you no friends?"

I explained that I had two brothers and two sisters and he seemed very much relieved by this. "You might go to them," he said, and we then fell into a long discussion of the ethics of family relationship. He knew, he said, what pride was. He knew how members of families usually looked on one another. Neverthe-less it was a great mistake in such a crisis not to go to them. I was doing myself an injustice.

"Why go to them," I asked, "rather than to the agents or representatives of the body politic to which I belong? Is it not as much the place of society as a whole to provide an opportunity in such cases as mine as it is for my brothers and sisters? I have done nothing for them. I have done my share towards sustaining society, both by working, giving in alms and paying my taxes. Why should not society do something for me?"

He did not know, but arguments on such points were useless. Society, as far as his organization was concerned, was not very effectively organized to meet the overwhelming demands upon it. They had no money or very little. They had no positions to offer. He could give me a letter or two which might secure me temporary work at a very low salary until I could find something else, but he would not be sure. As for aid until my salary should fall due they really had no money to give, and anyhow under such circumstances I had best look to my relatives or the people of the publishing world who knew me. He then gave me the letters.

I shall never forget how useless and ridiculous this whole conversation appeared to me. The whole organization of society seemed magnificently arrayed against charity and I was at bottom not sorry that it was so. I did not see how I was to come out but I knew that I had no real claim on society. I took the two letters he gave me and thought how the name of the charity organization label on them would look when presented by me. Then I thought what an attitude the recipient of them would naturally bear toward me, even if he gave me something to do. I had a horror of that. I tore them into bits and flung them in the gutter.

CHAPTER V

THE tearing up of these letters made a distinct impression on me. I knew it to be an act of vandalism in that it separated me, in my direst need, from a possible opportunity of bridging over my difficulties but strange to say I had a horror of charity even in that difficult hour. I did not care to be looked upon as an object of charity and I there and then decided that if I could not get a living any other way than that, I would not get it at all. I decided to go over to New York and look around, and so I walked over the bridge and up to 14th Street where I stood about wondering what I should do. On the way I had stopped at three newspapers and two business houses but they did not want anybody.

As I was standing at 14th Street it clouded up so darkly and the sky looked so lowery that I thought I had better go back. Then I thought of my sister living in Washington Square and decided that I might go down there. I had not seen her in three years. I had not exchanged a letter with her in four months—not since I had been living in comparative comfort in Philadelphia. I felt a strange hankering to see what she was doing. They were so comfortably fixed.

I decided after a time to go down there though I realized I did not look very good. My clothes were not any longer new and my shoes were not good, but still I felt that I presented a reasonable appearance. She would not be able to tell whether I was hard up or not and as for giving her an inkling I had not the slightest idea. I proposed to tell her that I was doing very well indeed, but that at present I was suffering from nervous prostration, which latter I consoled myself was the truth. She would not think anything as she had always known me as one who was thoroughly capable of taking care of himself and much preferred to do so.

The apartment which they occupied was a truly handsome affair in one of the large corner apartment buildings facing the park and its windows from both the east and north provided a most delightful view. It was arranged in the shape of an L with large lounging and sitting rooms and had about it that air of comfort and moderate luxury which those who have a little money can provide. Mr. B——, her husband, had been a fairly successful business man in his day and his idea of home comfort was always a solid one. He had handsome if not rich furniture and the hangings, the flowers, the music and the books always testified that here nothing was wanting to at least a comfortable life if one were inclined to be satisfied with enough.

This home had never struck me as luxurious. Hitherto I had often called here and thought it middle-class compared to some but now on this day when I called it seemed the height of the delightful to me. I walked through the hall after I had kissed my sister, looking at the rugs and the hangings and feeling, in spite of myself, that it was wonderful. To be able to live like this. To have a handsome home and flowers and books and music. To have plenty to eat. These after all in the last analysis, were the things that were essential.

Naturally she was glad to see me but surprised at my appearance. On the instant she demanded to know where I had been and what I was doing. "You're not well are you?" she asked, and I explained that I had been suffering from neurasthenia or nervous prostration.

On my announcing this I was overwhelmed with prescriptions by her which were certain to have a good effect in certain cases. For one thing she recommended rich milk and eggs with a touch of whiskey in it, and I thought of the last egg I had bought the week before. Then she recommended Panopepton, a remedy that costs a dollar a bottle, and wanted to know why I didn't go and see her Doctor Somebody, whom I knew to be a well-known physician who charged a very well-known fee. Lastly she demanded why I didn't come up to stay with them at a house they had in the country, and for which they were about to leave. Already she was getting some of their things together and they would begin seriously to pack on the morrow. This struck me as a very sensible and kindly proposition but I had no money to get there, and anyhow it was not a thing that could be taken advantage of for several weeks. I thought how I might overcome my fear of discovery of my state and go, but somehow the thing seemed impossible to me and I let it pass.

While we were talking Mr. B—— came in and then there were more explanations. He was a shrewd and intensely common-sense Irishman who had a fund of wit. He always liked me and this night he insisted on my staying to dinner. How was my book getting along and when would I come back to New York to live? They both thought it strange that I should go over to Brooklyn.

I stayed that evening and ate the first hearty meal that I had eaten in weeks—ever since I had left the boarding house at which I had originally boarded. There was a soup, a fish and a roast of beef, and I was gratified to see a salad and a dessert. It was but a normal dinner with them as it had formerly been with me, but now I kept contrasting it with the bread and milk that I was daily eating—a third of a loaf of bread with a third of a bottle of milk in the morning for breakfast; a third of a loaf of bread with a third of a bottle of milk for lunch; a third of a loaf of bread with a third of a bottle of milk for dinner, or supper, as you please with now and then a hot roasted potatoe or an apple if I could find one on the street. It seemed a sharp contrast.

I confess I listened to the conversation that was carried on with a touch of cynical interest. They were talking of the things that made life interesting to them,—the success of so and so, the failure of so and so, the usual trouble of getting good seats at theatres, the wretchedness of having to move and the like, all of which seemed like talking to a dying man of athletics to me. Theatres I thought, travels, clothes. Pshaw. What are these to the real things of life—the hunger, the nakedness, the cold. Outside here are men who like myself are slouching along not knowing where they are going to lay their heads tonight, and these people talk to me of theatres. I arose shortly afterward to go.

"What is your number?" she inquired when I started to go. "I want to write you when to come."

"414 Willow Avenue," I said, giving a wrong one.

I walked out and she called out an affectionate wish for me to come back on Friday before they should leave. Then I made my way down the stairs and out into the street, and then in the shelter of a neighboring doorway, for it was blowing up brisk and chill, I stood and looked at the windows. What a blessed way to live. When you had money how easy it was to sit and talk of doing things—to philosophize, but when in the words of a slang phrase that was then very popular you were "down and out" what an obstacle even the payment of a fare presented. For the want of a few dollars to pay my fare and keep up appearances I was to be debarred of the opportunity of taking a rest in the country. For the want of a few dollars, I was kept from giving my right address, so that they might come and see me; for the want of a few dollars I was, this night, standing outside my own sister's door, rundown, haunted by a horrible apprehension of sufferings yet to come and facing a long, lone walk to a cheerless room, where I would lie and worry about enough to eat. Truly my situation seemed to me to present a strange commentary on life and I began my journey Brooklynward in a gloomier spirit than ever.

My walk home that night or rather to the ferry, where I was compelled to pay three valuable cents for a passage, was a very unfortunate one for me. It had been raining but the wind had shifted to the northwest and it was blowing a very hurricane of cold. The wind whistled and the loose things of the city rattled and creaked and I had a hard time keeping my hat on. The latter was an old one, comparatively well-worn, but a serviceable one at that, and the only one I had. I had been treasuring it very carefully as

I did not know where I was to get another one. I walked along holding it with my hand and making a difficult progress against the wind when at the corner of 23rd Street and Fourth Avenue, just where the new subway, there building, presented the most compli- cated and subterranean appearance, a sudden gust of wind whisked it out of my hand and up into the air, and my hat was gone. I looked around and up in the air after it, peering vaguely into the night, and searched the sidewalk and the street between the open- ings, and, finally in my desperation went over to where the watch- man who was guarding that section of the subway was warming himself by an open fire and asked him if he would not help me look for it. He—a little old Irishman, with a most wrinkled and dissatis- fied face, looked at me in the most quizzical and indifferent way.

"Ye've lost yir hat ye say," he demanded just as though my bare head did not attest it.

"Yes," I said. "It fell down in the subway I think."

"Yah think," he said, rubbing his hands over the blaze but never moving. "It'll be a foine time ye'll have findin' it. Wait a bit. I'll go down and see."

He went off somewhere and stayed what seemed to me an interminable time. When he came back he had a smoky old lantern which he carried indifferently, and with which he descended into a hole opposite the way from us, disappearing into what looked to me like a shed below. When I went across the street to look in the hole where I fancied it had fallen I saw that he had not come over there at all and after a time realized that he was not coming. He had gone down in the hole but that was all. When I went back after ten minutes I found another watchman, who informed me that the first one had come up and gone home.

"You'd better come back and look in the morning," he said, also with a rich brogue. "There be many hats lost here in the night. Yer'll not be findin' it I'm thinkin'. The men usually picks them up and wears them."

I stood there bare-headed in the cold and sharp night wind well nigh beside myself with wrath and grief. I do not know when in life before any situation ever distressed me quite so much. Weak and run-down as I was I was afraid the chill wind would give me pneumonia, and poor as I was—I had exactly three dollars and thirty-one cents in my pocket, I did not see how I could afford to buy another hat. If I did so, and it cost me more than two dollars, I would not have enough money left to pay my dollar-twenty-five room rent in advance on Saturday which meant to me, that I must vacate the room. If I paid as much as two dollars I would be thereby expending all my spare change reserved for food, and then though I would have a hat and a room, I would have nothing to eat. I thought of the morrow and how it would feel to walk out empty-handed then, and I became somewhat horror-stricken. I felt as if I were surely being pursued by some malign fate that had my ultimate destruction in view and in my desperation and despair I gave myself up to the most awful feelings against life and nature. Driven and hunted as it seemed to me by every petty force in life, I turned with uncontrollable defiance. Let the winds blow. Let the sky rain. Let the night grow cold. What did I care. I would buy me a hat. I would expend my last money for one and go home. Tomorrow I would pack my trunk and leave it in the woman's care. Then I would go out into the street and see what the world would do to me. I would not starve—that was one thing sure. I would break a window or commit some deed that would give me an opportunity to publicly demand an opportunity to work. I would show this untoward fate how little it could rule me.

And then as I eased myself this way the old, oppressive, disheartening sense of the vastness of it all crept back on me. Who was I—what, to talk of defying life, the elements, society, nature. Me, a frail, sick little vessel compounded of water and a few chemicals raising my hand against a vast world of waters and a universe of chemicals. Me, a miserable little bark drifted this way by chance, by a tide that never thought once of any one bark or of all barks, but only itself—and mayhap not even itself. Me, a petty straw in the wind that today was and tomorrow would not be. How could I? Of what avail to do so? Who heard? Who cared?

Never in my life was the vastness, the indifference, the desolation of the world so terribly impressed upon me. It seemed now, as

I looked at it face to face, as if nothing but absolute resignation could cope with it and that I could not do anything but be resigned. To let it beat me, to let it drive me to and fro. To let it spit in my face and not to make answer—that was the way, and that to fight it, to defy it, to hate it and assume not to care, did not make any difference to it at all. It was vast, it was indifferent. It was incompetent to feel. I was just a flash of it, a facet. In all the waste and endlessness I was nothing. Only chance could avail and maybe not that, and yet chance might. I might. How incomprehensible—how maddening it all was.

I went to a hat store after due reflection, driven by the cold wind, and looked around for a hat. It occurred to me that in most of these stores I had seen little woolen hats or traveling caps, which sold for seventy-five cents or a dollar, which would answer my reduced needs. I found a brown woolen one which did not look good on me but which fitted me, and this I purchased to my satisfaction for fifty cents. Then I turned toward the ferry, wondering how I could go around anywhere with such a hat. It made me look like a freak.

CHAPTER VI

THE week that followed was a bitter one for me. In my tiny room that night to eat my bread and milk and still to feel that strange duality of person which I have previously described. I also suffered from wakefulness just as much and in all other ways my state was just the same, only now I knew that it was coming to a climax. On the Saturday following my visit I paid my usual one dollar and twenty-five cents for room rent in advance and found that I had just one dollar and fifty-three cents left all told. I sat down on my little bed to figure out how this was going to last me and discovered that by paying ten cents each day for milk and bread and spending nothing for carfare or ferry tickets I would have just eighty-three cents left to walk out into the world with on the following Saturday, if I went. If I cut out my lunches and made the loaf and bottle last for those other meals, as usual, I could save twenty cents more. This would give me one dollar and three cents on which to begin anew or in other words to have my trunk removed to some store house and stored, and my way paid to Manhattan Island, for I intended to go there. After my long illness Brooklyn seemed accursed to me and I was anxious to get out of it. I recalled the number of my house—113—and thought that some of my ill luck had something to do with that number—so superstitious was I. Besides I felt if I stayed there much longer that I should not even have ferry passage and then I should have to walk all the way around by the Brooklyn Bridge, which, from where I was located, was a good seven miles. I decided that I did not want to do any of these things—that I wished to get out of Brooklyn at all costs forever, and I decided that I would do just as I planned. Then— inconsistent—I went out as usual to see if I could not find some-thing to do and as usual did not find it.

It was a dreary week. I tried the old sugar refineries and coal packets along the water front. I went into my favorite market—the picturesque Wallabout, and asked at a wholesale bakery. I went to the watermen who have the canal boats, those queer little barges that go all around from Quebec and Buffalo to Scranton and Philadelphia, and asked if they would hire me. Many of them were getting ready to sail or *mule* as one should really say, for they are mostly towed by mules—to Quebec and Montreal pending the opening of navigation, and I fancied if I could get on with one as driver or any kind of a helper that it would do me a world of good. For three or four days I haunted these little inland water-ways asking this one and the other, but I could not quite connect. Three or four men owned their own boats but they wanted stronger men I fancy—men whom they could order about. They stood in awe of me. One of them insisted on thinking that I had money, and after refusing me work offered to carry me as a passenger for seven dollars a week. Then he expatiated upon the beauties of the trip.

Another told me plainly that I was too refined. All looked askance at me when I asked for something to do and I had to give it up.

The grimness of this to me was that it was the climax of a series of incidents that had been constantly revealing to me the wretchedness and inadequacy of my character. Why was it, I asked myself, that I could not impress these men with my willingness and fitness? I was not a lad. Were a pair of glasses and a wise look then such a bar that no ordinary man would have anything to do with me on account of them? Must I forever be feeling that these people who met me with refusals felt the inappropriateness of my coming to them and shunned me accordingly? Every one seemed to see or to insist that I was cut out for something better and that their work was unsuited to me. I think if ever the literary life, and the curious ability to examine the characters and motives of people, seemed accursed to me it did so then. "Talk about a man being able to go out and find work!" I exclaimed. "Let anyone tell that to me again. Some people can—when they are fitted to it, and not otherwise."

The approach of Saturday night or Saturday morning was punctuated by two events which made a marked impression on me. One was the arrival of a letter from my brother Paul which invited me to come over and see him, a request which I knew at once had been prompted by my sister for he visited there with her and the letter had been addressed to the wrong number I had given. It happened that the number I gave was a part of the same post-office district as that of my correct address and this latter had been pencilled on the envelope by the postal authorities and the letter forwarded to me. I saw from the wording of it that some inkling of my condition had been given him for he invited me to come over and see him, a thing I felt that he would not do, unless he knew that I ought to see him. We had quarreled over little or nothing a few years before and although I knew him to be the best of brothers and a man who had done more than all the rest of us for my mother and father, and for each one of us individually, yet in my vanity and self-sufficiency I had always looked at him askance, thinking that he should come to me. He was a celebrated song writer in his field and a successful publisher as well as a popular man-about-town in

New York but I had consistently avoided him and he in his natural resentment perhaps had kept away from me. So now I put his letter in my pocket saying that he above all others should not see me and went my way.

The second event was a message by a negro orderly from the battleship *Indiana*, to say that my brother-in-law, a young lieutenant in the Navy, had arrived in the Brooklyn Yard a few days before and having learned of my presence in Brooklyn through one of the magazines where he had inquired, now wished me to dine with him. This young lieutenant was a manly fellow and an ornament to his profession and I admired him greatly. He had but recently married and I had entertained him and his wife in Philadelphia, but because I knew him so well and because I had always appeared to him to be in better circumstances than I was now I was now most anxious that he should not see me in this small room. I felt myself fortunate to have been able to head his orderly off on the stairs and give him an answer before he reached my room, but after he had gone I realized that I was in a dilemma. I had no dress suit. The business suit I had on was really not satisfactory enough but would do and the hat I now wore was something awful. Three or four times since I had worn it street boys had commented on its appearance, and the people who met me all looked at it askance. I used to slip along trying to wear it, as one of my friends had once said of a very small and unbecoming style of straw hat which a season's fashion imposed upon him, "with an air of conviction"—but it would not do. It was ridiculous and everybody knew it. Myself most of all.

It may seem ridiculous, in connection with so serious a situation, to emphasize such little details but I can assure you that they grew on me greatly in importance and difficultness. For all my weighty philosophizing in the past I could not get away from the conventions. Some of us protest. The majority of us live sanely enough, but in every state, high or low, we find ourselves bound by the little things and we either accept them or suffer the consequences. I was suffering mine—unintentionally however.

Now however it was wear it or nothing and I decided to wear

it. I did have a frock suit and silk hat stowed away in my trunk but this seemed so inappropriate for a dinner that I donned my hat and went around. As of old he received me with the utmost cordiality and introduced me genially about, while I, for my part, looked forward with an almost painful delight to the opportunity of once again eating a decent meal.

As in the case of the previous dinner at my sister's, this one on the battleship touched me in the same way. I looked at these young officers about me, all handsomely groomed and well-nourished, and commented to myself on the way they had reached their positions. Most of them were the sons of good families who had seen to it that they had entered the Navy because it was an honorable and rather distinguished profession. They had been groomed in all the tactics of good society as well as those of war and were fit emblems of that social ease from which I was now so much a thing apart. In spite of what I had always deemed my natural sanity and toleration I now found myself brooding over the fact that they were provided for for life and were constantly moving about in an atmosphere of good manners, good clothes, good food, while I was poverty-stricken and hungry. Had they ever been hungry? Had they ever been cold? Did they know what it was to wander the streets half-dead from loss of sleep or ask at shop after shop for something to do, without getting it? No, they did not. They knew nothing about it and again I turned away in mingled wrath and sorrow.

Not at them. Mercy no. I did not put the blame upon any one little human being, or any swarm or mass of perishable mortals who would have their day or their hour, good or bad, but upon the Cause—that grim insistent Cause that willed life—or if it did not will it, as I sometimes doubted, still was it. A great moving infinite mass that had life in it and death in it; health in it and sickness in it; joy in it and sorrow in it, but that did not care. Variety was all it seemed to want—difference—and it might just as well have willed us all joy as pain—or could it? There I was back to the horror of the negation again.

I went home from that dinner brooding over this; wondering if they noticed how run-down I looked; wondering if his orderly had told him what a poor place I lived in, and wondering whether I should sleep that night.

To say that my weariness, my physical pain, the dread of the future and my depressed mental state constituted a horrible physical combination for me is but putting it mildly.

CHAPTER VII

THE following Friday, but two days later, my financial doom was so apparent that I could no longer deny it. Worry as I had, this long-dreaded conclusion had now approached and I had but one more day to go before the end would be upon me. Twenty-four hours. "This time tomorrow morning," I said, "I will have no place to eat and no place to sleep. I will have no place to go. What will I do then? Will I walk out in the country to a farmer's door and ask for aid? Will I break a window and get arrested? Will I apply at a police station, or the New York Charitable Bureau? Will I go to my brother's or my sister's? I will not. Then what will I do? I know that I shall not be able today to get work by asking for it. I do not propose to starve. What shall I do?"

As of old a dread terror came over me and I rose up and made one more desperate effort. With the fear of a real disaster impending I made a canvass of all the newspaper offices in Brooklyn and New York and several shops and factories by the way but to no purpose. I went to four different publishing houses. Although I had about abandoned the idea of convincing anyone that I could do labor, I still thought of the street railways and I made one last effort at the main Metropolitan station in New York, where a stout, ruddy brute of a man received me with the most rough-and-tumble address.

"What is it you want?" he called, when he saw me looking through the wire of the cage within which he was working.

"I want to see if I can get on the Metropolitan as a motorman or conductor."

"You?" he said, looking me up and down as if he were astonished.

"Yes, me," I replied defiantly.

"Well come around Monday. We don't receive applications today."

"Monday! Applications! Where will I be when my application is acted on?" I thought and turned wearily out again. As I was going however I paused to witness a most vigorous scene in which a drunken motorman, with three or four cuts on his face and a black eye, was laid off for a week for not reporting for duty on time. He claimed he was sick and the man who had been talking to me, said, "Sick like hell. You were drunk. You're drunk now."

"They are the people to get along in the world," I thought. "They can stand it. What does he care. What does anyone care so long as he is rugged and hardy." Then I thought of the awe these same people stood in of mind, of show, of so many illusions of which I was not the victim, and I did not know. To live was the thing however, rugged or frail.

That night I walked back to Brooklyn most weary and hungry. I stopped at a bakery where I had been accustomed to buy my bread and bought a fresh loaf which I carried away with me under my arm. As I was going down the street I said, "My last loaf," and tried to feel the significance of it but in spite of it all I couldn't. In spite of me I felt rather a feeling of relief as if the worst were over. A storm like this could not last forever. I was not dead and I was not going to die tomorrow. I would leave my trunk and grip here and go to New York, where I would look around and get something to do. Something would turn up. I ate my bread with a little salt and went to bed. That night I slept a very little, and the next morning I began packing my grip and my trunk and by ten o'clock I was all ready to leave.

The condition of the weather in which I was leaving and in which I had been living during the past few weeks had been one of reviving springtime. The weather had not been very cold—in fact it had been warm most of the time, with an occasional gray or rainy day, and a night of chill winds put in between. The flowers and grass had not been growing very fast, but there was evidence here and there that a luxuriant crop of foliage was about due, and any very really warm day may result in a great burst of green. About the city's streets, people had been walking without overcoats for some days and altogether the promise of the time was quite encouraging.

In this finish to my Brooklyn experiences I do not know what spirit of prophecy possessed me but I had a different idea of the outcome of my situation. I was not going to have the hard time I thought I was. I put a few letters from publishers and people of note in my pocket, solely to identify and verify my claims to a slight distinction, and with the remainder of my loaf and my salt done up in a paper started out. I did not know where I was going but I took the ferry and landed at 23rd Street, where I stood in the sun gazing about, wondering what I was to do next.

It was a most perfect day. All the way across the river I had been leaning out over the railing admiring the green salty water tumbling under a fresh wind and the gulls—the wide, white-winged gulls, soaring above it. How they poised. What ease they had. With what grace they wheeled and turned. "And they live," I said. "They struggle and fight like we do. Unquestionably they go hungry at times and die. But what a spectacle. I should not mind any state in nature so long as I had my consciousness and life."

Then I turned to the city. There it lay with its towers and spires and tall buildings. What magnificence. What difference. If one only had the key, the friendly word, how easy it would be to obtain a competence there. I had done so. Thousands were doing so. It did not exactly depend on fitness. Many a man not so fit as I was rolling in luxury. It had been given him. He had been born to it. Somebody had got him a position. And yet they talked of earning your bread.

How silly. In nature no such rule held as earning anything singlehanded. Each one was favored or discriminated against before he began. I was favored. I was given to write and no one had ever taught me. It came to me. Another was given to shine as a beauty, or a wit, or a financier. I had known a boy who had made a million at twenty-two. How could they talk of each one making his way, earning his distinction. As if the battle were equal. Nonsense.

And then I thought of another side of the question. How many there were to care for. How full every nook and cranny of nature is with a great mass struggling to live. You could not look anywhere on earth, in the air, under the waters, but you encountered a great mass of some form of life seeking to live. Nothing was wasted. Throw out a crumb—a bird would get it. Kill an uneatable animal, thousands of insects would pursue it. Drop your old clothes, some beggars would seek them or would go cold for the want of them. Everything was in demand. It was only a question of getting hold of the means of grasping something with a strong hand and keeping it; of having something which the world would buy— beauty, wit, strength, muscle—anything which nature provides and yet does not provide generally, and there would be no question of poverty. The most saleable I thought would be either beauty or wit, but of course I had neither and no means of procuring anything else.

I walked along, after reaching the New York side, thinking of these things and wondering momentarily what was to become of me when I thought of the Charities Society again. I had not given much attention to this idea since my first rebuff, but now that I was literally a penniless wanderer on the street I thought that New York's charity system might at least provide me with a night's lodging or a recommendation to some corporation employing labor, providing I should be willing to take it. Poor as I was—literally not knowing which way to turn, I was not at all certain that I would accept anything but was merely turning the charity organization over in my mind as a possible way. I finally reached 22nd Street and Fourth Avenue, having come through the "back way" of 22nd Street, and stood at the corner where the charity building stands and wondered what I should do. It wanted still a few minutes of twelve, and the place was not yet closed, as it would be in a few more minutes, this being Saturday. I looked at the building. I looked at the streets where people were already making for the street cars and depots, to get out of town, and wondered where I should be by the morrow. Could I get anything to do between now and night? Could I get anything to eat? I stood there hesitating until the few minutes remaining between me and the opportunity of appeal to the charity organization had passed, and then I realized that it was too late, and walked idly away.

In my stroll up the street another idea came to me, however, which I had not had before, and that was that I might appeal to the New York Central Railroad Company, the towers of whose depot I could see irradiating their presence ahead of me, and see if it would not give me something to do. An organization like that employed a great many men. The unskilled laborers were not doing anything which, if worse came to worst, I could not do. I thought of the General Passenger Agent, a man who made himself known to literary people by reason of his interest in literary matters, and decided that my appeal should be made to him. He liked writers and boasted of his acquaintance with some of them. I would go to him if I could get in to see him and state how I was situated. It might be that he would give me something to do. Accordingly I went up to the depot and after a time succeeded in locating his office.

The office of the General Passenger Agent, as I found, was located on the third floor, amid a veritable tangle of hallways which presented only ante-chambers and waiting rooms to those who were not initiated. I went into one of these where I was greeted by the invariable office boy who wanted to know what I wanted. I told him I was a writer and that I wished to see the General Passenger Agent, giving him my name. He went away but came back immediately to say that the Passenger Agent was out but his secretary would see me. Presently the latter came, a small, dapper, neatly-clothed man, who inquired very graciously what I wished. This time I did not say "work." Instead, I put on the air of a superior being and told him that I wished to explain my object. I told him that I had been in poor health and that I wished, in order to recuperate it, to obtain some form of outdoor work, preferably manual. Mr. —— was known to me as a man who was interested in literary people. Was it not possible that he would aid me in this matter?

The secretary doubted. There was no work outside of the mere picking and shoveling to be had and that was left to the foremen to provide as it was needed. Did I have any references? Was I known to Mr. ——? I was not but I showed him a few recent communications from publishers and others which seemed to make a marked impression on him. He invited me in, gave me a seat and heard me out with deference. When I was through he told me that he could not provide me any clerical position—those went by merit, the recipients always beginning as boys at the bottom and working up, but that if it were a mere matter of manual work—well, he would see. Mr. —— might give me a letter to Mr. F——, the Chief Engineer, who would arrange with me. It was a very interesting project he thought. The work was hard but it might do me good. He remembered another literary gentleman, a friend of Mr. ——, who had gone into a logging camp on a similar errand, supposedly through the kindness of Mr. D——. He was progressing finely.

This attitude was very interesting to me. It re-emphasized what I have always known: that to those that have—or seemingly have (the world is not discriminating)—shall be given, although I would not like to have said that the particular portion of the world represented by this gentleman would not have given me the place because of my necessity. You cannot always tell that. Hitherto however I had not received any consideration on account of my need and I considered myself fairly entitled to the doubt. I told him I would be glad if he could arrange it for me and he told me he would see what he could do. Would I come back in an hour? I would, and did, wandering about in the interim, highly excited about this sudden turn of affairs, but not knowing how it would come out. In an hour, exactly, I took my place in the antechamber, only to be received graciously and a letter handed me without further ado. I took it and went out in the hall where I stopped to read it. It simply informed Mr. F.—— that the bearer, Mr. Theodore Dreiser, "a writer and author," was desirous of obtaining some form of outdoor labor at which he could recuperate his health. He was troubled with neurasthenia and could not sleep. A favor to him would be a favor to the gentleman whose signature was affixed. It was that of the General Passenger Agent, without any *per* or anything else. I took it and hugged it to my breast.

CHAPTER VIII

To say that I was highly excited and gratified by this turn of affairs is but putting it mildly. I was fairly assaulted and overwhelmed. I took my letter and hastened, almost breathlessly, to the other office, a hall's length away, where I stood with assumed dignity and renewed courage while another conservative office boy carried my letter to the Chief Engineer, the person to whom my letter was addressed. That person did not come out, but the office boy did come back presently to say that I was to take a seat and that the Engineer would see me. Soon after, a clerk came out and went over the letter with me, explaining that his superior had no connection with such things but that he would give me another letter to another gentleman who would see that I got what I wanted. This other gentleman was the Engineer of Maintenance of Way, with offices in an entirely separate building, and he it was who had charge of all the work connected with the employing of men in a manual capacity. I should go to him, which I did.

This other gentleman, as I found when I reached him, was a very distinguished light in his own sphere although not quite as high as the Chief Engineer. He had, as he naively told me, thirteen thousand men under him, and could send me anywhere from the woods of Maine to the mining regions of Pennsylvania, or the plains of Ohio. He was a thin and pallid man, with a large, dark eye, a sensitive, firm mouth and coal-black hair, and looked very keen and artistic to me. He wanted to know at once whether I was a friend of Mr. —— and when I told him no, that I had appealed to him by reason of other connections, he seemed to be effectively moved by it. He told me that he marveled at my temerity, reached for a framed map and pointed to the various divisions of the road, discussed climate and labor conditions and wondered why I should choose to take such a radical step. "Why don't you try the Whitely Exerciser," he said. "I use that in my room every morning," and when I explained that I had tried it, without effect, as I had, he added with an innocence that had a tail of humor to it for me, that he usually found that a few weeks at a summer resort gave him all the strength he needed. He talked also of the hardness of the track worker's life and stated emphatically that he would not let me do it. "You can't," he said. "It may look easy to you from a car window, but it is very hard. You must give me a day or two to think of some suitable place for you. Suppose we put it over until Monday."

I said "Certainly," for I could not say anything else, and he bowed me out. When I was out in the fresh air of 42nd Street I wondered what it was that had created this evidently profound impression. The mystery of "attitude" and personality was greater to me than ever.

Now that I had the promise of a place however, I was really no better off than before, although I was greatly relieved mentally. I had laid aside my bread and salt on entering the General Passenger Agent's office, putting it on a window ledge until I should return, but when I went away I had forgotten it and now when I came back for it, it was gone. Some janitor or floor-sweeper had picked it up and I was without anything to eat. I turned and walked down Fourth Avenue thinking of the closed Charities Society and of the police station but unable to say how I should make out. The day was fine, the air bracing, and there seemed nothing for it but to walk and wait. I was very hungry and as you may believe, indescribably weak. I wondered truly how I should do the work when I got it.

In this crisis of course I thought of my watch but I had never put much faith in that. It was not anything that anyone else would want for it was very heavily and deeply engraved with my initials and the date on which I had purchased it. I had once asked a jeweler if that would not affect the sale or transfer of it even to a pawn broker and he had said, "Of course. But that is a thing you will never want to do anyhow." And I had thought so at the time.

Now however I took it out of my pocket and looked at it. It was a handsome watch, thin, neatly decorated and set in a closed case. It had cost me one hundred dollars. How foolish I was ever to have had my initials put on it. I looked around wondering if I could not get something on it anyhow.

While I was walking down Fourth Avenue I saw some lettering on a window which read "Provident Loan Association." During my investigations at various times in the past I had learned that this association was especially designed to aid those who were too poor to be left to the tender mercies of the average pawn broker. They were to be protected by it in that they were to be given loans on things which pawn brokers would not ordinarily loan on—trinkets and the like, the marketable value of which was not large. Now I wondered why I had not thought of this place before and after due deliberation took off my watch so as to have it in my hand and went in.

The place was not as painful as the average pawn shop would be to the average man in such circumstances in that it had the idea of helpfulness back of it. It was arranged somewhat after the fashion of a country post office, behind the tall partitions of which, and at small openings, clerks were ranged. I stopped at the first one and handed in my watch, asking him politely what I could get on that. He took it, opened the case, turned it over and examined the works with a glass and then said, "Twenty-five dollars." I could have fallen to the floor.

Twenty-five dollars! Why at that rate I could live for weeks. Twenty-five dollars! Now I could get my job and then wait patiently for my salaries. Railroads paid only once a month I knew but twenty-five dollars with the kind of economy I could practice, would last me that long anyhow. I decided at once that I would purchase me a new hat, get me a square meal and room and then wait patiently for my work to begin and my pay day to materialize. It seemed really a splendid prospect.

What a difference a small shift in circumstances will make in the buoyancy of some temperaments was here plainly illustrated, for although I was still very sick mentally, and very thin and threadbare, I was dreaming dreams of immediate recuperation. My troubles were now all over! I would soon be well. In a little while I would be restored to my literary position, and then—

I walked back along Fourth Avenue thinking, how for the day or two I had to wait I would have my trunk transferred from Brooklyn to the Mills Hotel, a large but inexpensive hostelry, where people were given rooms for twenty cents a night, and then tomorrow being Sunday, I would stroll out along the Palisades overlooking the Hudson and rest. This great relief, coming so quickly upon the heels of such intense disturbance, made me almost beside myself with a desire to lie down somewhere in the sun, where I could look at a beautiful scene, and rest.

CHAPTER IX

THE wonder at my luck was so great that I really did indulge in a thirty-five-cent meal before the possibility of my still not having plenty to go on began to dawn upon me and bid me be cautious. Twenty-five dollars was not much. Thirty-five cents for a meal, two dollars for a hat, sixty cents for my room for at least three days, anyhow, fifty cents for my trunk, my meals—at the very least forty-five cents a day, for my bread and milk diet had already palled on me so terribly that I was afraid it would do me more harm than good if I continued, and possibly a fare to some far-away station on the railroad—"Holy!" I thought. "Supposing they should send me to some far-off place where I would have to pay eight or ten dollars carfare!" How would I manage that? I couldn't. It would leave me scarcely ten dollars to live the month on, if so much. What a catastrophe. In a puff my recent joy went out like a blown lamp.

"Anyhow I can leave my trunk in Brooklyn. I needn't move that just yet," I thought. "I can get along without the medicine and as for the hat—well I must have that." My shirt was still clean for I had put a fresh one on that morning and to the last I had managed to pay for my laundry bills—all but the last two weeks, during which time I had been living on my accumulated stock. Also I had a shoe-shining outfit in my grip whenever I should get it. I could keep myself looking respectable and as for baths the Mills Hotel provided free shower baths. If nothing untoward happened in the way of a long-distance trip I might come out all right.

I started up Broadway after my dinner intending to go to a store over in Eighth Avenue, near 42nd Street, where I had once seen hats advertised for two dollars. I was thinking of my old one— what pangs I had suffered wearing it, how people looked at me, how they did now and what joy I would take in getting rid of it. When I came in front of the Imperial Hotel a handsome cab turned in near the main entrance and two men came leisurely out toward the sidewalk, both of whom I immediately recognized. One was a small, dark little hunchback in a black derby hat and long raglan coat, the fashion of the day. The other was a fat, ruddy man, very fat and very round, who had a light spring overcoat over his arm and an umbrella in his hand. His grip was being carried by a liveried servitor and he was laughing—a laugh that I had known and rejoiced in since my childhood, since he was my brother. I recognized him on the instant and his partner and was doing my best to hurry by unnoticed—it was too late to turn back—when he clapped his hand on me.

"Theodore."

"Hello, Paul," I said.

"Why I've been looking for you!" he exclaimed. "I was over to that address you gave Mame but you weren't there. Where are you?"

"I'm not over there anymore," I said. "I'm living in New York now."

He looked at me with his big soft blue eyes—the eyes of my mother. He pressed the lips of his big jolly mouth together in a way that I knew meant pain. He did not look at my hat but I knew he saw it, nor at my clothes, but I knew that he saw them too. He was looking at me, and when he said "Come over here," I knew that he understood and that he was going to offer to help me. Instinctively I felt a revulsion of feeling—a kind of hatred of his prosperity and of him. How could he be so prosperous when I was so hard up? How could he go on in his merry, comfortable way and have me slipping along in the side streets comparatively hungry. And now he was going to offer me sympathy—me, who had always walked so proudly alone. I drew defiantly aside.

"What's the matter, Theodore?" he asked tenderly.

"Nothing," I replied, with an assumption of indifference and superiority.

"Now don't say that, old sport," he pleaded in a tone of real feeling. "You know there's something the matter. Are you sick?"

"I have been," I said. "I'm all right now."

"Don't you need any money?"

"No," I said, drawing away, hurt by his crudeness.

"Listen, Theodore," he pleaded when he saw it. "You know I'm your brother. I don't want to infringe on your dignity. I know how you feel, but I am your brother and you oughtn't to let anything stand between you and your own flesh and blood. Now listen. I know you're not right. Let me do something for you. Let me help you."

"But I don't need any help," I insisted bitterly.

"Now don't say that, old man—" he insisted. "I'm your brother. You know I wouldn't do anything to hurt your feelings. Be reasonable. I'm going away tonight. I've got to go to Buffalo but I want you to let me loan you something until I come back. Now don't be unreasonable," he persisted as I drew away from him. "I know you're in hard luck. We've all been that way from time to time. Let me help you—here—" and he drew from his pocket, in the shelter of a window corner, a roll of bills, tens and twenties, which he pushed toward me. "Here," he said.

"No!" I exclaimed, determinedly. "No I don't want your money. I wouldn't think of it. You keep it. I can get along. Don't offer it to me. I'm all right."

"I know you can get along," he said. "We all can get along but you can't get along now. You're not well. Anybody can see that. Take it and let me see you when I come back. I'm only going to be gone a day. I'll be here Monday. Here." He pushed it out to me and tried to push it into my pocket, but I refused.

"Please," he said. "Listen to reason. For old time's sake. Just this once. For God's sake don't let your pride stand between us. I know you're bright. I know you are able. You can get along, but don't let me go away worrying about you. Take it and you can pay me when you choose. You can give it all back to me when I come back if you wish. Only take it now. Here," and he pushed it determinedly toward me.

I looked into his face and saw such a world of tenderness and affection there that it fairly swept me off my feet. He was so warm-hearted, so kind, he looked to me now so much like the loving brother, that I could not well refuse. Secretly I felt as if I could throw my arms around his neck and hug him but for the publicity of it. I took the money and gingerly stowed it in my pocket, looking at him the while and saying that I wouldn't use it.

"All right," he said, "but take it anyhow." Suddenly I saw tears glistening in his eyes and my own filled.

I stood there a moment trying to collect myself but it was too much. I turned and started to go.

"Will you come Monday to see me?" he called.

"Yes," I replied.

"Sure?"

"Sure."

I hurried away and as I did so, turning the corner, I saw him climbing into his cab.

"That is like him," I thought. "That is like Paul. The good brother. The best of sons. The only man I ever knew who was wholly and absolutely swayed by the tenderest of sentiments."

CHAPTER X

THE impact of this added good fortune was a moving thing to me. It took me out of my gloomy state and for the time being showed me the other side of the living question. Life with such a man as my brother in it was not so bad. My own future, with him to worry over it, was not hopeless. I would come out all right. I went up to the hat store and got my hat and then in a fit of exultation went down to one of the principal drug stores and had an old prescription, which I had taken when I first began to break down and which had done me some good, filled, a thing which afterwards I considered bad policy. I was letting the fact that my brother had placed so much money in my keeping—there was seventy-five dollars and more—influence me in the spending of my twenty-five—or twenty-one-something now, which, I had said to myself, even while he was forcing it on me, I would not do. This was a bad beginning and I decided to hold myself in check.

This prescription by the way was one of a series of twelve which had been prescribed for me by a very eminent nerve specialist in Philadelphia. They had cost me five dollars apiece and when taken in rotation had done me good, only, as the physician declared, they would not cure me. Nothing would do that he had said but outside work, but with that and these any cure would be accelerated. I had found that any one of them when taken regularly would serve to quiet my nerves and I was greatly impressed by them. When I found myself once more able to get one—I had not had any filled since my money first began to run low, I could scarcely resist the opportunity. I felt as if my recovery depended on it.

That night and Sunday and Monday nights I stayed at the Mills Hotel, a cheap but nevertheless imposing hostelry in one of the run-down sections of the city. It was a gloomy place to me, surrounded as it was by Jews, Negroes, Hungarians and a host of foreign life, but nevertheless it was cheap and comparatively clean, and had the added interest of novelty. My room was, like all the others, a mere cell, six by eight feet in extent, with partitions of marble resting on jacks which reached to within eight inches of the floor at the bottom and about three feet of the ceiling at the top. The intermediate spaces were filled in with wire netting through which you could see your neighbor's feet shuffling about on the floor if you chose to look below, or his entire room if you chose to get up on your bed and look over the top. It contained a very small bed, a single chair, a diminutive clothes closet and a single window, barred, which looked down past tier upon tier of other cells like it to the enormous court below, where a great crowd was sitting playing dominoes or reading newspapers. It was quite dim, being lighted only from the electric lights outside, and it had the smell of what was unquestionably a fine compound of all the other odors of the building, human and vegetable, such as might arise from the vile bodies, the pipes and the kitchens of men. It had such a bleak, depressing appearance that I thought I should die if I were compelled to live there always, and yet I was of it then.

This place interested me tremendously. It was such a curious thing in the life of the metropolis. Here it was a tall, handsome structure, finished in marble and wrought iron and decorated in the best manner and yet filled with such a company of wretched patrons as might have served to stock the almshouse of almost any community. They were all poor—old men, young men, middle-aged men, with such an air of run-down, hapless inadequacy as was disturbing to look on. There were some whose clothes, like mine, were in a fair state of preservation but whose looks indicated an exceedingly troubled mental state. There were others whose looks were comfortable enough but whose clothes were a sight to see. In between these were all gradations, from those who had only a poor hat or a poor pair of shoes or a poor tie down to those who had all things poor. They were truly a sight to see.

And the way in which most of them took their situation was a curious thing to me. They were not all down-hearted. You could see men—old men, young men, middle-aged men, walking about here with an air, as if they considered this a very excellent institution indeed. Then there were others who sat off in corners and moped by themselves as if they were tired of life and were anxious to be rid of it. Still others looked gloomily at you, out of aged or sordid eyes, or cast furtive glances as if they expected some untoward demonstration on your part. One of the attendants told me that not all who came here did so because of absolute poverty. There were some who liked the life of the place, and there were others who were too indifferent or too stingy to seek better quarters. This was cheap and was therefore good enough.

I cannot describe now just what effect this had on me at the time. It was depressing to me, I'll admit, and yet it had the element of charm which comes to one who is interested in the spectacles which his fellow man presents. During the three days, or nights rather, that I was compelled to stay there I was never weary of looking at this tremendous throng—there were fifteen hundred in all—and of picking out in a desultory way those who in my judgement were once situated better than they were now and those to whom this might be something better than they had previously enjoyed. Some of them, like the old men, were particularly striking, and I could never look at one old man, with a fine, intellectual face and distinguished white hair who used to walk the floor there without feeling a positive pain. He was such a clean-looking old gentleman, his intelligence was so apparent and yet his poverty was so great. It was all very sad.

The first night that I was there I could scarcely rest for the noise and the strangeness of it. My room, being open as I have described, let in the sounds and the odours from all the others and gave me a strange sensation as if I were sleeping out in the open air or under some immense roof, without any enclosures. All of the guests did not sleep by any means and this alone was sufficient to create a disturbance for you could hear quite plainly everything that went on for a long distance off. Some of them seemed to sit and commune with themselves in an audible, self-explanatory way, as if they were worrying about something. Others tossed and turned in

their sleep as if it were some wretched nightmare they were enduring. Still others got up and prowled about until hoarsely commanded by some disturbed neighbor to lie down. One old man quite near
me complained of the condition of his bed and the indifference of
the attendants and another one advised him to "chop it off,"
meaning to cease of course.

The next day being Sunday and my brother being out of the
city I decided to go for a change up to Fort Lee, a point on the
Palisades, overlooking the Hudson where I could sit and look at the
river and the boats and enjoy a little rest. I had been so long
enduring an intense nervous strain that this opportunity of going
out and looking at a beautiful scene without being dogged by the
shadow of want or the thought of where I was to get the next meal
was a means of infinite relief. I took an L train to 125th Street and
the ferry to Fort Lee and then idling in the sun, for it was another
perfect day, walked and climbed to one of the most picturesque
rocks, several hundred feet above the water, where I lay in the
sunshine, my old winter overcoat under my head for a pillow, and
looked at the lovely expanse of water below me. It was a beautiful
scene. The gulls, a dozen or more, were circling gracefully on their
wide white wings over the river. The yachts and shapely steamers of
which there are always so many on this perfect body of water were
sailing as gracefully by. Before me in delicately reduced outline was
the skyline of the city, towers, spires, minarets and smokestacks all
gracefully arrayed looking like some glittering toy which the clever
hand of someone had prepared. It was a beautiful scene and it
touched me so that I thought I should die rather than go back into
the gloomy life I had been leading. "To think of Brooklyn," I
thought, "of those gloomy, horrible streets. And to think of the
Mills Hotel. Thank God I have youth and a little life left. My mind
is not utterly dimmed to this yet. I can respond to the sky and the
waters and the clouds when these are beautiful. I can love and
rejoice in a perfect day."

And then I turned with an anxious and yet hopeful face to the
future. Tomorrow I would see my brother. Tomorrow I would visit
the dignified Engineer of Maintenance of Way—the ruler of thir-

teen thousand men. Tomorrow I would go forth and acquire something and would turn my back forever I hoped on want, and wretchedness and hunger and pain. Tomorrow—but even as I was dreaming the day was drawing to a close and it was necessary for me to return to my restricted quarters in the Mills Hotel.

CHAPTER XI

THE next day being bright also—a part of a series of sunshiny mid-April days, that revived my heart, I tried to shake off the gloom of the Mills Hotel and determined that I would reject all advances of assistance and go on in the way I had recently planned—that of taking care of myself. The night had proved a bad one however and I was doleful with the weight of poverty I saw other people bearing. To be down. What a horrible significance that word had come to have for me. To be so poor that you could not buy a decent suit or a good bed or a truly nourishing meal. To have to live in the Mills Hotel with its ruck of want and ignorance, or to be pushed into so small a room as I had occupied in Brooklyn or here—it was fearful. It really seemed to me as if I had been caught in some deep, dark, painful depth and was but now just feebly attempting to crawl out. I was not out yet. I thought I might slip back. Supposing I never recovered my mental strength again? Then I am doomed to it, forever. Oh dreadful ending.

I went up through Washington Square, Fifth Avenue and Broadway to the Imperial where my brother was stopping, all the way contrasting the freshness of the life I saw about me, with my own. These clean streets. This handsome park. The fine hotels and homes clustered about. Yes, a life with money was the thing after all. Say what you please there was nothing in life without it. You must have some money, enough to live on as you wished, anyhow. Enough to be clean and decent and mentally at rest.

When I reached the Imperial my brother was not down yet but he sent down word to have me shown up. I went through the handsome lobby and the thickly-carpeted halls thinking of the difference between this and the place I had just come from. Here was the luxury and the comfort which made life worth living. No worrying over food here, no ordering about by officious attendants as I had seen at the Mills Hotel. These servitors were respectful if not obsequious and the conditions dignified and conservative. If I had ever been able to lay enough aside I should have liked to live in a place like this or something like it, I thought. I was weary of poverty and the other side, however conventional, seemed wonderful.

When I reached the room my brother was there to greet me. He rose when he saw me and exclaimed: "Well Theo, old sport! Dear old flesh and blood. How are you?"

"All right, Paul."

"And how have you been?"

"Fairly well," I said.

"Well I'm mighty glad to see you old man," he said. "And now sit down and make yourself at home. Tell me about yourself. What have you been doing of late?"

I told him that I had been sick but that I had been hoping all along to get better. It had been a little hard with me but now I was on my legs again or nearly so, for I expected to get a job that would benefit physically, and then I told him of my visit to Mr. —— and the letter he had given me. "I am going to work on the road as a day laborer," I said.

"Work, nothing!" he exclaimed when he saw it. "You'll do nothing of the sort. Why man you're not able to work. I've got the thing for you," and he picked up a telegram which he had laid conspicuously on the dresser and handed it to me, adding, "You to the sanitarium, do you hear?"

The telegram was from the originator and head of one of the most unique and famous health resorts in the country, which I had often heard of before, and simply said: "Rooms reserved. Will expect you Tuesday."

I stood there looking at it, amazed at his generosity, while he kept repeating in his mock-authoritative and yet affectionate way, "That's right. You to the sanitarium, sport, and not a word out o' you. Tomorrow. To Muldoon's, do you understand, and I hope he pans the life out of you—good and hard. It'll serve you right."

"But, Paul," I said.

"But what?" he exclaimed in his mock-serious and very humorous way. "But nothing. Don't 'but Paul' me. I know what you're going to say. You may be able to hornswaggle the public with your cheap literature but you can't hornswaggle me. I've got it all arranged and you go tomorrow. Tomorrow do you hear and there's nothing left now but to bow your head and receive the paternal—I mean the fraternal blessing. Bless you my children," he said, sticking out his fat hands like a preacher and rolling his eyes to the ceiling in the most sanctimonious way. "I hope he knocks the life out of you when you get there."

I listened to all this thoughtfully for I knew Paul of old. He was the most enthusiastic, the most jovial, the most childlike of men. Once started this way there would be no kindly way of stopping him and I thought I had best make a determined stand but it would not do. He simply laughed and joked, insisted that he was the older brother and ought to know and to every argument I offered returned an obstinate reply.

"Why won't you?" he demanded insistently. "What good will refusing do? Will it be any more credit to you to accept a place from the railroad than it will a vacation from me? You know they're not hiring you for your strength."

"But that's a railroad," I said.

"Yes and 'but' I'm your brother and blood is thicker than railroads you know, Bill."

I had to laugh, and whenever I laughed he would catch me up and joke me into silence.

Finally I said, "But I really oughtn't to do this, Paul."

"Never mind what you oughtn't to do. This won't be the first thing you'll do that you oughtn't to have done. You to Muldoon's tomorrow, and you don't get out of my sight until you promise."

"Well then," I said, "I fancy it's all up with my railroad work temporarily."

"Permanently, Bill. Permanently," was his rejoinder and I laughed again.

I should say here that at this time my brother was in a most successful position financially and was easily capable of doing as much for me as he chose merely as a matter of personal gratification. He was at the top notch of his personal fame as a popular songwriter while his publishing business was growing by leaps and bounds. His songs were selling at a great rate and he had a host of friends and such a following of admirers and pleasure seekers as made it difficult sometimes to get at him. Blessed with a genial and witty temper he had always been able to make his way comfortably and yet he never lost that tenderness which could make him see into such a predicament as mine. Ever since I could remember he had had someone on his staff helping him and I was but another. Only in my case family affection came in to draw him and he was a little bit more lavish of his kindness.

The remainder of this day was given to the most hurried preparations. This excellent brother would have no rest until I went with him to a great clothing house where he bought me shoes, a suit, some underwear, some linen—always on the plea that if I did have plenty a little more would not hurt. He insisted on my coming back to stay with him that night and as for my returning the money he had given me he would not hear of it. That was a gift and more besides, though if I insisted—to quiet me—he would take it back sometime—not now. He ordered a lavish breakfast, wanted to take me to the theatre and did everything else that the most extravagant tenderness could suggest. I was both astonished and ashamed,—astonished that he should show himself so mindful of my unworthy self and ashamed that I should be compelled to accept it from one whom I had drawn away from in the past—held to a certain extent in egotistic disdain. Truly I thought our chickens come, sometimes, home to roost, and I grew immeasurably in the perception of human nature.

That same day in the afternoon I went to pay my respects to the Engineer of Maintenance of Way,—the distinguished gentleman who was trying to find a place for me. He was as affable as ever, moreso if anything, and I am sure my demeanor had strengthened itself somewhat. Once more he was about to reach for his map and survey that vast area of mountains and plains which his roads' ramifications represented when I interrupted him with an explanation.

"I have decided not to go out on the road just at present," I said. "Instead I am thinking of trying a sanitarium for a few months. If you have no objection I will wait until I return from that. It is just possible that I will wish to go then."

That was an excellent idea, he thought. The sanitarium might build me up better than the railroad. Anyhow it would not do me any harm since the work I would have to do on the road would be quite hard. He would try and find something reasonably easy, but chances of anything like that in the railroad business were slight. He bowed me out and I saw a strong man in a velvet demeanor.

That same evening I went to Brooklyn to get my grip and trunk. I went across the ferry and up the dismal street where only three days before I had walked so lone and so seemingly forgotten. There was the house with silent red front, the curtains drawn, the same air of meagre desolation. I knocked at the door and was admitted by my landlady, thin and cat-like and sombre, who was pleased to see me again, but sorry to see me go. I went up to my room, empty and cheerless now, that horrible room, and picked up my grip. Standing by the window I looked out into the street and wondered. Here I had suffered, here I had been hungry, here I had been hopeless. If it had not been for human sympathy here I might have been even now, only worse, but tenderness, that great, mooted, doubted quality, had rescued me. It had lifted me out of the slough of despond. It had made me see that it was existent. Without it I would have been helpless—without it unhappy. In so hard and stony a world what else was important? Oh kind, genial, light-hearted brother—not wise perhaps, not dignified, not tender—, but soft-hearted and sympathetic. Truly through him and him only did I learn the wonderful lesson. He with his foolish, affectionate simplicity had burned it into my very soul.

I took my grip and walked sorrowfully out.

CHAPTER XII

THE next day being the eventful Tuesday we started for Muldoon's. This gentleman had long been known to me by his fame as the ex-champion, or as I afterward learned from him to call it, the "retired" champion wrestler (undefeated) of the world. He had been the boyhood idol of one of my brothers and I had often heard the latter speak of him as a wonderful man. Now I was to come in personal contact with him for he it was who had the recuperating establishment or "human repair shop," as I once heard him call it, where I was to take up my temporary abode.

This establishment was located at White Plains in one of the prettiest stretches of hill country that it has ever been my fortune to visit. It was situated on a knoll, several miles from any village, and commanded from the piazzas and balconies by which it was surrounded, such a stretch of country as the ordinary pedestrian does not often see. For a score of miles in every direction the green-covered earth rose and fell in undulating beauty and the roofs and spires of nearby villages might be seen nestling peacefully among the trees. Far away to the east, the land sloped to the blue waters of Long Island Sound, where was to be seen in fair weather a constant procession of snowy and toy-like sails. To the west and the north-west were visible the tops of those distant hills which shoulder each other near the waters of the Hudson. On the south there was a suggestion of water and some peculiar configurations of land which by day seemed to have no significance other than that which attaches to the vague in outlines of a distinct beauty. By night, the soft glow of a myriad of lights emanating from a region to the south, identified it as the body and length of the merry night-revelling New York. Northward, the green waves repeated themselves unendingly, until they faded into a dim green-blue, and the eye could follow them no longer. This was the site of the Muldoon Sanitarium.

On the morning that we started Paul was still in the most jubilant spirits. You would have thought that I was the missing sheep in the ninety-and-nine legend that is so beautifully rendered in the churches. He was constantly telling me how much of a man I was, how often he had predicted great things for me and was sure that just as soon as I recovered my health all would go well with me.

"You will see," he said, as he leaned back in the cab which he insisted on taking and placed his arm affectionately on my shoulder. "You're going to shine, now you mark my word. All of us have to have our ups and downs. Now you look at me. See how long I was dubbing around. Why my boy, when I was at your age I thought the world was against me, too. I didn't have anything. But things change. You've got to go through a certain amount of suffering before you can amount to anything. We all do."

"Well Paul," I said, "I've had my share recently."

"That's right, old sport. Only don't worry over it. Remember I'm your brother. I'll see you through. Now don't you worry," and he looked at me as if he were afraid I would.

I laughed at his innocence and good nature and marveled that he should seem to see in me what I used to think I saw in myself. Vanity was still with me. A certain amount of egotism. If I could just get well, I thought, I might still shine.

We reached the 42nd Street depot and there he bought the tickets. In the baggage room where I went to check my trunk he followed and looked at my luggage outfit suspiciously. On the train he talked of nothing but old times, our country home out in Indiana, our father and mother and the other members of the family. Al was in Chicago, Ed in New York with a well-known actor. Rome, alas poor Rome, but that is family history. At White Plains he hired another carriage—the very best in the place, and when we were on the road sang me snatches of his latest songs and told me of his prospects. The business was getting better every day. His latest song looked liked a decided success. Someday, he said, when we were both famous—I as well-known as he was now, we would go back to our old home and surprise the natives. One of them, an old neighbor of ours, had pressed forward amid a crowd to shake his hand the last time he was out there, and it would be much more imposing when we both went. Such innocent dreams! I marvelled that the heart of a man so well along in middle life could retain those charming ambitions of unsophisticated youth.

When we reached the sanitarium the distinguished proprietor came to greet us. He was a very powerful man, magnificently developed, who looked as handsome as Hercules in his riding breeches and tight-fitting coat. He was evidently well-known to and affectionately fond of my brother for he shook his hand warmly and whispered something to him. They went off together and presently he returned to say that the servant would shortly show me my room. He invited us in to lunch and we were served in a corner by ourselves—the regular meal being over. Then we walked out on the gravel walk and I was treated to many more injunctions not to worry. He would come out and see me. I would be all right. There was nothing to do but to stay here and take it easy, doing just as I was told. Then he departed after throwing a parting injunction to the gladiator to treat me well—which brought only a reserved smile.

That same hour I was given a room. The house was a great roomy affair, beautiful because of its height and breadth and because of the airy freshness which pervaded it. It was oblong in shape, with a large hall running down the centre on the second floor, lined on each side with small rooms. These rooms opened out again at their other ends onto a general balcony. At either end of the hall were great rooms, the one at the north being used for a general lounging room. That at the south for the private chambers of the host. Below stairs, on the ground floor, was an immense gymnasium, beautifully finished in varnished oak and shining like a mirror. There was a large dining room near it, a bath room, and out on the lawn a smoking room, or partition. Farther off, over a beautiful sweep of green grass were the stables about the eaves of which house-martins were flying, and within the doors hostlers and servants were visible. My room was a very clean little chamber fitted only with a bed, a dresser, and a chair. A rocking chair stood outside on the veranda and as rocking was my favorite occupation I liked that very much. The porter brought up my trunk. I opened and unpacked my things and then went into the great lounging hall to rest, where the other guests were idling.

I should say here that this institution was not entirely unfamiliar to me. Two years before a brother-in-law of mine—Mr. B——, had been here and a year before my brother's partner. I had learned through them or through family gossip of the nature of the treatment, which consisted, as I understood, of a kind of sharp personal supervision by the owner, coupled with a very normal course of exercise and diet; ball throwing in the gymnasium, horse back riding in the open air; walking or running over a given course and so on, coupled with strict discipline as to the hours of rising, retiring, dining and the like. It had been described to me by my brother-in-law as hard, but I did not fancy I would trouble over that as I approved of the idea. He had characterized the proprietor as "Bulldoon" instead of "Muldoon" which struck me as very humorous. I wondered just how much of a slave driver he was—if at all. The thing which seemed to have stuck in my brother-in-law's crop was that this man had lorded it over him in some way.

CHAPTER XIII

THE room that I entered when I first visited the general lounging room was well filled with a company of men whom I instantly recognized as being of that order of intelligence which considers itself more fortunate if not better than the rest of the people of the world. They were all comfortable-looking souls of from twenty to

forty years of age with a manner so suggestive of place and possession that it was almost obnoxious. They were inconspicuously
dressed and there was an evident attempt to appear natural and
simple but the manner they employed in addressing one another
was so plainly self-conscious that it was as good as a revelation.
It consisted, if one may attempt to portray it, in a certain ill-
concealed assumption of superiority, coupled with a mock simplicity of manner, which was most easy to see through. They seemed to
be saying to themselves, "I have it. I am wise. I am powerful. I am
as good as anyone, if not better," while at the same time pretending
not to think so. This was coupled with a very evident contempt for
any assumption or show on the part of their associates, the same
being met with cold sneers if not open comment. It was as if each
and all of them were constantly fencing for social recognition and
distinction, and constantly being disturbed and enraged because
they were not getting it.

And the air of the room breathed it. No one looked up when I
came in—that is not immediately. That would have been a form of
admission that an arrival was of some interest. Instead they went on
with their reading. One gentleman played a gay melody on the
piano. A second discussed an auto-mobile trip. A third looked idly
out of the window. It was perhaps fifteen minutes before a kindly-
faced young scion with a nature which I afterward learned to be
charming though weak came over and greeted me with, "A stranger
here?"

"Yes—" I said.

"You'll find it very interesting. The boys are all pleasant. My
name is Kennedy."

"And mine is Dreiser," I said thankfully.

He called a young man who was leaning against a book case
near me and introduced us. So my general acquaintanceship began.

The general introduction over I fell back into my normal
humor of spectator and looked critically on. I did not consider
myself particularly worthy of attention though not deserving of
neglect. I was more interested to see how these people would treat
one another and found ample confirmation of my original impres-

sion as the afternoon wore on. Horses, dogs, theatres, automobiles, stocks, Europe, the latest books, the most celebrated actress—all informed me that the group of men with whom I was now associated had money and knew how to spend it. They were used to the things they were talking about and spoke in the most affected and disinterested way of all these things. It was not as if any of these topics were lugged in for show, openly, for they really were the possessors of them. Still the pride of place was over it all and one so poor as myself could not help being aroused by it.

And the way in which they at once assumed that I also was of it, or should be, if I presumed to associate with them was charming. I have a natural distance of manner, which has served me in many a trying circumstance and in this instance it seemed useful as a curtain which protected me from a too close inspection. I sat off watching the whole thing as a spectacle while from time to time someone would make a slight overture towards sociability. To my shame I must admit that I did not always avail myself of them with the freedom that I might have. This accursed element of pride keeps us so indifferent.

During the afternoon a French housekeeper who seemed to have charge of all this gladiator's affairs came to me and doled out my portion of wearing apparel. I was given a suit of woolen tights and a sweater that I was to wear in the gymnasium, four suits of gray woolen underwear, four coarse blue woolen shirts, four pairs of woolen socks, four crash towels, a pair of gymnasium shoes, a pair of road shoes and a bathing robe which I subsequently returned, as I had a very excellent one of my own. These I carried to my room but was duly informed by my host later, that I was to take the gymnasium suit, a suit of the woolen underwear, a pair of the woolen socks, my sweater, one of my blue shirts and the gymnasium shoes all down in the great bath room and hang them up on two hooks, the numbers of which he gave me.

"Those are to be your hooks," he explained, "and now tomorrow, after you have had your bath, you take off your old things and hang them out on the fence to air and put on these clean things. As long as you are here you will wear wool. And every morning you will change from your dirty clothes to the ones you aired the day before."

I listened to this with great interest for I knew that his regimen of diet and exercise was strictly enforced and that I would be expected to carry it out in the least details. I did remark that I had never worn wool whereupon he tartly exclaimed, "Never mind what you've worn! You'll wear it here."

There was something so curt and self-sufficient in the man's attitude that it irritated me, but I said nothing.

That evening I was inducted into the great dining room and took my first meal with the crowd. It was a very ordinary meal—beef, potatoes, spinach, a salad and a dish of boiled fruit, but all excellently cooked. I had wondered what novelty in food would here be enforced as essential but was surprised and rather pleased to find there was none. The main thing as I soon discovered was to get to your meal on time and to eat what was set before you, a thing which had many humorous exemplifications. I myself was caught up sharply at that very meal, for asking for a second glass of buttermilk which I craved very much.

"We eat what is put before us here Mr. Dreiser," announced the host from the centre of the room where he dined all by himself. "If anything more is intended for you, it will be brought without your asking."

Naturally, before so many strangers I collapsed in silence.

That night and the next morning were worryful periods for me. I had heard of the strenuous exercise that was enforced in the gymnasium as well as on the road and was troubling as to whether I could fulfill it. Muldoon, as several made quick to tell me, was a hard taskmaster. He would not take into consideration anyone's weakness and he did not hesitate to enforce his commands with oaths and even blows. He made everyone get up at six and go down into the gymnasium where they exercised for forty-five minutes on an empty stomach with the light and heavy or, as some of the others called them, "large" and "small" medicine balls. Two men had to stand together, one on each side of the room, and throw these balls to each other—throwing them so that they would strike the floor directly in front of their opponent and bounce into his hands. If you didn't throw them right they were hard to catch and if you didn't catch them Muldoon would get after you. Then he would swear, or would sometimes take you for his partner, which was the worst of all.

"Wait," they told me. "You'll see for yourself how tough it is."

I confess this was not very reassuring.

The next morning after a pretty bad night I awoke before six and lay waiting for the fateful knock at my door which I knew would surely come. Muldoon they told me called all his patients with his own voice, or rather by the knock of his hand. He came down the long hall in his dressing gown and tapped twice at each door, the terrified pupils issuing immediately forth and following him meekly, like lambs to the slaughter, down to the gymnasium. There the exercise began at once, or as quickly as they could get into their gymnasium suits and that was very quick. He would allow no loitering. Woe to the man who did not hurry, or who stayed behind in his room. The thought of what would follow seemed quite dreadful to some of them.

I waited my turn, my head aching and my mouth having a bitter taste in it as it always did those days, until at last I heard the fateful knock, dim and distant, far down the hall but steadily approaching. I jumped up and slipped into my dressing gown and shoes and grabbed my clothing—road shoes, bicycle trousers, coat and tie, and started to the door ready to step out the moment he should knock. When he reached me, he knocked at my neighbor's door and the one beyond me but passed, without knocking at mine.

"This isn't right," I thought. "I'm a new man. He has forgotten me."

I heard the others trooping out and down the hall after him and I decided that it behooved me to follow. I hurried out and down after them, looking in wonder at the tousled heads, the yawning faces and the sloppy gaits of those ahead of me. I hustled up and went into the bath room, going up to my hooks, when I suddenly heard the stentorian voice of Muldoon.

"Who told you to come down here?"

"I thought you wanted me," I said. "You forgot to knock."

"You take your things and go on back. I'll call you when I want you. Don't get so overzealous."

I gathered up my things and in the face of a secretly grinning throng sneaked out—as red as a beet. It seemed to me as if I had disgraced myself unnecessarily and permanently.

CHAPTER XIV

THE next three-quarters of an hour brought me my turn and I was called by a servant to come and join them in the bath room. I went, and there enveloped in dressing gowns and still wearing their gymnasium clothes I found the whole company breathing and perspiring like engines. They all looked exhausted—greatly so—and sat dully gazing at the floor.

"You can drink some hot water now," he said to me.

I joined with the others in drinking as much hot water as I could, which he doled from two pitchers he had by him on a small table in the centre of the room. He then let us sit and sweat awhile and afterward ordered us into the bath.

The latter consisted of two closets or retreats, open toward the room, in which two men could stand and wash side by side. Over the head of each was a shower. While the others were undressing and entering by turns he explained to me that I had but one minute to take my bath. Ten seconds in which to jump under the spray and get myself thoroughly wet, twenty seconds in which to jump out and soap myself over, ten seconds to get back under again and rinse all the soap off and twenty seconds in which to retch and dry the skin. He also cautioned me to put my first towel down on the floor after I had wiped myself with it and use it as a shield for the feet against the cold floor while I was drying myself. While he was talking he looked to me for all the world like some stern old monk of the Church, the hood of his brown cowl drawn over his head, and his tall, perfectly-proportioned form standing as straight as an arrow. His eye was as clear and his jaw as cruel as a tiger's.

I confess I tried as earnestly as I could when my turn came to fulfill his injunctions but I was not very successful. When I jumped under the water I began splattering myself aimlessly but he soon called me to a sense of order even in this, in rough but not unkind words.

"Begin with your feet," he said. "Wet your left foot. And leg. Now your right. Wet your right. Now your chest. Let the water run on your chest. Now your back. Step forward and let the water run on your back. Now your arms. Let the water run on your arms. Now your head. Wet your head. Now get out and soap yourself all over. There's the soap. Up there in that little box. Put it back there when you're through with it. Quick, now."

Like a child being directed by a mother I followed these injunctions as quickly as I could, but I could not do it as he wished.

"Faster," he said. "Faster. You're mighty slow. Haven't you any life in you? Quick now. Get a move on you. There's the soap there right where I told you. There. In that box. Now begin within your left leg, just as you did in the bath. Now the right. Soap your toes. Don't you ever soap your toes? I never knew a man who ever came here who seemed to know how to soap his toes. Now soap your chest, your back, your arms—left arm first always, now the right. Your neck, your face, your head. Now back under the water again."

I was fairly panting.

"Same process over again," he called roughly. "Don't stand there and catch cold. Your left leg first, you know. Your right. Chest, back, arms, head. Quick. Hell, don't you know how to put any speed into your movements?"

I was nearly frantic with excitement.

"Come out now," he called. "There's Graves laughing. He doesn't remember what an ass he was when he began. Take your towel and dry yourself." (I saw Graves' jaw close like a trap.) Begin with your feet again. Left foot. Same foot. Same process."

It was all very funny and yet very trying to a beginner.

I got through at last however, not without being shown how to pull my woolen shirt over my head without opening the buttons and to do that first of all, and then I went out to hang my clothes. It was a gray day, and windy, but in my new woolens and from so refreshing a bath I felt quite good. I hung them out like all the others and went in to breakfast where I enjoyed my meal. All the time I was wondering what so strong a man should think of so weak a body as mine. Anyone with so much strength must have a royal contempt for physical weakness.

After breakfast I found that the crowd gathered around the back door outside the shower room to await the orders for the day. These included the possibility of walking or riding and I was told that it did not lie with the patient whether he was to do either or neither. This man was monarch of all he surveyed here and no patient had any privileges or feelings which he did not delight in over-riding. It did not strike me as a very pleasing prospect.

That morning he came out and announced that all but a young man named Sherman, and Kennedy (the man who had introduced himself to me the day before), and myself were to ride.

"Can you ride, Dreiser?" he asked me.

"No sir."

"Well you can walk if you wish. You three," he said, turning to Sherman, "do the short block." Then he turned after the others, who were already making for the stables, and followed them. The two young men with whom I was to go started off at once.

I learned on this occasion that the "short block" so called was anything but short. It was a stretch of road, traversing various angles and one loop, which covered about five miles and which was quite hard to do in the time allotted—one hour. It led by farms and pretty country houses where people were sitting on verandahs and reading and where farm hands were toiling monotonously in the fields. I fancied it would be quite easy at first and boldly announced that I was quite good at walking, but I soon changed my mind. The thick dust of the road clogged my feet, my woolen shirt and underwear became insufferably warm and in a very little while I broke into a profuse perspiration which wetted me all over. I soon grew tired also, and when we reached a cool well, half-way round the block, drank eagerly. Then we took up our trot again and I thought I should drop before we finally cantered into the yard.

On this trip I learned a great deal more than I had previously surmised concerning the men who were keeping me company here. One of them as young Sherman made quick to tell me, was a Vanderbilt, a scion of one of the main branches of the family, who owned a very well-known theatre in New York and who was sent here by his mother to recover from some very wretched indiscretions which bid fair to wreck his constitution. Another was a rather well-known clubman whom I had heard of in my day—a gentleman who came here not because he was sick at all, but because he wished to tone up. He brought his own horses. A third was a Philadelphia light, very rich and very good-natured but given to drink, and this was his way of sobering off. With us in the house then was a famous actor, a well-known physician suffering from morphine poisoning, two unknown ones, a judge, a few merchants and several gentlemen of leisure. Young Sherman, as I was afterwards told, was himself the brother of a very wealthy hardware merchant of Rochester who had contracted some eruptive blood disease which was very dangerous at first but was now fast being cured, and my young friend Kennedy was the possessor of a fortune in his own right, with a horse, a yacht, an automobile and so on, at his immediate command. On this very first morning he gave me fairly good evidence of his tendencies for he was for cutting across lots and lying under a tree to smoke some cigarettes, which was against the rules, and he finally did. When he was not smoking or complaining of being "overtrained" he was talking of the soubrettes he knew and the fine times he had with them.

CHAPTER XV

THE bath on this occasion was a repetition of the one had in the morning, only that this time we three were alone. We had time to drink our hot water leisurely and to bathe as we chose though all chose to do as directed. The young man Sherman exhibited his remaining ulcers which were numerous and ugly and began to expatiate on the value of water and how wonderfully this treatment affected him. He spoke of "sweating it out" and the value of plain exercise, without medicine, Muldoon not allowing any on the place. I remember hearing him say this with surprise, for I did not know that plain water drunk so freely as here ordered and exercised out in the way of perspiration could cure so malevolent a disease. He seemed to be quite sure of it however and spoke of four more weeks "fixing me just right. That'll be the end of nonsense for me," he added. "I'm going to work."

The other young man, expressed no doubt about it and said, "I've put on eighteen pounds since I've been here."

"Eighteen pounds!" I exclaimed.

"Yes, eighteen," he rejoined. "Why?"

"I should think such exercise as we had this morning would pull you down." I felt very weak myself.

They laughed.

"You think so," put in Sherman. "It acts just the other way. If you're fat it will pull off flesh and if you're lean it'll put it on. I've gained sixteen, but I guess I've reached about normal for me. I haven't put any on for three weeks."

"How long have you been here?" I inquired.

"Seven weeks."

"At fifty a week," I thought.

We dressed,—I in another outfit of new woolen, for I had soaked the one I had brought down the night before, and hung this

out on the railing. Then I went to the balcony and drew up a
rocking chair, in which I rocked and tried to make out the distant
Sound. At noon a great clatter resounded on the walk and then,
thirty-two horses strong, the riders of the morning arrived—
Muldoon like a general at their head, and the main exercises of the
day were over.

For that day and many others I was kept busy learning interesting things about this man and his wonderful treatment. He
seemed to me so far as I could judge on so short an acquaintance a
wonderfully impartial man. At first blush he seemed to have no
respect for either wealth or poverty, but to have a profound contempt for weakness—physical, mental, moral. To him the weak
man was the wretched man and the strong man, without good
judgement, the worthless one. He would glare at some of the scions
of aristocracy in the most contemptuous way, and in so far as
dignity was concerned he had no respect for that either. He was
constantly on the lookout as it seemed to me to shatter it. I
wondered whether his scheme of treatment, including as I had
often heard, mental dominance on his part of the wills of all those
present, was an expression of self-generated idea, born out of a fine
philosophy, or if he were merely a brute, and this fine idea was an
after thought. It might readily have been so, it seemed to me.

The first morning I went into the gymnasium with the others I
got some light on this, for there for the first time in my life I learned
what true exercise was. This room as I have said was equipped with
two kinds of balls—one a small air-inflated leather sphere, about
the size of the human head, weighing three ounces, and the other a
large, pumpkin-sized missile stuffed and weighing about three
pounds. The former were tossed—two, three, four and even five at
a time—between two men and caught on the first bounce. The
others were tossed singly and caught, being hard to throw and hard
to stop. The time devoted to work in the gymnasium was divided
equally between these two kinds of exercise.

It was difficult to say which was the harder or more trying.
Two men as I found would have a hard time keeping two of the
light balls going nicely, for it was an art to lift one above your head

with both hands and toss it and then reach down and catch the one coming to you, before it should bounce past. It was also an art to throw the large balls with any precision, as they whirled peculiarly. Shirking was not possible as the eye of the master was always on you. He seemed to be able to tell, whether he looked or no, whether you were working or not and also he judged by your perspiration at the end of the game, and your other conduct in and out of the gymnasium, as to whether you were conducting yourself properly. If you did not, and were not conducting yourself properly his rage seemed to become enormous, and he would threaten to tear your very soul out.

On this first morning I considered myself quite a star for a little while when I first went in because I found that I could make things go. I had fallen in with a very genial society man who was inclined to take things very dignifiedly. He was one of the sort who tries to display a reasonable amount of dignity on all occasions but his efforts in this respect were more pitiable than otherwise and he only made me laugh. Drink and high living had stiffened him up considerably. He would look at me in the most amiably reassuring way and try, as I thought, to express consideration, whereas I was really pitying him. Suddenly the voice of Muldoon, broke in with "Heath, to me," and then I saw his face change, and an agonized look of helpless weakness spread over it as he dropped his ball and ran.

I did not have so very much time to watch what happened to him after he left, as the man whom he replaced was very energetic and kept me busy, but I heard the language used and caught some glimpses of him as he floundered around in what looked to me like a cyclone of balls. Presently he crossed our line in an agonized scramble and with him came a veritable avalanche of abuse and hoarse commands, which completely upset me.

"Hurry, now! Faster! Put the ball back to me. What the hell are you standing there for. Put it back you God damned ninny. Here," and before he could get a line on the difficulties besetting him, he was struck once in the neck, another time in the chest, a third time on the head and a fourth time on the back—all in the space of a moment or two. I was astonished.

"Don't stand there, Dreiser," he yelled at me. "This isn't a place to yawp. If you can't do the work, get out."

I fell to immediately.

Then he began on my hapless partner again and it was only a minute or so before he had him floundering in the corner, hope-lessly bereft of all his senses and vainly wringing his hands amid an avalanche of balls, saying, "Well, I can't go any faster than I can, can I? I can't do any more than I can."

"Come! Come!" he shouted. "You're no baby. Don't stand there like a fool," and then he gave him a little time to recover his senses and thereafter dropped him for another. It was so that he exercised his patients.

The fact that men would take such treatment and pay for it was an amazing thing to me. It seemed rough and brutal and to begin with I had not only contempt for these men but for the man who treated them this way. What a silly thing, I thought. How much more preferable it would be if they would go out and work. I was for leaving and doing so myself, but I was in very poor physical shape and reasoned that this might fit me some for the harder work I was to endure later. I therefore stayed.

During that day and for many others—in fact all the time I was there, I witnessed more of these same exhibitions of temper or assumed wrath as I eventually learned it to be. I never knew a man who could work up so great a rage in so short a time and get such excellent results from it. He was positively appalling in his fire and fury at times and came tearing after us like a roaring bull. It was all coupled with so keen a wit, such showers of bitter truths, about laziness, indifference, contemptible weakness and the like that anyone with any sense of humor could not fail to be aroused. He seemed, as I looked at him, in health and action a startling and bitter commentary on my own inefficiency and weakness. What a thing to be strong. I think if I ever envied anyone anything in this world I envied this man his magnificent brain and body.

And he did have a fine brain. It was not the largest in the world when it came to sweeps of thought but it was full of vitality and direction and he knew how to act, and act quickly. He would stand in the centre of the room and keep his own exercise going, handling four and five balls as fast as they could be put to him while at the same time driving his opponent into a perfect frenzy of excitement and watching all the room besides. He seemed to have on his mind each man's peculiar weakness and he would burst out at times in the most salient comment, calling attention to someone's actions in words which showed the depth of his own insight. Thus he had a merchant there, a Hebrew who was the employer of five hundred men in his own sphere, but who was a perfect dunce when it came to exercise. He did not seem to manage anything with any activity.

"Do you mean to tell me that man has a wonderfully fine mind?" he shouted one morning in front of the whole class, pointing him out—"that his brain is a marvelous brain? I suppose he thinks so. I'll bet if you could see him down in his own little business house you would imagine from his conduct that he was the wisest person alive. And now look at him. There he stands with his mouth open—a big, thick-headed ninny. Two balls flying in the air before him are enough to upset the thing he calls his brain completely. If it were a question of doing somebody out of a few cents though there's where he'd be at home. His mind would be active enough there but here—why this is something he never did."

The man merely looked at him as if he felt it to be so.

That same morning he took a new man, a distinguished jurist by the way, and put him through the paces he had put me through the day before only he was not quite so gentle. This man was very dignified looking, but not overwise I fancied, and in a very much deteriorated physical condition. He was slow and weak and Muldoon sent him under the shower with an impatient injunction to hurry.

"Don't stand there," he said. "You haven't all day, you know."

The man moved.

"Why don't you rub yourself," he said to him, when he came out and looked helplessly around. "Rub your chest! Rub your stomach. Rub your legs. Damn it rub your legs. I swear you're the slowest old poke I ever saw."

"But I'm rubbing as fast as I can," protested the gentleman.

"Fast nothing. Look at that," he remarked sneeringly to the others. "He calls that fast." Then seeing him reaching slowly for his toes he added, "Now he thinks if I'll give him a week or so he'll rub his toes. Funny isn't it."

The man was evidently dumbfounded. He was so overawed however that he said nothing. Finally his master, growing weary of his slowness, shouted, "Here, you wash your toes!"

"I am," said the other.

"I'm not talking about the outside of them. I should think a man as old as you are ought to know how to wash his toes."

"I would have you know," said the other, straightening up with a most inappropriate air of legal dignity, "that I am a gentleman."

"Well if you are," replied Muldoon, "you ought to know how to wash your toes."

This ended the matter for the time being but there was the most ridiculous clatter about "outrageous" and "positively shameful" which sounded like opéra bouffe to me.

CHAPTER XVI

FOR some time thereafter I was kept busy and amused watching the development of this health treatment. For one thing I was taken out on a horse back ride, whether I could ride or not, being simply ordered to do so, which cost me many pangs. I could not ride and I was very much afraid to try, but I was given a fat little pony of a horse, which was set in fat little ways, and this I mounted with great difficulty, my long legs hanging down the sides like flails, and my arms reaching readily to the horse's ears. I used to sit and think what terrible things would happen if the horse should run away and I should be thrown to the ground and killed, whereas the beast no doubt was constantly figuring on how it could do the least work. It had a funny little trot, one of the worst imaginable for riding purposes, and I was near bounced to death, before I could learn any method of easing myself, or could become hardened. At the same time I was constantly called upon to watch the motions and obey the commands of this wonderful leader, who had a thousand tricks for keeping us nervous cranks from thinking about ourselves.

"Look at him," he observed, pointing at me when I was jogging hopelessly along. "He thinks he is very wise. He thinks he is a philosopher. Let a selfish ass get that bee in his bonnet and there is nothing under the sun that will get his mind off himself. Now you sit up, you long-legged ignoramus, and pay attention to what I am talking about and the orders I am giving, or I'll give you some exercise worth talking about."

His eyes fairly flashed fire.

I confess that this sort of language was bitter to swallow, but I had sense enough to see that what he said was true. I was long-legged and I was selfish, and I had thought that I was somewhat of a philosopher. It might be true that I was an ignoramus after all for who can tell. Anyhow my mind was riveted on myself and I was having a hard time getting it off. Besides he was big and strong and trying to cure me and could have cracked a dozen such men as me together and broken our heads.

His railing had the advantage however of not being special. He played no favorites. If I was held up to scorn this morning it was not because I was any worse than the others. Everyone came in for a share of his abuse by turns, the weakest as well as the strongest. He seemed to fairly love to take the man who considered himself immune or superior and show him for a ninny or a coward or a dunce.

I remember one morning we had all started to walk Rye Beach, a thing which we sometimes did, Muldoon riding behind us on his horse, and a new man had come along, a very pompous, self-opinionated-looking merchant who was quite stout, and who seemed to think that his social or financial position gave him some special standing with the owner of this institution, an idea which newcomers occasionally entertained. The gladiator was not in a very good humor however, and although he allowed the newcomer to walk near his horse he did not say much to him. The latter talked volubly on however until ordered quite curtly to move up in front, which he did.

We had not gone a mile or two however before he began to drop back and finally fell even behind, complaining that he was tired. He also spoke to several of dropping out entirely and waiting until the procession returned, which was not permissible. He was evidently not out of the eye of the gladiator for the latter eventually rode back and demanded to know what he was falling behind for.

"I'm a little bit tired," he said ingratiatingly—as much as to say this is all good enough for the ordinary run of your patients but between us—you and me—some easier arrangement will be more acceptable.

"You'll have to keep up with the procession," replied Muldoon sternly. "You can't drop behind this way."

"But I don't care to walk over there, Mr. Muldoon. I don't have to walk if I don't want to do I?"—this with an engaging smirk.

"You certainly do. Come now and catch up with the others."

"But I don't want to."

"Never mind what you want to. I say you must."

"This is an outrage! I will leave the place!"

"You may leave the place, but you'll walk to Rye Beach and back if I have to get down and push you every step of the way."

The man was astounded. He looked at this tiger-form gladiator, then at the crowd, and seeing that he was really up against the necessity of making a fight or walking, he walked. That night he packed his trunks and departed, but the gladiator did not mind. Instead he made some humorous remarks on the fun some people expected to have when they came here, an idea which seemed to have quite a humorous side to him.

He would not give us a moment's rest but was constantly changing the gait of the procession from a trot, to a canter, from a canter to a gallop, from a gallop to a walk and so on, and as constantly shouting orders to mount or dismount, to change the manner of holding our lines, to run or walk or stop, and when dismounted leading our horses, which was very tiresome (but as I subsequently learned very beneficial). At the same time he would rage and swear at us, taking the slightest defect or action for an excuse and railing away in front of the whole company until you were only too glad to hide your head in shame. He had a wonderful way of hitting the weaknesses of each and would readily pick out some person's failing or vanity which he did not hesitate to harp on.

This exercise was an excellent thing for me. We rode all over the beautiful valleys lying about his institution,—up hill, down dale, through thickets where green limbs scratched our faces, by the shores of lakes where the cool breezes fanned our hot bodies, up dusty roads where we ate loads of dust that gathered on our lips and back by splendid estates where the elegance of man was set forth in magnificent parks and beautifully gabled and turreted houses, scenes of life and beauty such as few of us enjoy. One of the estates we crossed was a composite of seven hundred acres of hill and water country—set every yard of it with flowers and rare trees and closely cropped lawns which it must have taken dozens of men to look after. The house, a wonderfully ornate and beautifully arranged affair, was set on the top of a hill and commanded a wide range of country. It was closed, however, as I learned and the owner had not been here for two years. He was traveling in the Orient. Meanwhile the grounds were kept in perfect condition, but never opened except to special acquaintances, such as the owner of our health factory, who had permission to take us through now and again. The owner of it I was told had come into possession by marriage.

I recall this fact largely because it struck me forcibly at the time. I was so new and fresh from want that I could not help thinking about the chances of life. I used to ride through all this country listening to the talk of how this land was held for value, and how, before very long, without doing anything but hold it, the owner would be very much richer, and how this gentleman here (for our host seemed to know all the history of the country and was good enough to retail it to us at times) was the son of some other gentleman, who had died and left him all this magnificent estate.

And here, on our left, was the magnificent property of the so and so's, bankers, or railroad owners or trust magnates, who were worth so and so much—fabulous sums which never mean anything at all to me, since I do not know how to reckon above a few hundred dollars at a time when it comes to expenses. And here on the right of us was the home of so and so, famous for balls and parties—who once had apple blossoms brought from Florida at an expense of hundreds of dollars to celebrate a wedding, all because apple blossoms were the daughter's favorite flower—expenditure which seemed like lavish wastefulness to me.

And then I would ask myself how these things came to be so, and whether such conditions could not be improved upon, and would be led off into those endless mazes of speculation which for me end nowhere. I could not unravel the whyness of things nor offer a rational solution. Only the wretchedness of men weighed on me and I would ponder by the hour over the suffering and the hunger in New York alone, the crowded tenements, the sick babies, the people sweating under undue loads this very summer day and the women sewing, sewing, way late into the night.

Back in Brooklyn was my wretched chamber, probably occupied by someone else. Down in Bleecker Street was the Mills Hotel, crowded with its company of grim, lonely men; and here set upon a horse and gamboling along amid green trees, green fields, beautiful flowers, and beneath a lovely sky was I, so recently snatched as by a hand from the maws of want. It was a curious condition, truly.

And the attitude of these men was a thing that interested me greatly. Some of them, the young ones, particularly those not so wealthy, were excited to envy by the very magnificent estates. One of them, a very young man with a large head and a thin body, who was sent here by his father to have his body built up before he entered business, was wont to exclaim—he was my riding partner for a time—"'Cush' is the thing! The long green for mine!" and he would look over the grounds and tell, how he would have some money,—"a million or two at least" if his health held out. He was quite well-to-do, the family being one of the richest in Springfield, but merely enough was ridiculous to him. "I want the coin," he said one day confidentially, "lots of it. All I can get."

"And what then?" I asked.

"Never mind what then. I want it. It's necessary to have it if you want to amount to anything today."

This frank materialism rather pleased me. I did not admire him personally. He was cold and stingy, but his honest confession was always well worth hearing and he looked exactly like someone who would have it.

There was another young fellow, a "society" young man, who was so dull and so shallow, that I wondered his boasted riches were not taken away from him quickly by someone. He was forever talking about the "plagued" something of something "donche-know," the poorness of his saddle, the monotony of the ride, and the wretchedness of "the beasts"—they weren't horses at all. I am quite sure I never heard a single remark from him worth remembering, in all the five weeks I knew him, unless it was that a college was the place to form your friendships for life—"to pick your company, doncheknow" as he expressed it. And as for what we passed on the road it was all commonplace to him. He did not notice it.

Among the others there were many who were not so dull but few who were less material. I could mention a Hebrew who was always talking about his "trobbles" and his "vorries"; another Hebrew, whose wife insisted as he told me that he lacked "that touch of indifference" which constitutes the true money-maker; an iron manufacturer, whose nervous doubts about his health had made him twice take out an insurance policy, solely because he wished to see if he were sick enough to be refused. He had heart trouble or fancied he had, and this was his way of seeing whether he was really right. And a young broker, connected with a great banking house, who was possessed of the most perfect manners and style but nothing more. All of these men and about thirty others of the same calibre rode and chatted with one another, keeping as it seemed to me a cold, selfish watch on one another, for fear one would do or say or look something a little better than he himself did. It was very interesting and I watched it with a critical eye—"me," as Walt Whitman would say, "the coldest, most selfish and meanest of them all."

In these days I think I took about the bitterest view of humanity that I have ever had. It was not that I had not felt and observed the cruelty of life before—I had, but here the spirit of criticism was roused in me by what I deemed the materiality of these men. I would sit and watch them by the hour, their airs, the secret pride they took in their positions, the way in which they reserved a dignified silence for fear their own sense would be questioned, the readiness with which they leaped forward with a sly comment or a sharp thrust, whenever there was a chance to do someone else an injury, and contrast it with sickness and death and the changing and shifting of things in life generally. What was the use? And then the assumption of virtue, or rectitude, or superiority—all these things galled and irritated me. Like the others I was ever ready to say something mean, to come in with a sharp dig and to cut as deep as I could only I did not count myself very vile in doing this. Once or twice I said something which provoked a bitter snarl and I was put down by some, I know, as a crank. I did not fail to see at the time that I was doing this, but I had reached the place where I blamed it all on nature—the devilish scheme of things, and let it go at that. Surely if I was no better I was no worse, and they were all in the same boat with me. At the same time I would console myself with the idea that in the main I was not as bad as they were—not as cold and unfeeling. Ridiculous, isn't it?

And the man who was training us came in for a share of my judgement. I criticized him also, finding fault with his materialism, his brute strength, the fact that he did not see that he was no better than anyone else. One day when we were out riding together, for he took me many places in one or the other of his fourteen fine vehicles, I took him to task for his attitude.

"You think you are strong," I said. "You talk as though you

were self-made. You don't seem to realize that you were given your strength—that your magnificent constitution was inherited. You didn't make it. It wasn't your exercise that developed it. The thing was there and developed into you, made you want to exercise, made you grow, and do as you did."

"You mean to say that I didn't have a thing to do with it?" he demanded.

"Not in the least. You are what you are by virtue of inheritance and you ought accordingly to be gentle and tender. The glory of the strong is their gentleness."

"But I don't agree with that!" he exclaimed crossly. "I've worked for what I have. I've exercised. I've carried halves of beef as a porter, and unloaded tons of ice as a stevedore in my time. I've danced naked in the open air in December, when I was in the army, in order to dry myself, and keep clean when I didn't have a towel, or a way to wash my clothes. I could have gone dirty and lived but I didn't want to. I wanted to exercise and be strong and I was strong."

"You wanted to," I said. "That's the point if you will only see it. You wanted to. Have you any idea what made you want to?"

"Why what are you talking about? The sight of dirt, and the idea of being strong made me want."

"But what made you dislike dirt?"

"What a question!"—he exclaimed.

"Yes, but it's deeper than you think. Do you mean to say that you made yourself dislike it?"

"Of course—" he said.

"Get out!" I replied. "It's plain that you don't see anything of the forces behind yourself. You don't see life. You can no more make your likes or dislikes than you can fly. They are innate."

He looked at me in a puzzled manner as much as to say "You are crazy," but as it was plain that we did not understand one another I did not continue the argument. It was not possible to make him see I thought, and I let it go at that.

CHAPTER XVII

DESPITE my mental attitude this exercise had a beneficial effect on me. This man, whom I deemed such a brute, was nearer right than I was for he saw through my dreary indifference to the nervous weakness that was producing it and did everything he could to shake me out of it. Out on the road, in the gymnasium, in the lounging room and dining room, he was constantly ding-donging at me to do this or that or the other or not to do it, which made him seem a kind of a scourge to me. He used to come in where I was sitting, thinking, and say, "Now you get out of here. I don't want you loafing around the house," and when I would go out anywhere, strolling off by myself, he would immediately demand to know where I had been and what I was doing. "I don't want you traipsing off without my consent," he commanded me one day. "You want to remember that you are under orders here and I want to know where you are and what you are doing. Don't you leave this yard without my consent."

I followed this order for a few days but it was not long before he changed it again, hounding me, as I thought, in many other ways. He kept me afraid that he would assail me in the gymnasium, worrying me with thoughts of what he would do if I didn't observe this or that detail and in other ways showing that splendid insight which made him a wonderful figure to me. He and his actions began to get on my brain and in that fact alone I found some relief.

To my surprise, at the end of the first week I found that I had gained three pounds and at the end of the second two more. In the course of two or three weeks I found that my nervousness was beginning to decrease and that the displaced angularity of things had been modified somewhat. Whereas I used to sit on the western balcony there and try my optics on the western landscape trying to figure out why the landscape did not look level, and how soon, in the course of the treatment, it would, or when it was very bright and warm go out and lie on the grass, trying to adjust myself—my nervous entity to my physical one, now I began to take an interest in things outside of me, and to feel as if life were not so bad. People were all wretched and greedy as I had imagined, but so was I, and why not accept the conditions? If I had a better way, a higher example, out with it. Otherwise take things easily and quit railing.

From the time I began to take a slight interest in the institution and to brood less gloomily on the worthlessness of my companions, I began to improve, though very, very slowly. There was one man who came there shortly after I arrived whom I liked exceedingly, a thirty-eight-year-old Hebrew, who had a most estimable sense of humor. He used to make the most droll remarks concerning the fiery nature of the steed which he was riding, a very testy brute that showed its teeth and liked to bite, and it was through my laughing at him that we became friends. We used to stroll off together talking over the question of nerves and the characters of the occupants of this institution and Muldoon and finally we came to have a real feeling for one another, which helped to divert me a great deal. He was an employer of men, many hundreds of them, but was at present a little weary of the details of his business and had come here to rest. He was never weary of telling me of the fight he had made to establish himself and the difficulty he had in maintaining himself even yet. All his life had been given to the building up of this one thing, his business, and he was restless when he was away from it. "You know," he said one day, "I get so that I can't sleep unless my mind is busy during the day. I want to have something to do—my things to do. I want to rule and direct. It's a habit with me now and I have to have it."

Another man was a charming jewelry manufacturer from Providence. He was only thirty-five years old and from a boyhood spent in the cotton mills, where he had contracted the weakness of lung which eventually produced the disease from which he was suffering, consumption, he had eventually risen to the place where he controlled his own wholesale jewelry business and enjoyed an income of ten thousand a year. He was humorous and boyish, with a fund of anecdote that was inexhaustible. When he got on the subject of his youthful laziness he was simply irresistible and he would lie on the balcony in the sun and kick his heels, or roll on the grass of the hills or fields thereabouts and tell how he went photographing for a living or how he tried to bring a cow home from a pasture once and got tossed over a fence for his pains, until his sides would shake at the remembrance. He did not seem to be depressed by the fact that he was going to die, though at times a seriousness came over him, which made it plain that he was thinking of it. Once he said, "You know, I ought to die just to round out the tragedy of my life, don't you think?"

"Well that's one way to look at it," I said, "only I'd rather it would be someone else for awhile yet."

There was another man who was a case-hardened society-man—born, as he used humorously to say, "of rich but honest parents." This good fellow hadn't the slightest conception of life outside of college, his boon companions, the life of the cafés and hotels of New York and his money interests but he was genial to the point of weariness. He used to want to go off and get something to drink on the sly, and when he failed in that, for want of companionship, would complain of the unsociable nature of people, and how little they appreciated the necessity of these things. He used to lie on the balcony also and talk of his past love affairs and what a miracle it was he wasn't married. One day a telegram came for him however and he was driven away in a showy trap, and that was the last I ever heard except that he had been seen drunk in one of the most opulent hotel bars of the city.

These acquaintances and observations produced a singular effect on me. I had never associated so closely with men so richly endowed with money as most of these were and on the whole I was not charmed with the spectacle they presented. With the exception of the manufacturing jeweler and the Hebrew wholesaler, they were exceedingly sordid and so narrow and conventional in their views that I could not get along with them. Money was the main object of most of them, money and nothing but money, though some of the social lights professed to ignore it or at least to look upon it as a natural accompaniment of the human state. The latter flocked by themselves, talked of people and places of whom and which I knew nothing, and made occasional excursions to the city from which they brought back quiet references to stocks and bonds, the great hotels, the arrival and departure of friends and so on, all of which interested me as a spectacle. I tried to adjust these things with what I had long conceived as the normal condition of life—variety—but somehow my boasted toleration failed me. While I was still willing to admit that the greatest variety might mean the greatest happiness, these people with all their fine things excited my envy. I was sick of poverty, or worse yet want, and would have gladly exchanged my end of the bargain for theirs, or for at least a competence. As for the pleasures in which they indulged I am quite sure I could have dispensed with most of them.

CHAPTER XVIII

THE passing days brought an urgent desire to be up and doing. Though I had accepted this outing in a spirit of nervous doubt of my ability to do manual toil, I was nevertheless sick of the idea of having accepted it as a gratuity or rather temporary loan. I wanted to be rid of the stigma of charity, and though I felt that my brother's intentions were only of the best—he was calling me up on the phone daily and constantly manifesting the keenest interest in my progress, I was nevertheless dissatisfied and felt it was vile to accept it. I was not experiencing such wonderful benefits from my stay but that I could afford to give it up for morality's sake. The nervous troubles that I had when I came were still partially with me. I did not sleep soundly, and my eyesight still manifested that tendency to see things at a wrong angle. I worried because I was still up against the proposition of making a living in a new way and did not know how I should succeed. Authorship was a long way off from me then, and in the main it had never afforded me anything more than a mere competence. What a way to go through the world, I thought.

About the end of the third week I wrote my brother that I was thinking about leaving and that brought him out on the next train. He would not hear of it. I must give the treatment a fair trial. "Don't be a crank!" he exclaimed. "Don't think because you don't get well in a day that it won't do you any good. You notice a little improvement don't you? Well then give it a fair trial. Stay."

And to please him, more than anything else, I stayed.

During the next two weeks I observed that I did gain a little principally in flesh and I slept somewhat better. I found a great relief now in walking in the wood, where the leaves were green, and in sitting by a favorite spring down in a hollow, where the gnats whirled in spirals and where a large frog used to make his home. I used to slip away from the institution and go down to this spring where on a sort of bench of stone I would sit and look in the clear, cool pool and at the clouds and trees mirrored there, and listen to the birds. There was one bird in particular, which I had always known and admired, but which here filled the woods with so much harmony that it put me quite beside myself. It had a perfect voice, a compound as it seemed to me of all the echoes and harmonies common to a woodland depth, pure gold and silver, all colors, all forms, all tones, the voice of the wind, the peal of a bell, the murmur of a brook. I used to listen in rapt silence, and once or twice, I say it without shame, my eyes filled and I cried. There is something in these things far beyond reason. They belong to the vast sweep of elements to which we shall all someday return.

As my final week drew near and came to a close I began to bestir myself in order to face the world, from which I had been so providentially withdrawn, with some reasonable means of sustenance. I wrote a note to the head of thirteen thousand saying that I would come to him for a position shortly, and then to my brother saying that I intended to work on the railroad. I did not know what else I could do, as I had no skill in any manual trade, and no training in any professional one. The Hebrew gentleman who had been so friendly to me had been kind enough to suggest that I could

come and work for him—I had indicated my intention of supple-
menting this by a term of physical labor,—and another gentleman,
an iron manufacturer, also staying there, had suggested in a joking
way that he would hire me, but I did not see any real avenue of
physical betterment in these. Both places were in the cities, and
both indoors, and I fancied both offered as a matter of kindness. I
had it in mind to work outside if I could. I also thought that
I preferred to work among total strangers and I fancied that so large
a corporation as the one I was looking to would arrange that for
me. I had some faint dreams of a track far off in the Adirondack
Mountains or the Blue Ridge where I should be seen picking
away through a long summer's day earning my bread by the sweat
of my brow. It was a pretty scene to me. It had flowers in it, and the
smell of the green fields, and a touch of blue sky that I could not
keep out. Obviously work on the railroad was the thing, and I
firmly resolved, before the week was out, that it was the thing that
I was going to do.

Naturally my brother objected. He did not see how that would
avail me, any more than a longer stay at this institution, or, if I
would work, a light place in his establishment. Why did I not wait
and let him get me a place in some city position—there were such
to be had and he thought he had influence enough to get me one. I
thought I knew better, but anyhow the idea did not appeal to me
then. I wanted to work on the road and that was the end of it.

When my final day came, I took my departure from this
institution with a rather heavy heart. I was not sorry to leave it
exactly and yet the charm of its luxury and location, contrasted
with the life I had mapped out for myself, was rather appealing. I
looked at the three or four men remaining of all those who had
been there when I came—the others had departed and been replaced by strangers, and felt a pang at the thought of leaving them
and of being shortly forgotten. No one was remembered here or
elsewhere. The outgoing guest was quickly replaced. All those who
took his place commanded forgetfulness of him by the necessity of
attention to themselves. It was as if man had no place in nature, no

entity. "That today is and tomorrow is cast into the oven," came to me. Oh the inexplicableness of it all. The shift, the change.

When I went to say good bye to the host of this excellent institution he shook my hand warmly. He was a thoughtful person for all his storming and raging and the tragedy of life did not escape him. I had often thought that I had seen him turn a fleeting look of sadness when some one or other of the many excellent guests had left, and I fancied that he did not make an exception in my case.

"You've done very well, Dreiser," he said, gripping me firmly. "You've tried to do your best. That's something. When you're away from here, you'll see perhaps that all my browbeating isn't as bad as it looks. It has to be that way, though I sometimes think the game isn't worth the candle."

"You're mistaken there," I said. "So far as any game is worth while, this is, and you are an able man. You may not think you do good, but some of us cannot help but be better for having known you. I know I shall be. Anyhow I shall know how to wash my toes."

He smiled grimly.

"It's more than most will ever learn."

I stepped into the vehicle ordered for me and was driven to the station three miles away where the sharper of a stableman duly swindled me to the tune of three dollars. He knew that the rate was exorbitant but to my protest merely replied that the others paid it. What did I think? He also tried to look the scorn he felt for anyone who would come from such an institution and protest his fare. Truly I could be only some faker in disguise—some beggar masquerading as a man of wealth.

The great city on my return seemed a harder place to gain a foothold in than ever. As I walked down Madison Avenue, the hot asphalt-paved street with its tall accompaniment of closely sealed houses, the owners of which were abroad, seemed more heartless and forbidding than ever. Why should people flock to cities, I asked myself. What could they gain here? It was all taken up. The ways were sealed. You could not gain a foothold. All it did was to offer a fine spectacle to the eye—to wave a Tantalus bunch of pleasures before the eye, but forever beyond the reach. All these years I had been contemplating this magnificence but never once tasting it and yet I hung on. Was it with the hope of doing so? Obviously I had no basis for it. Better abandon desire and retreat. Be satisfied with the humble life. It was the only way.

I reached my brother's and he was sorry that I had come without notifying him. He wanted to meet me. Since I was here he would abandon everything else and talk it over. Didn't I want to go off and rest somewhere for a few weeks? Didn't I want to wait and see if I could get something better?

"Here, old sport," he said, "here's a hundred. And more when you want it. Draw on me."

"No more," I said, waving it back. "Once was enough."

"Come, come," he began, but I hushed him this time with a look of firm determination.

"Nothing more, Paul," I said. "You have proved how good a brother you can be. Now let me show you how I can go it alone and pay you back."

"But you're not well yet."

"Never mind. I can get well. And as for money I have plenty of that which you gave me. If I find that I can get along without it, I will return some of that."

He shook his head, reproachfully. "You're the limit," he said.

"And you're the best of brothers."

"Well I'll see that you don't want if I have to come up where you are and live with you."

It was so that I burned my bridges in that direction.

The next morning, after a visit to a friend in Newark, I went to see my captain of thirteen thousand. He was as suave as ever, as distant, as cold. He took down his glassed, framed map once more and said: "Now I've thought this all over and I've decided to send you up to a little shop we have on the Hudson. It's not very large and it has a variety of work. I'll arrange it so that you can do a little of each kind, inside and outside. You'll get an idea of what we do in the way of preparing materials and then a little later if you like,

I may be able to send you out on the road with a construction corps. That will be about the best thing for you."

He paused as if to see what I would say and I naturally felt that I could do nothing but approve. What he offered seemed excellent. I wondered what he would pay me, but as I had come to him under such exceptionable conditions—mistaken ones in fact, I could not very well say anything. I thought that I would try it, whatever the wages were, and waited while he had his chief clerk dictate a letter, one of those short, curt, documentary affairs, which read for all the world like an order from a general to his next in command. It was addressed to the Chief Engineer, at Waverly, gave him my name and recommendation and ordered him "on presentation" to put me to work in the company shop at Spuyten Duyvil. This was signed for him by the clerk and handed me without more ado. When I asked if Thursday would do, he replied, "Any day," and I walked out.

It was so that I made my entry into the railroad business.

CHAPTER XIX

THE division offices at Waverly, which I visited after three days of sight-seeing with my brother, I found to be a collection of dingy affairs in a commonplace brick building located in a rather desolate neighborhood, near the local depot of the company, a few miles out from the city. It was filled with a crowd of rather zealous-looking clerks who looked at me in an imperative way and one of whom took my letter, leaving me standing. When he had read it he went inside, to another room, and presently returned with another letter saying that I should present it to the Supervisor of Buildings. This gentleman I learned was in the same building, a little farther on in this hall, but in control of an entirely separate department. I took the letter, read it, saw that it was just such another imperious order as the first, and presented it. There I was received by another clerk, who took it, read it and eventually advised me to have a chair. I could see by his manner that he was slightly overawed by my appearance, though his own was aggressive, and I laid it to the combination of dress, my own sense of equality with all the world, and the mention of the name of the Engineer of Maintenance of Way which occurred in this last letter, where he was spoken of as my "sponsor." This clerk went into an inner office also, where another man was sitting, a broad-shouldered, broad-chested man with dark hair, dark eyes, a firm jaw and an aggressive manner, who looked it over and laid it down. I could see from the door that he was puzzled by it, and that in all probability he objected to it. Here was a man being forced upon him by the reigning powers whom he did not want and whom he had no use for. It was probable that I would prove intractable, or at least not subject to the same severe discipline enforced upon the men. It was folly and he pondered (I am quite sure of this) whether so silly and disorganizing an adventure could not still be nipped in the bud. As with a puff of cold air the grimness of this life dawned upon me, and I realized that these men dealt with the hardest kind of facts and only such. All dreams of a fantastic nature were here laid aside or better still were rigorously suppressed. A keen, disturbing sense of unfitness assailed me, and I realized that I would have to make myself useful or I would not be able to stay long. I would have to show this man that I was perfectly willing to accept his authority, to bend myself utterly to him, or he would take means to have me suppressed. There was to be no foolishness in his department.

After a few moments I was called in and then I realized that what I had fancied was true. He was reserved, exceedingly. He wanted to know whether I had ever worked on the road. I had not. This was for my health, he had been advised. I told him only partially, as I would have to work at something anyhow, while I was recovering my health. He did not seem to like the idea. Hadn't I better reconsider? This work was hard. There was no easy work on a railroad. "If you are not used to it," he said, "you had better not try it."

"With your permission, I believe I will though," I answered determinedly.

"Very well," he said, with an almost animal smile, it was so negative. "If you think you can do the work I'll let you try. There's not much harm in letting you try."

"Is this the reception my letter brings me?" I thought. "I would have fancied that a man of so great a jurisdiction as my sponsor could have secured me a better reception than this."

I fell back while he discussed places and needs, just as though one specific place had not been mentioned and he finally observed:—"How would you like to be time-keeper for a construction gang? Have you ever kept time?"

"No, sir."

"It's not easy. This place isn't anyhow."

I told him that if it made no difference to him I would prefer to do manual labor. My brain, as Mr. Hardin's letter stated, was in no shape to do complicated clerical work at the time, and I was very much afraid that if I undertook it, it would be to lose ground. I suggested that as Mr. Hardin, the Engineer, had suggested, I be allowed to do light physical work to begin with.

"All right," he said to his clerk. "Send him to Spike. I guess we can find enough to keep him busy."

The young man, in his reserved, intelligent and self-confident way, suggested that I come with him, and he in turn dictated a letter, this time to the Shop Foreman at Spuyten Duyvil, which read as follows:—

Mr. F.A. Strang, Foreman.

Dear Sir:

This will introduce to you Mr. Dreiser whom you will put to work doing general labor around the shop and outside, paying him fifteen cents an hour. He is a man recommended to me by Mr. Hardin and is completely run down mentally. Mr. Hardin requests that we keep him busy at general labor in order to build him up physically. You will put him to work at once at the amount specified.

Yours truly

R. P. Mills.

I took it and went, the nature of my prospective general labors filling my mind.

The location of this shop, as I found when I reached there, was one of the most ideal that could be imagined. It was situated on a little point of land reaching far out into the Hudson, just where the latter joins the Harlem, and was opposed, on the south, by a beautiful green hill, thickly covered with trees, between it and which the Harlem ran. On the west and north stretched the Hudson, a beautiful expanse, showing the Palisades and the distant tops of the Kaatskill Mountains. Just outside, for it was enclosed as all shops for some occult reason seem necessarily to be by a high yellow fence, was a pretty little depot, nestling against the side of another high green hill which looked down on the shop like an immense head. In front of this and paralleling the track and the side of the fence was a pretty plot of green grass and some beds of flowers. Outside in the river some yachts were riding at anchor, and above on the hill crest several cottages were visible. I decided that first of all, before presenting my credentials and going to work, I would take this day and the next and get myself comfortably located in the immediate vicinity if I could. I therefore went up on the hill and tried to find a room among the many pretty cottages that I found there, but it was not to be.

All of the people there were of a very exculsive turn being mostly people of the city who had their summer homes here. I was directed with much reserve to the hollow below where some small cottages were located but these also refused me admission. They were above boarders. Then I went to the station agent or rather his associate the freight agent, a small, vapid-looking man who, with the air of someone who was doing me a great favor, offered me the joint occupancy of a room in a miserable old ramshackle of a house set under the hill. It had once been a mansion but was all run to decay and was occupied by four different families. My unknown but proposed sleeping partner was a freight handler, who worked at the adjoining freight house. I was to have this room and board for six dollars a week, but no bath! Naturally I declined.

My next venture was along a green, shaded road ornamented with occasional cottages where people were sunning themselves, but no one wanted me. Then I walked down to a station below— one of the northernmost of the many hundreds of streets that make up New York, hoping to find something with a view and clean, but no rooms were available, and particularly none with board. About nightfall I turned my steps wearily up a road which led back toward the Harlem and at last came to a bridge, beyond which was a hill attractively covered with private houses—perhaps as many as two hundred of them.

"Here surely," I thought, "is a place where I will find something." I crossed over, stopping to admire the hurrying tide of salt water and the view west, where, in line with the restless bosom of the river, the sun was sinking. It was a beautiful picture—composed of a green hill in the background, a great steel mill, with many black stacks midway, and the silvery, glowing bosom of the stream in the foreground. Overhead the sky was a steely blue but in the west it was red, fading into electric yellow at the top. It was soft and summery and to me tender. I do not know that I ever lingered more soulfully or with deeper feeling over any scene anywhere.

The hill, as I subsequently found, upon traversing it, was not only a hill but an island also, made by a small division of the river, which here ran in two glimmering streams about it. It was quite high, of pure white sandstone, and partially covered in an irregular and pleasing fashion, with homes. The streets, as I found when I reached it, went round in a ring, and the lowest one kept the waters of the divided river in view all the way. Pretty frame houses ornamented with grass plots and flowers and shaping themselves into peculiar angles because of the curve of the streets, lined the ways. At the cross streets and openings, lovely views flashed upon the eye—nearby rises of green heights and distant suggestions of green-covered slopes, and all about were the waters of the river, with the phosphorescent gleams and sparkling daubs of color which the dying light of day always lends to water. It was in my poetic and perhaps exaggerated fancy one of the loveliest places that I had ever seen, and I thought if I could get a room here, I would be, if not happy, at least fortunately enough situated to warrant my being so. I had never fancied that being what I was, an excitable and high-flown sentimentalist, I could be happy in the long-contented sense of the word; but as for bliss, that ecstasy that seizes one at the sight of a beautiful landscape, that flows in with the possibility (fancied) of peace, that rises like bubbles to the brain when the night falls in beauty, or the birds sing in peace—when love and life and pleasure crowd as nascent possibilities upon the brain—I have had that all my days.

CHAPTER XX

THIS hill as I discovered was more hospitable. After traversing it and finding a road house situated on one of the main roads that lead up from the city, where if I chose I could get a meal later on, I went around to a Methodist minister's residence whose church I had seen standing on one of the curved corners, and made inquiries as to whether anyone on the hill was known to let rooms. I knew, or fancied that I knew, so much for human vanity that my personal appearance would commend me, and as for references I had plenty to give.

The young girl who met me at the door did not know. She fancied there was someone, but only her father could tell me. Would I come back and talk to him later?

I would. I went around and had a moderate dinner at the hotel or roadhouse where I had a table out on the balcony overlooking the river, and then went back and met the minister, a grave old gray-headed gentleman, tall and slim, who listened very kindly to what I had to say. He seemed to take a real interest in my project

and was desirous of helping me. He did not know of anyone here,—
they were all private families, in comfortable circumstances, unless,
unless—he bethought himself—it might be the Wollestencrafts
would take me as a favor. They had once taken one young man—
only he believed the latter was a relation come to think of it. I
might go and see however. It would do no harm. I could say that he
sent me to inquire.

I thanked him very much, and after listening to a long disser-
tation on Wesley (he happened to be writing a sermon about him at
the time) and some erudite commentaries on labor I managed to get
away and visit the Wollestencrafts. I knocked at the door of a pretty
house, overlooking the Harlem, and was greeted by a tall woman,
gray-haired and handsome, who wished to know, in a very direct
manner, what I wanted. I explained to her, as politely I could, just
what I wished, and why I wished it. She looked at me critically, and
I fancied approvingly, out of the most experienced of eyes and
finally declared that although she was ordinarily opposed to taking
in strangers she might make an exception in my case. Certain
credentials that I had seemed to impress her. Let me come back
tomorrow and she would let me know. I went away with a distinct
impression that this was the place I would eventually locate,
though why I should feel so or why she should choose to take me I
could not say. The house looked like that of anyone but one who
would choose to take boarders.

On the morrow I returned for I was anxious to get settled and
go to work. My money was not any too plentiful and I had several
things to do before entering the shop. One was to get my working
clothes ready and the other to confer with the foreman and find out
what, if anything, I would need. The lady was decidedly affable and
told me at once that I might come. I immediately went to the local
depot and ordered my trunk to be brought up when it should arrive,
sent word to the downtown post master where to readdress my mail,
then got on the train and went to Spuyten Duyvil, which was the
next station above—about three minutes' run—and entered upon
the scene of my future labors.

The shop, as I found when I got there, was not so agreeable as the scene which enclosed it. The yard as I entered the gate, revealed the fact that it was made of cinders, dumped in upon what had recently been submerged land. The building was two stories high and of wood, painted a dull brick-red for the lower half, and shingled, with dark green shingles, for the upper. It had a red roof and was rather pleasing. On its left as you approached were a half-dozen tracks loaded with all sorts and conditions of cars and in the back, near the rear fence, was an unsightly pile of rubbish, telegraph poles, iron bridge sections, semiphore arms and whatnot. On two or three platforms, small green watchmen's huts and outhouses were being constructed by a force of carpenters who were working in the sun. A fine, inspiring whirr of a great plane came from within the building, and I could see workmen at all the windows working at lathes, or fitting window sashes together.

"What an ideal place to work," I thought. "They have a cool breeze and a beautiful view. It will be a pleasant place to work anyway, however confining."

The shop, as I entered, revealed the customary array of machines and tools. In the middle of the room was a great plane revolving at a tremendous rate and eating out the edges of some large pine planks that it was grooving. Two men were standing beside it, one at either end, the first feeding, the other receiving and carrying the planks away. The room was full of wood shavings and flying wood dust. At one point in it a band-saw was revolving and by it was a man cutting out some blocks. In other parts of the room and along the sides were other machines—a great rip-saw, a cross-cut saw, a moulding machine, and a large grind stone, not all of which were running, but some of which were attended. The man who was receiving the lumber from the plane was shielding his eyes from the flying chips by holding his head down and by pulling his hat low over his eyes. He seemed to have a sensitive face and I thought a sad one. All the others had a hard-working look, though not remarkable enough to be attractive. I looked through an open door leading back and saw a blacksmith at his forge, the sparks flying high in the air. He was beating a red-hot piece of iron with a masterful stroke.

On the second floor, where after due inquiry I learned that the office was, I saw another scene of labor. Here was a chamber, perhaps fifty by one hundred feet long, fairly crowded with machines and men. There were carpenters at turning lathes, more carpenters at jack planes and small rip- and cross-cut saws. Long benches extended along the centre of the room, and at the sides, facing the windows, and before these, and in full view of all the magnificence of the Hudson and the Harlem, were men working, making desks, tables, cabinets, window frames, window sashes, doors and door frames and what not. Outside, in one part of the yard I could now see a gang of Italians unloading a car and another gang loading one. There was a long Pullman train speeding, without slowing down, about the platform of the depot. It was a busy scene, and while I was wondering at the enthusiasm of it, I was also already reflecting upon the confinement of it. Outside was the world. Outside was life. Outside was something that was not toil. It was as if I were reflecting the mood of a new world, as if already I had caught the spirit of the place and was complaining against confinement.

The foreman as I learned upon inquiring at the office on the second floor was not in—he was sick of mumps. The young man who was acting in his place was a dark, intelligent-looking lad, who eyed me in the most sullen fashion. He seemed to be in the dumps about something and when I told him that I was coming to work here and that I had a letter for the foreman, he merely said, "Yes?" I explained that I wanted to know whether any tools or anything special in the way of dress were required—an apron perhaps.

He shook his head. "Let me see the letter," he added, and when I gave it to him, he opened and read it. He then gave it back to me. "Better keep that and give it to the foreman when he comes," he added with a peculiar—I thought cynical—smile. He then told me that I needed nothing except old clothes and possibly a suit of overalls. I thought once that I would ask him the exact nature of my work, but decided not to. I put on my hat again and walked out, the beauty of the world outside being wonderfully enhanced by my little excursion. Why was it that I felt so? Was it that the mere sight of work was so offensive to me? No, I thought; rather it is beautiful, but there is something there, uneasiness or dissatisfaction or the old human ache that makes one wish to be somewhere else, and that is what I feel.

CHAPTER XXI

THE rest of that day and the day following were spent in getting my things to Kingsbridge, for that was the name of the place in which I had located, and getting my room arranged. I found that I was to have quite a nice chamber, small, but neatly furnished, and that my home life was to be all that comfort could desire. The house was large, the furniture excellent, and in good taste. In the dining room, whither I called at dinner, I found a handsomely decorated table, with one or two silver pieces, a large and ornately decorated sideboard, and a half-dozen high-backed chairs, attractively turned. The floor was stained, and the walls hung with appropriate pictures. A mantle with a large mirror reflected the furniture of the parlor, beyond. It was possessed of a screen that shielded a door at one corner. The table itself was spread with an appetizing array of food.

If I did not quite understand my reception to this house in the first place it was not any clearer to me now. The occupants were apparently anything but in need of the comparatively trivial sum I had to offer, and yet I was received with the greatest deference, and allowed to sit at table in the most social way. The mother as I quickly learned was a widow, possessed of a daughter, who was not present at the time, a widow also, and a nephew, who was looked upon in the light of a son. There was a cousin also, spoken of as expected to dinner but I did not see him then. Only the nephew arrived, a genial, airy person, slender and good-looking, but very pale, who made a most agreeable impression upon me. He was not what I would have called a learned man, but apparently of sound business sense. He seemed inclined to make friends with me at once and we reached a very agreeable understanding before the meal was finished. The mother also showed a depth of insight and a degree of experience and observation that captivated me. She was well informed on almost every topic worth talking about and had read often and met some of the most celebrated persons of her day. She seemed to like literature and art but to prefer the practical and natural in both and discussed all things freely. I was decidedly impressed with her as a strong personality and wondered why she had not been heard of in some capacity.

The cousin, as I learned the next morning in dining and riding downtown on the train with him, was a very different sort of person. He was cold, I thought, hard and unscrupulous with a degree of ill-concealed conceit that was offensive. He was a medium man, not tall, rather thick-set, with a round, gray head, gray eyes and a sinister, unnatural smile. He talked with a degree of affected warmth of his relatives but I could feel no sincerity in it. He spoke of his business interests in a way which showed me that he had something—perhaps less than he wished to indicate but plenty at that. His interests were in the mining line, but I could never quite understand. I went on about my affairs, confident that I did not like him, and by night had all the details of my clothing ready.

That night as I was sitting out on the porch after dinner, looking at the water as it rippled through the low marshland below, (screened by a grove of trees that grew between it and the street on which the house fronted) and speculating on the solvent nature of all water, its vastness and mystery, the daughter came out and sat down. She was a weary-looking lady, rather pale, I thought, with dark hair and a wide, fine eye, but healthy. She had a sensitive mouth, arched and full, and round cheeks. She looked rather comfortable to me—easy-going, and introduced herself with much grace. "There is no one here to do it for me," she said. I accepted this without much comment. We talked about the neighborhood and the scenery, and the local life in New York, and then I expressed the fact that my life had been a thing apart from it for some time. She explained that hers had been the same for a year or more, living up here. "However," she added with a touch of comforting philosophy, "you can be happy anywhere, I find—if you can be happy."

I looked at her as much as to say, "What wise bird is this talking—at twenty-five?" And I saw that I had a person of sense to deal with. It crossed me a little to think that she should assume to philosophize so smartly in my presence, in the face of my recent experiences, and I returned, "Oh, yes. Theorizing about life is easy. We can all do it from an easy chair."

I was sorry I spoke afterward for it was plain that she had taken it as a personal thrust. She leaned back in her chair and looked at the water.

"It's pretty bad I know, but we do have to make the best of it, or die you know."

"Yes, or die principally," I said. "That's the point. I some-times think it's the only solution for most of us."

"Not for all of us. There's a little consolation. Do you know the Brightons?"

I confessed that I did not, but we found other things to talk about and presently she got up, having drawn me out of my mood, and went in. "She's a bright girl, and a pretty one," I thought. "What hair!"

Then I fell to my musing again, watching the water, silvered by a new moon. At nine I went in and to bed and the next day being Sunday, I spent upon urgent invitation with my brother.

On Monday morning my real labors began. Sunday evening I had arrived home (as I thought of my present abode) early and got my things together. I had laid out an old gray suit, worn in places, but still fairly presentable, the cheap hat that I had bought in New York, before going to Muldoon's, the old pair of road shoes I had used at the sanitarium and one of the rough blue shirts I had worn there also. I had also a suit of overalls, blue, and a glass flask in which I proposed to carry coffee or tea. I had wanted to get me a lunch box, but had forgotten it, and was now doomed to carry my lunches in a paper until I could get where I could buy one again,

New York most likely. I laid them all on a chair and once more cautioned my hostess that I must be called at a quarter of six, a thing that seemed to amuse her.

"I always get up at half-past five," she said. "I couldn't sleep later, if I wanted to," and indeed, for the two mornings I had been there I had observed this with some surprise. Seven had always seemed a goodly hour to me, and in my run-down nervous condition, eight and later was agreeable. At Muldoon's, six had been a constant millstone around my neck, but five-thirty! The fifteen minutes more I gave myself was precious. "I'm glad for my sake, that this is a habit of yours," I said.

"I have done it all my life," she said.

The next morning I arose at her call at five forty-five, though I had been wide awake and trying vainly to sleep for two hours. The course I had mapped out for myself, was to go through some five minutes of calisthenics prescribed by Muldoon, drink three or four glasses of hot water, which would be ready for me, jump into my bath and then dress and breakfast, after which I would walk to the depot and catch the six-fifty-seven train. When I returned at night I proposed to take another bath, change my working clothes to my good ones, and spend my evenings in respectable leisure. In the morning I proposed to change my underwear and other garments to fresh ones, and so alternate with my first garments until my week should be out. Then I would take all these to a laundry or washwoman and begin fresh on a new set, just as I had at Muldoon's. I wanted to make a fair test of this work and cleanliness proposition, so far as my nerves were concerned, and to be therewith, gentlemanly and clean.

On this morning I found it a hard pull to get up and go through the calisthenics alone. I was depressed with the idea of toil and my own inefficiency and hurried only because I knew it to be absolutely necessary. My bath freshened me up some, but my hot water taken so early, and so quickly before my meal destroyed my appetite. I had no hunger anyhow these days, so early in the morning, and could barely force a little oatmeal down my throat. When I looked at the clock and saw how quickly the time was passing, I grabbed my hat and my lunch so kindly prepared for me and hastened away, just in time to make my train by running three blocks, for as I then discovered, railroad trains are as like to be a few minutes ahead of time as behind. This one was four minutes early, and I only caught it by falling aboard. Then I climbed into a car literally packed with pipe-smoking Italians and workmen of all degrees of intelligence who gave me a short glance but nothing more, and I sat down.

CHAPTER XXII

THE shop as I found it on this morning was not exactly as I conceived it from my point of inspection on the hill top or on my first visit of inquiry. The day was gloomy and gray and the sight of the cinders and rows of battered cars standing on the tracks within the yard betokened anything but a pleasant life in toil. There was a suggestion of opposition about the men whom I saw lagging in along with me, a touch of weariness and regret, as if they had long had their fill of this. "Work, work!" I thought and I wondered whether I was taking an extra gloomy view of this, or whether it was really as I suspected. I went into the shop and up the stairs where I was greeted by the young man whom I had seen Friday and who told me I could go down stairs and wait. "I'll send someone to show you what to do," and then as I went down the plain wooden stair, the wheels started. There was no whistle. Only the increasing swish, swish of the belts and the clicking and whirring of the wheels. In a few moments there was a full tide of life rushing over all these axles and wheels, and then a young man, red-haired, fair-skinned and very strong, came to me and said, "I'll show you where to put your coat and box. Then you go with those two men there."

The two men pointed out to me, after due process of stowing my coat, were two brawny sons of labor who looked for all the world like twins so much were they dressed alike. They each had on a suit of brown overalls and a large-brimmed, dirt-soiled black hat, and each had a mustache. Each had a browned, leathery-looking skin and each walked with a slow, measured gait. Each looked to be the same age as the other, and about the only difference that I could detect at first was that the right eye of one of them fixed me with a glassy stare. I confess that I was not very much pleased with them. They looked to me somewhat like automatons. There was something too of the relentless and the indifferent that characterizes nature's grosser mood—of the slow, grinding force of a machine that has you in its grip, crushing you, and does not know it is, and could not stop, if it would.

"Come on, new man," said the man with the glass eye, motioning me. "Follow me, if you're going to work with us."

He led the way, with what I thought was a showy swing, to a pile of long ash posts, about eight feet long and six to eight inches thick. They were covered with bark and slightly wet, and looked to me as though they were very heavy. "Are they going to ask me to carry those things?" I thought.

"They want a lot of these up stairs," he said, and picking one up in his big brown hands rolled it over on his shoulder, and walked away. The other man did the same. Only before he walked off he said: "Let me show you something," and then added with an illustrative motion, "catch it in the middle, and balance it this way. It'll make it a heap easier for you."

I went up to it and tried to pick it up, but I found that for me it was an exceedingly heavy weight. I swung it around and by dint of pulling got it in position and my shoulder under it, but when I first lifted it I thought I should stumble and fall. A sharp pain shot across the muscles of my back and down my legs. I found myself straining for breath, and with the greatest effort I dragged myself along, trying to look as if I could do it. "I mustn't say that I can't handle these," I thought. "I wouldn't last an hour at that rate," and with every muscle in me straining with pain I crawled up the stairs and into the front part of the room where I let it fall with a thud, by some more of the same kind.

The man who was running the lathe nearby, for which these were being supplied, a querulous, self-opinionated old fellow, whom I afterwards came to dislike, said, "You don't want to drop it so hard. You'll break the floor through."

"I couldn't help it," I replied, almost savagely, and walked off. Down the stairs I went, not knowing whether I could carry another or not but determined to try and at the foot of the stairs met the two dromios already returning with two other posts. I went out and shouldered my second, and eventually got up with it and so my third and fourth. When I was about ready to conclude that I had done myself some irreparable physical injury the man at the machine said to me, "Tell them men not to bring any more. I have enough now."

I heaved a heartfelt sigh of relief.

"Thank God there's the last of that," I thought and went below.

The two men who were carrying up others when I came down received the message in silence. They went on up and came down, going off somewhere and then the red-headed man who had first spoken to me came up and said, "Now you can carry out that saw dust."

He pointed to a modest pile of shavings, and showed me where there was a bushel basket, and a large, long-handled iron scoop. I took the basket and filled it and started back to the engine room, where I naturally supposed they belonged. On the way I inquired of the smith, however, and was told to go straight ahead. Once back there I found the engine room, and a large, fat, comfortable-looking engineer, who looked very good-natured.

"I'm your new shaving boy," I said in jest and by way of greeting. "Where'll you have 'em?"

"In here," he said, pointing to a large bin, and I dumped them in.

The appearance of this engineer was in pleasing contrast to that of the other men I had thus far encountered. He was a large man, five feet eleven if he was an inch, with a great fat body, and a round, rosy bullet of a head. He had on a suit of blue—overalls and jumper, and the sleeves of the latter were rolled up to his elbows. He had a jolly face, fat, kindly, with a good-natured, intelligent blue eye. On this first occasion he greeted me most cordially.

"Ain't used to this sort of work are you," he said.

"No," I replied.

"You'll find it kinda hard first off, I expect. It's always that way when you just begin. You'll get used to it after awhile. It'll come a heap easier, when you're used to it."

He followed me to the door once or twice, and after I had carried a number of baskets advised me to sit down.

"There ain't anyone goin' to see you out here," he said. "The boss ain't here today. Besides you're workin' hard enough. It'll be a heap better for you if you'll take it kind of slow to begin with."

I thanked him for his kindness but kept on my way, as I preferred to work. The baskets were not very heavy and I fancied I could work all day in this way without getting very tired. With a lively step and a good-natured feeling that I was now launched upon a recreative career of labor I went walking to and fro, to and fro, filling my basket and humming a tune by the way, although at times the grimness of it, and the continued ill drift of my fortunes, came back to me with an icy bitterness.

"Carrying shavings!" I said to myself over and over. "Carrying shavings. And that and one-fifty a day. The miserableness of it. Gee!"

In about an hour the shavings I had had piled up before me were all gone, the last "smidgeon" of them, and then I had to report to the acting foreman, the young farmer-like lad with the red hair, who had given me this second job to do. He was up on the second floor, among the carpenters, and I went there, looking curiously at the rows of industrious men the while. They looked at me also, the curiosity of my being there looking clearly back at me out of their eyes. I felt glad to have something to do in connection with the foreman and hastily addressed my request to him.

"You go out to that car there," he said, pointing through the window to the yard, where besides the dull rows of splintered cars could be seen the distant glory of the hills and waters framing them like a picture, "and let them show you how to pile the stuff. That'll be something." I went down stricken, for I had seen my first two associates of the morning carrying good-sized planks to a car and shoving them in. I went out and informed them that the red-headed man, Mr. Simmons his name was, had sent me, and the one who had the glass eye, John Carder, exclaimed to the other who was named John Hicks, and who was in the car, "Well get down John!" and then to me, "Get up there."

I thought his manner was slightly dictatorial but I did not like to say anything. He volunteered no further information and they both went away, presently to return with some two-by-four sixteen-foot joists. "Pile 'em in the corner," said he of the glass eye, "top o' them others," and he shoved his two in, nearly in position. I laid hold of them in the middle, but the other John, coming up, called me to take it by the end.

"Just pick it up by the end," he said, "and shove it along. Wait. I'll show you," and seeing me inexperienced he climbed in the car, and began a few lessons in piling. I was always to pick a plank up by the end, and shove it along into position while piling in a car. It made it easier. I was to lay a stick of wood on the floor so as to form a rest for the planks under which I could get my hands. I was to look out for my fingers, and splinters, and never, under any circumstances to try to lay any piece of lumber down with my fingers. "Drop it," he said. "Drop it three feet from the floor. It'll fall into place all right. If it don't, shove it along with your foot. Don't ever try to hang on to it. It'll make it easier for you."

I did as I was told, and found that the work though hard, was not beyond me. It offered some diversion in the number of piles to be arranged and the tally to be kept. I learned how to handle two-inch planks and six-by-six-inch posts, and found that the burden of lifting could be modified considerably if only one knew the tricks of balancing. The work was steady though, and for me, so unused to it, wearisome. I found after a time that my arms and back were beginning to ache again, and that my fingers were smarting from splinters. Once I caught my middle fingers under a plank and then I doubled up with pain. However I managed to adjust things and keep the work going when all of a sudden a whistle blew.

"There she goes John," said the glass-eyed worker coming up, looking in. "Better get your dinner now, new man."

I climbed down, weary enough, and saw the wheels dying down to a stop as I entered the door.

My lunch consisted of a few sandwiches and some fruit. I ate gloomily as I sat on a pile of lumber. Many of the hands came down from above, painters, carpenters, tinsmiths and what not, and lined themselves up in a row on lumber piles and benches. They talked of work, and the number of men being laid off, and some little things relating to their homes or their wives, or the foreman's health and so on, but nothing of general interest. Some read their papers, some maintained a moody silence, some joked, with rude jokes about their wives or their companions. Two or three joined in a pointless political argument, so barren of ideas that it was painful. I studied them all, looking at first one and the other and trying to make out their characteristics, but finding few if any that I could admire. They were hard-working men, and their toil I thought was in their favor, but the same vapid comments ruled here that ruled among the well-to-do at Muldoon's. It was not so spirited here as there, and there was not so much wit, but the subjects were of the same importance, not more so. The only difference that I could see was that here the conversation was about meagre things, while there it was about showy ones. The old clothes, the old lumber, the old dirt and a less tidy state of everything made up the difference. Here commonplace ideas dealt with grim conditions, where there commonplace ideas dealt with fortunate ones. In what way were they worse?

CHAPTER XXIII

THE whirr of wheels, growing gradually louder, put an end to my reflections and then I returned to the car, where I had labored so wearily in the morning. The idea of more work of this kind—hourly work—daily work—yearly work, had an appalling effect on me and I looked away wistfully over the high board fence at the green hill opposite and the swirling waters of the river outside, marvelling at the beauty of it. There was life, there was peace, there was sweetness outside—as it always is,—life the beautiful, the elusive, the forever distant. The cars about me looked grimmer, the men duller, the yard bleaker than ever I had imagined anything could look and I wished from the bottom of my heart that I was safely out of it.

And yet in the midst of these very reflections there was something infinitely sweet about these reflections. I am such a lover of life—its lights and its shadows are so appealing to me, that withal nothing could be wholly bad. I looked at these brown-clad men plodding solemnly, I might almost say indifferently, to and fro, and the vast scheme of nature with its insistence on law and order came over me with an appalling weight. Here was an illustration of the meaning of life, of its insistence on energy and force. Man was made to work. He was made to fit in with the great scheme of labor and nothing but labor was satisfactory to it. To be rough, to be indifferent, to be pitiless seemed the very essence of it. There was nothing in the world but that. It seemed constantly striving to undo the softer and the tenderer side of life.

And while I worked these men talked—a little.

"Gee, this is a wet one, this is," said the one who was named Hicks, the more genial of the two, as he came tramping under a great piece that seemed to fairly strain his back. "I tell you that's the time they weigh heavy—when they get wet," he said.

The other man plodded sullenly, gloomily. He seemed to me to have a sour, pugnacious view of life and looked at me out of a gloomy eye. Such a stare. What a way to take the world. I felt for the time being as if he had some grudge against me and yet I felt too as if it were an innate, subconscious discontent—the struggle of a flesh-bound essence, recalling in some dim way the pleasure and joys of another state, struggling here in some wretched, voiceless way to be free. Ah blind nature. Mother of all that is. How we trust and mistrust thee all in the same breath.

The afternoon wore on and during that time I began to see the subtle connection that exists between skill and experience, in anything—even in so humble a task as this of piling up wood, one piece on top of another. These men, so dull to the ordinary matters of importance in life were nevertheless skilled to the point of extreme usefulness in this matter of piling lumber. They knew or seemed to know exactly how and where to lay hold of a piece of lumber and how and where to balance it. They had an art of walking and an art of turning which made it almost impossible, to one not accustomed, to see how they did it. They had a way of picking up a plank or post at the end and shoving it along the floor which took off two thirds of its weight and they had another way of placing one end and then lifting the other which made it quite easy to handle what to me, at first, seemed enormous pieces of lumber. There was a trick they had of dropping lumber, which pleased me greatly, for it allowed you to get great boards into position which otherwise might catch and smash your fingers. There was speed in their tricks also and I came to have a great admiration for what I conceived to be the skill of the thing, for it *was* skill, and to feel that I had already added considerably to my sum of practical knowledge. Altogether I was thoroughly and practically benefited by what I saw, and when I was through I was truly glad that I had the experience.

The remainder of the day, when this car was finished, I spent in sweeping up the second floor, which I was told would require my attention. It was literally covered with shavings and blocks and sawdust to a depth of six inches. I never knew until I got in there that lumber waste could take such varied forms. There were lumber shavings that looked like young girls' curls and there were others that looked like hashed spaghetti. There were lumber chips, and lumber blades, blocks, splinters, nubs and sticks. All the trash of a day was here piled up, and I thought as I looked at it, and all the machines under which it was scattered that I should have a job cleaning it up if I managed to do it that day yet. I secured a broom, a pusher or rake, a scoop and a basket however and began to gather it up, dumping it into a bin hole that led from beneath one of the carpenter's benches at the west end of the room to the floor below. Here I encountered an old Irishman who was very crusty about letting me disturb him. He claimed to have lost some tools by having the stuff swept down this way and cautioned me to close the lid when I was through.

"Sometimes," he said, with a peculiarly owl-like batting of his eyes and a marked accent, "men'll be comin' along here and they'll jist, unbeknownst ye know, knock a tool off. If it goes down in that hole it's not likely it'll ever be found again d'y'see. It's not the first tool I've lost that way—not the first. So if ye'll aalways be careful just to close the hole after ye're through I'll thank ye and we'll get along very well indeed."

Here is some old crank I thought who will make trouble for me if I don't look out for this, and I tried to take good care, not to offend him. I went on with my work and in an hour or so, completed it. Finally at five-thirty I saw the men taking off their overalls and getting ready to leave. I put my broom and shovel and rake away also and went below where the Irish millwright proffered me the use of a piece of soap and a towel. I washed myself and donned my coat and at five-thirty-five when the wheels stopped I went out to the station platform to await my train. In ten minutes more that came along and at six o'clock exactly I walked into my room, at my new home, tired, dirty, feeling as if I had been dragged through a thresher. Decidely this method of earning my living did not appeal to me, but I consoled myself with the thought that I was helpless and this was the only way.

CHAPTER XXIV

D URING the next few days I was kept very busy doing the work that was demanded of me at Spike, and I can truly say that I found it very hard. My strength was not much—a mere bagatelle compared to that of some that worked there with me, and the labor imposed upon me was frequently all but beyond my strength. I was compelled to carry shavings, to sweep the floors and remove the accumulations of blocks of wood and sticks which littered the milling department, and the carpenters' room above, to load and unload lumber to and from cars and to carry in lumber, which to me was the hardest of all.

This room in which I first worked was a perfect maw for lumber. It contained all the implements with which lumber is originally milled and the quantity consumed by them was something to see. I was compelled to carry planks hour after hour and day after day, at times supplying the material for orders which to me seemed to come in with amazing and painful regularity. There was a freight that plied between 30th Street on the North River, and Mott Haven Yard at 138th Street, which appeared regularly in the morning at nine and again in the afternoon at three and shunted four or five cars in, and took as many away again, which immediately meant that there was more lumber to load or unload. True there was a yard gang, composed of from three to fifteen Italians, according to the pressure of work, and an American foreman who were supposed to attend to this work, but even they were not always capable of coping with it. In times of pressure the two men whom I have described as the two dromios, and who were usually employed in loading cars exclusively, were added to their gang, and then carpenters, millwrights and helpers in general according to their immediate usefulness or their power of rendering better service.

Not infrequently I was called out to aid in this, but my services were not of the best. I could not handle these things as well as some, and for the most part I was left inside.

During this time I was given much to brooding, and for the time being it seemed to me as if my state had fallen about as low as that of a human being well may. To be compelled to rise thus every morning at six or rather five-thirty, to eat a lonely and rather desolate breakfast and to hustle out through a damp atmosphere while others were still drowsing seemed the height of hardship to me. "What kind of a world is it," I said to myself, "wherein one is always struggling to keep his head above water. What a pity that there is not enough wisdom vouchsafed the human organism to keep itself well balanced and in health. To be driven about this way like a slave—to be whipped and scourged." Truly I built up a very interesting picture of myself, and bemoaned my fate accordingly.

At the same time I was learning some very interesting things concerning life and the conditions of the laborer which I had not known before. This village of Kingsbridge, with its rows of pretty, peaceful houses all supported by labor, had an impressive effect on me, now that I saw it through the eyes of one who works with his hands. Whether viewed in rain or shine it seemed altogether lovely. From the depot a winding, tree-shaded road, led up, across Broadway, and by the banks of the Harlem to a little clump of houses and stores set down in the valley adjoining my hill, which was the very picture of revolutionary days. It had a church or two and a library, a few grocery and feed stores and a coal and grain dock, all lined up in a drab and yellow block where quiet reigned. There was a little launch-building plant and one wretched hotel or inn set down on the water's edge, and facing a road which led due north from New York and where a fine collection of automobiles and vehicles of various kinds sped past. About and around, on the north, the east and the west, were a number of green hills forming a kind of ridge which enclosed this valley. The little river, which here turned in a circle about the island-hill on which I lived, was dotted with rowboats, and the sight of the many frame houses nestled among the trees created a most agreeable impression of home.

As I walked along this evening viewing these things I was deeply touched by them. For the first time in years the simplicity and the seeming hardship of the underworld came to me and I dwelt with a softening eye on all that I saw. This was labor. This was what it was to work hard and come home after a long day to a comfortable home. These houses on the hill—how they loomed up with that atmosphere of tenderness and comfort which appeals to the home-loving instinct in man. Toil and the comfort of the night— how these loomed large in the hour of weariness. I could not handle these things as well as some and for the most part I was left inside.

During this time I had a chance to broaden my knowledge concerning manual labor, which I had no choice but to accept. These machines and cars so constant in their inpour and outpour, and so deafening and disagreeable in their noise and dust were the centers of the most varied and profitable activities. The planes for instance did the work of hundreds of men in planing, the moulding and jigging machines, did that form of delicate carving and shaping,—a fragment of which a man could not hope to do in a day, but which one of these machines would turn out by the hundreds of lineal feet every hour. The ripsaws and cross-cut saws performed herculean feats in cutting and shaping and surprised me by their speed and accuracy. I had been used to seeing these things through windows and open doors, and listening to their noise from some comfortable vantage point where they sounded like the drone of distant bees, but here, close at hand, where the work was being actually done they took on a new significance to me.

"What a task," I thought. "How continuous. What a profit there must be in the control of labor. How much it is that they individually yield. This vast sway and sweep of elemental energy— how does it come that the few have put their hands on it and control it while the many serve and wait?"

The actual observation of labor at close range had a varied and peculiar effect on me. At times, when I was not too busy I was inclined to look on it with a gentle and melancholy eye. This constant carrying to and from, while not a comfortable labor, had its relieving aspects. It occupied my mind. Then too I was never weary of studying the characteristics of those about me and wondering at their condition. The regularity with which they came to their work in the morning. The sameness and at times the indifference with which they prosecuted their work all interested me. At times I was appalled by the monotony of it. At others by the uselessness or rather unprofitableness of it all. To what end did it lead, I used to ask myself, and why was it necessary? What profit and who obtained it? Surely not these.

That these speculations were not good for my mind nor profitable in themselves was quite well known to me and yet I could not resist them. Life just at this time was a vast and appalling phantasmagoria to me—a strange and mysterious problem which would not let me be. I was compelled to think of the weirdness and peculiarity of it, and the more I thought, the more inexplicable it became. I used to turn to my work after one of these intrusive flights of fancy and hope that I could get my mind off it and on my work. If I could just stop thinking, I thought. If I could just forget everything but the fact that I have my work to do. It seemed as if my mind had been laid bare as if by a scalpel to mysteries of the universe, and that I was compelled to suffer, blood-raw, the agonies of its weight.

About two weeks after I had been there I was greeted one morning by the foremost of the two men whom I had worked with the first day and was told to follow him. I went out into the yard and at his direction climbed into a car which he and his partner then began to load with two-by-four joists, smooth-planed, which were fourteen and sixteen feet long. It was not hard work, nothing like the painful experience I had had with them on the first day, and I began to think that I had been mistaken as to the total character of their work. Everything they did was not hard. I was rather glad that I was able to do it so actively, and was thinking that I should like more of this if it was possible, without getting into the extremely heavy work, when the man with the glass eye, John Carder by name, addressed me with an unusually cheery greeting for him.

"Howya like this work?" he inquired.

"Very well," I replied. "It's not as hard as I thought it would be."

"Better'n workin' inside there ain't it?"

"Well, it's certainly cleaner. I don't like the dust in there very much."

"It'll do you good if you work outside here once in awhile," he continued. "It'll be better for your lungs. I hear you're not feelin' very well."

"No I'm not," I replied, slightly wondering who had told him. This gossip of course, as to my reason for being here would go from man to man, but I did not expect to hear it from him. From the little I had seen of him around the shop he struck me as a taciturn, distant man, rather inclined to be self-willed and opinionated, and with an exaggerated idea of his usefulness. Why I thought this I could not say for no one had ever said a word about him to me. In fact none of them had become friendly enough with me to pass any comments.

He went away, coming again with more lumber on his shoulder, and looking doggedly into the car.

"A queer creature," I thought, "dull and thick. He may not be any of the things I think him, and I may be simply nervously exaggerative in my temperament. I ought to try and be friendly with him if I can."

Thereafter I laid myself out to be pleasant to him and I think he noticed that there was an atmosphere of kindness and goodwill for he also became less taciturn.

CHAPTER XXV

THE fact that I was thus safely ensconced in the labor world for the time being had a very depressing effect on me. Used as I was to the freedom of the world outside, to better clothes and more extended range of thought than could easily be here employed, was a thing which weighed heavily upon me. For all that I saw the advantages of health and the slow recuperation of my financial condition involved I nevertheless felt like an outcast, and as I wended my way homeward this evening I went over in my mind the various afflictions of my recent days and wondered whether I should ever really recover from them. To be maimed as an insect. To get a hurt that would not heal. How disastrous it was in this or any order of society or in any place in nature. There seemed, as I viewed it then, a kind of immorality in it, which debarred one from broad and pleasant social contact. He is injured. Therefore he is not morally whole. Let him go forth and wander by himself. He does not any longer belong to the sane and healthy order of society.

The house when I reached it, was a pleasant stop to these reflections. It was situated, as I have described, on the westernmost segment of the lowermost circle of streets, overlooking the waters of the Harlem, which here flowed in an alternating current first six hours in and then six hours out. The opposite bank from that on which I resided was occupied by a range of low, yellow, wooden tenements, the homes of a number of foreign workmen, who were employed in the steel mills beyond, and back of them again was the bank of a huge hill which towered like a leviathan above them. They were so homely, the little tenements of yellow. They snuggled so humbly between the green wall of earth and the hurrying current of the river. They looked by day like some brown patchwork left over from a preceding autumn of glorious color and by night like some jewel-studded stuff of velvet, or some wall of ebony set with diamonds. High overhead, above the crest of the hilltop shone the stars, and far below lay the water, gleaming and twinkling with rays which the tenements cast. I remember looking with a soulful, heartfelt awe upon the beauty of the scene and wondering whether I should ever be able to describe it and whether I could ever make anyone feel what I was then feeling.

Fragments

This part of the mss consists
in the main of random notes
about the various workingmen
in the shop at *Spike*—no sequence
attempted—
> Author

I. The Illness

I should say here that mine was a serious case of neuresthenia—or nervous prostration. It had begun with the conclusion of a novel which I had written three years before and which exhausted me greatly. It was enhanced by various physical indiscretions which it will serve no purpose to enumerate here and the general stress and worry incident to earning a living, as well as by moving into a neighborhood entirely unsuited to my nature. The latter had been done in pursuit of the idea that one could live anywhere and be happy so long as the interior condition of the house was satisfactory. But I found out different. The drearyness of the neighborhood into which I moved—it was on the East Side, facing the East River—the wretchedness of the poverty and the sight of the gloomy Blackwells Island on which were housed the sick, the criminal and the insane of the city had a most depressing effect on me. I continued there working and brooding trying to make both ends me until finally went South on a publishers contract and got rid of that terror anyhow.

However by that time my physical condition had been pulled to a very low state. I was morbid, had fearful dreams, slept very little at night and ended at last in Philadelphia with notable symptoms and aberrations. For one thing I found that I could not ten thoughts scarcely consecutively. For another that I was constantly most gloomy and depressed,—almost to the state of tears, the world looking exceedingly grim. For a third my nerves began to hurt me, particularly in the ends of my fingers in which I felt genuine pain and lastly, I began to have the idea, or the almost irresistable impulse to turn around in a ring. That is, if a I were **127** sitting in a chair I would want to keep turning to the right—an involuntary nervous discharge of will force almost making it impossible for me not to do so. Then too my eyes began to hurt me and I felt as if the columns of the paper or book I was reading was crooked. I even went so far as to consult two occulists on that matter who assured me that there was nothing the matter with my eyes or my glasses and I also put myself under the care of a celebrated nerve specialist who treated me for three months without much result though he pointed out the course by which I subsequently recovered. When I was through with him and my other experiments I was possessed of exactly 32^{00} dollars and no means of obtaining anything more unless I should write and that very quickly something that would sell. Anyone who knows how difficult it is to sell to magazines and how slow they are in making up their minds to accepting anything can have some idea of my situation as I viewed it then.

It was not however as hopeless as it seemed. (I:115–17, 122, 138)

. . . dreaded to think what I do when my money was gone.

I should say here that my nervous condition had made a coward of me. Extraordinarily sensitive to what the world thinks, particularly of the beggar, when in the best of health, my nervous feeling on this score when my health was so poor and resources all but gone was racking. Although possessed of relatives and friends, in the way that relationships and friendships go in this world, I nevertheless felt that I could not turn to them. What would those who knew me as a modestly successful author think of me should I come to them asking for assistance. What would my brothers and sisters think, who knowing me as a rather selfish and self concerned individual, should I come knocking at their door and saying I am ill and without means of support. What would the world in general say seeing that I was not absolutely ill in bed should poverty force me to ask for a means of livlihood. Me without trade or calling save the one at which I could not work. I pictured myself, tall, dignified, rather thoughtful and with black rimmed glasses on my nose entering shops and stores and saying to the average clerk, "I want work."

"And what can you do."

"What can I do? Anything or nothing. I have no trade, but I am not a fool. I will do anything that might will allow me to do."

"Yes. Well we haven't anything at present."

And what a recommendation of oneself—"Anything I can do." Me without any physical strength. Without any real mental energy to do the thing which I had been by nature cut out to do. In that hour I wished a hundred times that I had learned some trade which I could now turn to. It would have saved me so much pain.

And yet without my illness I did not consider myself utterly worthless, even physically. I realized that I could work as a clerk, a conductor or motorman, a railroad hand or a most anything which did not require special training. I was active, quick, willing, once I should be forced to take it and I felt that if I tried hard I might be able to get it. Still all these things were so much apart from the life which I had been leading—they represented such a different order of existence that I felt I should be out of place in them. I could try, but what, if I could by any means regain my skill as a writer, a waste of time to turn to them. No I thought. I must write, and in that thinking I was continuing the worst error of all my many.

The weeks which followed proved the truth of this. (I:121, 119, 135, 131–32)

―――――――――――――――――――

. . . the docks reached far out into a very peaceful bay of the East River and where hay and straw and apples and ice were being continually loaded and unloaded. Others took me far north along the East Shore of the East River where great sugar refineries, iron foundries, and tall manufactories crowd the waters edge. At other times I wandered willingly amid the endless maze of resident streets where three story houses of one design shouldered one another and where people seemed to be living out a just existence in a passive commonplace way. At other times I found myself strolling in the sections of wretched poverty where narrow living and narrower thinking were combined with dirt and squalor general. These were sad pilgrimages and depressed me even more than I was able to say.

During this time I did my share of philosophizing concerning life. (I:118, 120)

. . . was no exception. I soon found my money supply reduced to fifteen dollars and then ten dollars and then I saw that I had but one more week to run before I would be unable to pay my board or room rent in advance and myself put out in the street. In the dread of this I got up and on several days made desperate tours of the city looking in this window and that, hoping to find courage to do something. I had been thinking if worse came to worse I could get on some street car line as a motorman or conductor. I was not so frail but that I could do that I reasoned but now on the morning before I broke into my last ten dollars I went down to the headquarters of the Street Railway really worrying over the necessity of finding where I could put in an application and when, for a position. When I reached there however my courage failed me and for an hour and more I walked the streets adjacent to the general office trying to go in. I was so distressed at the figure I cut that I could hardly find words to tell the man what I wanted. The crowd of motormen and conductors who were there being measured for new suits or answering to complaints of various kinds looked at me with curious eyes. Some of them stood aside for me in such a deferential manner that I felt as . . . (I:128, 123)

And so it was with a score of other applications made about that time. I rose each morning and went to breakfast at seven. Here after eating ravenously of all that was put before me—a large appetite is characteristic of nervous prostration being due to the systems extreme efforts to recover itself—I would slip a roll into my pocket to serve me as lunch. Then I would go out and walk or ride to some factory or business where I fancied I might get something to do, buoyed up on the way by my extreme necessity which made it absolutely essential for me to do something. On the way I would say to myself "now I must do something this morning. I must go right in. Never mind what people think of me. Their acceptance of me as something better than I am will not keep me alive unless I get something to do" and then I would hurry and get within fifty feet of the door, when suddenly my courage would pass out with a rush. I would find myself hesitating and saying "what will they think." Suddenly I would find myself involuntarily retreating and exclaiming "no I cant do it. They wouldnt have anything there for me to do anyhow. How would I look being sent away after a shop girl or boy had informed me that the manager did not need anyone, or that he was so busy he could not see me." It produced cold sweats on my body. It made me feel at times as if I would have to drift and starve.

And here I should like to say that this sense of personal inappropriateness now took a very firm hold on me and I began to see why it is that some people succeed and some fail. While I was thus wandering around it came to me that the reason why I was so unhappy in my efforts was that I was physically and mentally unfitted for the thing I was seeking as well as personally conscious of my unfitness for the thing I was seeking. Thus the person who has a trade or a profession—who feels called by some inborn sense of ability or capacity in any line has no fear to ask for work in that line. It is an honor to him. I have no sense of unfitness in going to a publisher to ask him to publish my book, nor any in applying to a magazine editor to publish a story. I have never hesitated to ask for anything anywhere, when I thought I had something valuable to give in return for it, but this proposition of the hands was something very different. The world I realized was not giving something for nothing. It was not going to allow me to go to work unless I looked as though I was fitted to do the work. And this I was not.

What reason had I for applying I asked myself. What work could I do? To the former I could only answer "self preservation." To the latter—none. I was not particularly interested in anything I applied for—in most cases bitterly opposed to, and yet, necessity driving me I was coming to ask favor. Hence I was largely a burden on the person or institution who or which listened to me and unless my merely manual strength should worth something when hired I might have looked upon as an object of charity. Why should I be hired? Why indeed.

People and institutions feel these facts. They know when you are valuable to them and when not. In most cases all those to whom I applied percieved that I was out of my element and perhaps thought that I should go where I belonged.

I remember suffering a very bitter hour on this score. (I:133, 130, 129, 137, 124–27)

II. The Mills Hotel

. . . be to obtain a competence there. I had done so. In Wall Street were tons upon tons of gold. In the banks and shops any amount of clothing and food. The groceries and restaurants were full of food. People were paying extravagant prices for all sorts of things that did not appertain to the immediate sustenance of the body at all. Why should I want. Why should anyone want.

That night and Sunday night I spent at the Mills Hotel, where I came in direct touch with another phase of human misery. This is a hotel situated in one of the once fashionable sections of New York, Bleecker Street, but now a very badly deteriorated tenement house region, where Poles, Hungarians, Jews and Negroes swarm. It is however a handsome structure of cream colored brick and gray stone, nine storys tall, with an overhanging roof of dark red tiles and an entrance way of most imposing proportions. I had often seen it and read of it in my wandering about and living in New York, but I had never been there and now that I forced to go to it in a way I was rather curious now to see how it was conducted. I went down and asked for a room and being assigned by the clerk to a chamber on the fifth floor went up to it.

The conditions I found there were anything but pleasent. The room assigned to me (and all the others were like it) was a tiny affair, 6 by 8 feet . . . (IV:148–50)

. . . of men. It had such a bleak, depressing appearence, and I thought I should never get well if I were compelled to live there and I lay in bed that night thinking of all the people who were compelled to live there and wondering how I should stand it if I were old, or sick beyond recovery or had no watch to pawn, no brother to seek me, no friends to go to, no letters of importance to identify. Supposing I had not, as I had thought I had not, even money enough to come here. What would have become of me then. Where would I have been this night.

I lay there in my wretched bed for it was not clean and thought of the life about me. Here it was, this vast host, come up or down out of so many phases of life and at last on this night, this day, this year perhaps for some, quartered here like so many straws in some little by pool of a great river. Outside the world was rushing by. The theatres were full of people, the streets full of life. Shops were still open, vehicles rolling, familes preparing a comfortable outing for the morrow, but these—these were cast aside. They had no homes no money to go anywhere, no friends to see. They were pushed in here by the rushing current of life, while it raced a joyous course outside.

And then I listened to the various sounds that came to me during the progress of the night—the strange echoes of life, that in my nervous condition seemed to make it uncanny. All of them did not sleep by any means. Some seemed to be sitting and communing with themselves in an audible, self-explanatory way, as if they were worrying about something. Others tossed and turned through the advancing hours as if night could not bring them any rest. Still others got up and prowled about until hoarsely commanded by some disturbed neighbor to lie down, while others yet made complaints of the condition of the beds, the indifference of the attendents. "They dont ever fix em," said some one near me. "They'd let me sleep on the same sheets for a month. Its an outrage, thats what it is. Its a d—— shame."

I listened to this with open ears. I had been complaining of my own bed to myself.

"Why don't you kick," said the voice of a sympathetic neighbor.

"Kick! Huh, a lot of good that'll do you. Haint I kicked.

"Chop it off. Chop it off! came from some one who objected to this midnight colloquy.

The morning brought no surcease of all this, but only the sight of grizzled men prowling around the halls in their shirts and trousers, suspenders down and of crowds washing and shaving themselves in the big washrooms on each floor—the rooms offered no opourtunity for private ablutions of any kind. I made my way like the others to . . . (IV:151–57)

. . . recovery had now truly begun. With this and my new job and my extreme desire and determination to get well I would soon do so. I went down to the Mills Hotel where I took a room for three days at twenty cents a day. Then I went over to Brooklyn and got my grip and with it returned my little cell. Here I bestowed myself looking out through my barred window down into the great lobby where hundreds of poverty stricken men were sitting around playing dominoes or reading the newspapers. It was a gloomy institution to me, sad, narrow, horrible but I could not help it I thought and went to bed. That night I scarcely slept a wink, thinking all the while of Paul, of my watch, of my job—all all the things that had befallen me so rapidly. Could have been that my feeling about the ending of my wretchedness that I had experienced the night before had been a premonition, a psychic, subconscious forcast. I wondered.

The passing of Saturday night and Sunday and Sunday night brought me a new insight into the possible miseries of human life. Although I myself was partially extricated the sight of this vast hotel with its burden of want and misery was enough to keep me wretched. (IV:162–64)

. . . idlers, loafers, stingy people, theives and then at the old men those queer old men who rove the city by day and gather here at night and wondered how they stood it. To think of being caught in such a maelstrom of want as I had endured at say sixty or seventy. To see your strength gone, your hope gone and to be compelled to sit in such a place and wait. For what? For a little food, a little clothing, a little something to keep on living here and then to die. Awful. One of the hallboys told me that out of the great throng of 1500 who live here some one is taken away every day sick and to die. The majority of them never returned. A great provision against would be suicides here was the open condition of the rooms, the wall or partitions of each only reaching high enough and low enough to conceal the main operations of ones toilet. The rest of the distance was protected against entry by an open wire netting. There was no chance to turn on the gas here because there was none. (IV:167–69)

III. Kingsbridge

CHAPTER XXVIII

IT was during my introductory observations in connection with the conditions in this factory that I was led into a more extended intimate study of the life and atmosphere of Kingsbridge. This village, set down among green hills, and partially encircled, as the island portion of it was by green hills, was one of the fairest and most pleasing pictures of earth that I have ever witnessed. It was a quiet old place, bereft by the flight of time and the near approach of New York of all that had once made it interesting and busy as a village and yet superficially endued with a kind of buoyancy and enthusiasm which came from the fact that although New York had killed the old life, it had all but created a new one. From the depot, as you dismounted from the train a winding, tree-shaded road led up accross Broadway and by the banks of the river (the Harlem) to a little clump of antiquated wooden houses and stores, which served at once as the remnant of the old life and the nucleus of the new. It was surrounded on every hand by long tree shaded lanes of houses which clustered together in curious isolated groups and then left the roads bare again. Houses covered the island opposite, which contained the cottage in which I resided. Houses covered the green side of a nearby hill to the eastward, which when the sun shone on them, stood out from their green setting like little white structures of card board, and houses decorated the tops of a hill or two to the westward, which were always visible by daylight by their white colors and at night by their lamps. Immediately about this tumble 137 down centre of old life were a few churches and schools, some half awake business enterprises such as a coal yard, a launch building establishment, and a small hotel, set close down to the waters edge and in the distance, over the waters of the river to the south and on the distant top of a hill stood a notable nunnery its pinnacled roof surmounted by a handsome gold cross, and its imposing array of windows gleaming in the evening sun like burnished gold. When night fell and the lamps shone forth, the hills and valleys, rising and falling in darksome rythm, revealed a world of seeming peace and prosperity gathered in little gleaming groups which made it all the more appealing for that was under the extended vault of heaven, and looked down upon by billions of scintillating stars.

The house, as I have indicated, whenever I returned to it had a most summery appearence. The awnings were nearly always down and the various red and yellow and blue jardinieres flourished with plants and vines upon the porch. Inside all was airy and clean and I invariably made haste to divest myself of my old clothes and after bathing to array myself in something clean and cool. I had a neat blue serge suit as well as some outing shirts and a pair of low quarter shoes—the remnants of another summer, and these with a fresh collar and tie made me quite presentable. I came down after a time ready to enjoy the view which the porch offered, and was called with much cordiality to dinner.

The family on these occasions was always composed of all its members and a lively conversation ensued. I was questioned as to my labors and gave a truthful account. It then turned to work in general and the characters involved in it, and finally one evening some mention was made of a Miss Abbrechinna, who was also a character in the village. She was they said the daughter of a rich Italian banker, resident on the Hudson a few miles more, and noted here for a certain form of ostentation which my hostess and her nephew seemed to consider out of place in a village like Kingsbridge. Comment was made on the way she rode her horses in the village, the number of equipages she displayed, the frequency with which she changed her costumes—daily in fact, and their gorgeousness, and the fact that she drove her father to the station every morning and came for him again in the evening. "I saw her the other day", said the hostess, and she had on a stunning gown of lavender silk, with hat to match, and a long white plume. She looked very charming but I dont see the point in wearing it up here. There is no one to see it and its out of place."

"Let her alone", said the daughter, who seemed to have a vast toleration for human weakness. "She hasn't anywhere to wear it, why shouldn't she wear it here. She has the money and I dont see why she shouldn't use it that way if chooses. It is no ones business.

"Its peculiar, thats all," said her mother.

"Who is she, anyhow", I asked. "It seems to me I have heard that name."

"Oh, you know," said Miss Wollestencraft. "Her sister ran away and married a coachmen. It was in the papers. Her father keeps a very close watch over her and she has no one to go with except him. Its real sad. She is beautiful.

"Is her conduct so marked," I inquired. "I should think carriages and dresses anywhere near New York would not be considered very remarkable.

"Oh I know, but hers are exceptional said the daughter. "She really does overdo it. She courts attention and gets it. But I dont blame with her, poor thing. She hasn't any other way of displaying her beauty. Dresses and carriages are pretty poor consolation for want of companionship."

"And is she so companionless?" I asked, in surprise.

"Apparently" said the mother. "She doesnt seem to have anyone to go with. They are a very wealthy though. It is a kind of tragedy."

I thought of this as I sat out on the porch that evening, viewing the flying and worked up a fine philosophic contrast between myself and her. Here was a woman who had money and health and was unhappy, and here was I without them, in the same state.

"Evidently it is not the result of any particular thing, but just the want of variety, something new," I thought, and dreamed over the swirling waters, running in the moonlight below. This lady with her wealth and her uncomfortable solitude had taken a very firm and interesting hold upon my imagination.

Nevertheless, for all my musings, I was not destined to be happy here. This life, beautiful as it was, contrasted sharply with my working state and my physical condition. I could not help winding up my soliloquies concerning the beauties of this life with thoughts of my own fallen state. How far I was from any realization of my own ideals. How long it would be (if ever) before I could reclaim some of the pleasures of the world that I had known. I was as I had often said to myself, without money. There was no assurance that I would ever completely regain my health. And if I did not, then truly life was a failure for me and I was destined to go down to some unheard condition which would keep me miserable to the end of my days.

During this time I was interestedly looking about the village and one evening, as I was coming from work I noticed a open [   ], standing near the depot, its polished body and luxurious cushion reflecting the wealth and comfort of its owner as its mettled horses and handsome caparisons reflected his taste. The front seat was occupied by a lady who from the appearence of her dress and beauty of her face instantly recalled to me the account I had heard retailed at the dinner table of the wealthy heiress who was making herself conspicuous by her want of discretion in thus arraying herself where the simplicity of the occasion called for something less conspicuous.

She was a beautiful woman—about two and thirty, I should have said, with dark, lustrous, shadowy eyes, a full mop of raven black hair, and cheeks and chin that instantly appealed to you by their piquant roundness, the formerly healthily colored with red and latter softened into an egg like whiteness at the turn, which left the impression of perfect contour. She was well formed and stately, or perhaps I had better say self conscious, for she seemed as I looked at her, innately alive to every attribute of charm about her.

Her arm were encased in long suede gloves, which set off their plumpness to a turn. Her hips and torso were beautified by a close-fitting dress of the most delicate coral hued velvet and her hat was a study in the same color, large of brim, beautifully turned at the left with an immense ostrich feather, dyed the color of her dress, and a buckle of gold, that seemed to hold it fast in its clasp. At her throat was a radiant bow of gauzy ⌊   ⌋ which set off her throat and the delicacy of her face, and she seemed altogether a vision of lovliness.

"Not wholly tender", I thought, as I viewed her. "Rather self-conscious—too much so, but beautiful and with a look in her eye that may mean either sadness or coquetry. So this is the lady that is noted for her showy equipage, her fine dresses and her lonliness. I dont suppose she would ever dream that a creature such as myself, would ever be capable of thinking and judging of her by her appearence. She does not know that I exist, even though I pass so directly within her gaze.

I do not know how it was but this woman was thereafter, in some indefinable, subtle way, linked with the beauty of Kingsbridge to me. The fact that she was connected on this particular fashion with the gossip of the village and that her face had that indescriable look of weariness about it gave her a peculiar charm in my eyes. Her beauty and her clothing were decided attractions, of course, and the fact that she was reputed to be wealthy something also. I was not at all averse to contemplating these things though I confess that her beauty was the main object. Wealth had its charm. It provided the proper set, like the gold that holds the diamond, and made it if anything more delightful. (IV:34–58)

IV. Workers

. . . liked the smell of the smoke and the ring of the anvil, and whenever I would pass I would make some comment on it. He seemed pleased that I should be interested and began at once to explain the points of his trade which were numerous and interesting. I learned that morning for the first time what tempering meant, and how it was accomplished and how iron was wrought. He told me too of wages and how blacksmiths began there careers, and added that a railroad was a poor place for a blacksmith to work, since it did not offer a full practice of the profession. He had one helper, small, grimy, solemn looking who was one of the funniest little lads I have ever seen. He wore a blue gingham shirt and old soiled trousers, just the color of oily soot, which were about twice to large for him in width. His hair was long, and unkempt and his ears enormous. He had a big mouth and dirty, yellow teeth, two of which were missing, and big hands, much too big for his size. His eyes were small and he had a sort of battered face, something like one sees in satyrs cast in bronze. Nevertheless he had a smile which made up for some of his defects and a laugh which could be heard all over the shop. He was constantly running back to the engine room where old John was sitting and when I first came there, was nearly always to be found perched upon a box, talking to the big engineer, whom he seemed to like. His friendship for the the blacksmith was not so great—in fact as I subsequently learned there was a good deal of feeling between them, and he was averse to staying in the room with him—when he was not working. Nevertheless, they made an interesting picture when they were together drubbing a peice of iron, on the anvil, and when the little helper was gazing out of the window into the bleak yard, where the cinders and rubbish was he was sometimes a pathetic sight. (IV:7–10)

While I was working in the shop I remember dwelling most interestedly upon the characteristics which made these people good or bad workingmen. One I remember struck me at once as a particularly good workingman, for he was constantly to be seen plodding about at the same gait and doing his work with smiling good humor. He was an American, a carpenter by trade, and as I afterward learned, a resident of Kingsbridge where I lived. He had been living there ever since the war—some forty five years before. He was a middle-aged man, as long lives go, fifty-five years or thereabouts and slightly lame in one foot. He was also well built and plump and of such a smiling good humor that one could not help liking him on sight. I noticed him building sashes and door frames, and at other times watchmens houses, and small freight receptacles, in the yard and he was always in a good humor. He was the first, and for a long time the only one to give me a cheery good morning, as he did to others.

There was another man whom I subsequently came to admire and sympathize with though at first I did not quite understand him, and that was an old German, a Lutheran by faith and a cabinet worker by trade, who seemed to be looking out on the world with a sour dissatisfied air though as a matter of fact he was simply sad, or nervously morbid, like myself. He was a thin man, thin and spare, with a deep lined, hollow cheeked, hollow eyed, face and a sort of a cat like movement who looked at your furtively, out of burning black eyes. He occupied a bench on the second floor where he turned out some of the delicate peices of work in the shape of grill partitions, ornamental cabinets and the like, intended for the handsomer stations and offices of the road. He was constantly looking around as if he were afraid of something, and I could see that it was a real grounded fear. What it was I shall detail later, but at present I shall only say how struck I was with the way he worked. Day after day, hour after his nimble, thin fingers, waxy in their color, were busy fitting these delicate peices of wood together, and forcing the light panels of walnut and oak and rosewood, with which he worked into position. I was never tired when I passed of looking at this man. He was so frail, so delicate so earnest. His whole life seemed to be burning itself out in some vast effort to get something accomplished. And yet he was only a cabinet worker.

Still another was a long, lank American who was a sort of a spiritual descendent of the long nosed Yankee of literature, a peeking, prying, weasel-faced creature, who constantly talking in superlative, exaggerated sentences, and handing out stories and bits of advice which were as trite as they were rediculous. He was instinct with a self-complaisent vanity which made him feel quite sure that he was a wise as men are usually made and as fine a carpenter as could be created. He began talking to me the first day I saw in a condescending and yet confidential and advisory way, which amused me greatly. I looked upon him at once as some one I might well beware of for he had a touch of secret maliciousness in his eye, that indicated to me that he would hesitate to say unkind and unjust things about if he could. I tried to be as pleasent as possible, but there are things which are not endurable to our various temperaments in nature and this was one of them, to mine. He made me smile, but I was afraid of him—afraid, in the sense of not wishing to stir up opposition.

Still another was big John the engineer. He was such a comfortably built creature that I use to marvel how he got anything done. He was forever sitting reading his paper, or waddling out to the side gate which opened from the high board fence on the South side of the yard and looked out on the waters of the Harlem. Here he would stand when the necessity of firing or oiling did not require his attention and gaze at the small oyster boats that here plied their craft, planting seed oysters and gathering them again and looking at the green hill, which raised its beautiful green head opposite.

Big John, as I could see, was not much interested in nature as a spectacle, and could not philosophize for a moment concerning its meaning. He was interested in life, in the movement thereof, and so long as anything or anyone was passing in action before him his mind was occupied.

I think for the first week or two, despite my illness, and peevish examination of all that surrounded me that I was really charmed by this life. It was so new, so strange. These people were so different. It was useless to think of talking about anything that I had previously been accustomed to talk about for they did not understand. I remember starting various discussions in a mild, interlocutory way after I had been there a few days, but no one seemed to understand what I meant or to follow the drift of my argument. You could get good sane comments on how to thread a pipe or plane a board but when it came to the ethics of anything or the possible means of anything they were all in deep water. Children of nature all of them, following their little rounds of duties according to their lights and working as nature probably intended them to work without questioning how or why. (IV:16–33)

. . . should not, all at once, concieve the impermanence and changefulness of it and seeing it go mad, or dissolve. It was a critical period.

During this time however I found a strange satisfaction in the work. It was not a comfortable labor and it did not suit me very well, but this carrying to and fro had a relieving aspect. It occupied my mind. I could not thus lift and carry and think of myself or the world. I had to give some attention to my work and in doing so I lost thought for the time being of my physical ailments. Sometimes, quite frequently in fact this problem of the infinite would creep in between me and what I was doing I and I would up against that insoluable problem. It had a terrifying effect and I fled from it as I would from an evil personality. I tried my best to stop my thoughts and turn my mind, but I could not always do it.

One of the things that aided me however was the presence of these men and strangeness of my situation. Not being used to this workaday world and having a natural love of character I turned my attention to them and found some relief. I looked at the men who were working about me, and took almost delight in adjusting myself to my new relationship and in trying to see the thing as it looked to them.

One of the most interesting characters in this connection was the foreman himself, who arrived the second day I was been there. He was a tall, lank, thin man, with a comparatively long growth of limp red haid, and a red mustache, a large one. He had an angular body, strikingly so, with arms and legs that fairly seemed to dangle, and he face was peaked and bony. His eyes were large enough, but of a long, slanty, Chinese variety, with a touch of faded out blue in them and his mouth and ears were enormous. He had a cruel leer and a shifty, uncertain glance, which struck you treacherous. On our first meeting I took an innate dislike to him which served to distract my attention considerably, for he had no method of looking at me. When I handed him my letter he took it in an uncertain gingery way and read it without a word. Then he shoved it in his pocket and walked away.

This reception troubled me a little at first. I saw that he did not like me, or at least did not know how to take me, and I felt that he might make it very disagreeable for me if he chose. With that foolish self-consciousness of the neuresthenic I ran ahead looking for trouble and wondered how I should come out. Being anxious to hold this place I had naturally long for a slight touch of consideration as I felt that without it—without some modification I would not be able to hold my place at all.

None was shown me however, as far as I could detect. I was left to do my work, just as it had been originally mapped out for me and I can honestly say that I tried to do it. Despite numerous suggestions, which had been made principally in the absence of the foreman I kept doing all that I could, and noticed, that whether this was best policy or not all those of were of a serious turn of mind did so also.

There was, as I soon discovered however, a serious opposition to his steady round of toil in the minds of some. Thus on the first day that I had been here, one of the workers, Michael Cronin by name, head of the milling department came to me where I was industriously filling my basket and said:

"What are ye workin' so for hard. Cant ye see what the others er doin'. Look it about ye. Why man, if ye work as hard as that all day, ye'll be as tired at night as if ye had been workin'."

Another, Joseph Hays, a long, lank, weak eyed, shock headed youth, who had a peculiarly mild voice, and an uncontrollable habit of nodding his head like a duck when he walked came to me and said:

"Never worked at this kind of work before, didja?"

"No", I replied.

"Well—I jist wanta tell yah somethin' to begin with", he went on. (IV:59–69)

Old Henry too and John Caffey were fascinating characters. The former was a little old German night watchman, who formerly had been the engineer but who had become so old and so uninfluential that he had been pushed out his job and went on duty at seven and quit at seven, passing the long dreary night alone. He had formerly been a shaving boy also. Before he had got this job, and had carried shaving in zero weather, up an icy plank into cars that were waiting to recieve them for 13½ cents cents an hour, or $1.35 a day. He had a wife and a son living in Hoboken where he went daily and some of the men seemed to think he had saved a little money, though no one could tell. He used to slap me on the back mornings in a friendly innocent way and say "hart work, eh. Carrying shafings iss hart work. Dese fellows arount here tink not, but I know. Hart work."

The other man, John Caffey, was a solid, chunk of a carpenter with one of the kindliest most contented faces I have ever seen. He was slightly crippled, but when limping about the shop in the most good natured way. During all the time I remained there I never saw John Caffey anything but contented and good natured though the conditions under which he worked were perhaps as bad as you would find anywhere from one point of view. (IV:88–91)

There were others here who in the process of my labors took my eye. One of these was the foreman of the Italians a soft pudgy, easy going American, who was somewhat of what is colloquially known as a "rube." He was a fairly large man in girth, with a doughy face, and an eye devoid of anything save a rather vapid amount of craft. It was his one desire to appear easy and self-sufficient but he did not look the part and he had, as I noticed a way of slapping some of the underlings not under his command on the back in a spirit of mock bonhommie. I had not been tramping to and fro very long before he came up and wanted to know how I liked my work.

"There was some talk of giving you to me" he said, but I guess it must a' fell through. You'd a' been all right you'd a' come with me. I got the Italians".

I looked him over smilingly enough but I did not like him. He was too showy and too weak. It was plain to me at once that he was never born to rule. (IV:92–94)

. . . with increasing effort. When the cars would pour in and the work would pile up, the foreman would be around urging the men to greater energy. He would hurry from room to room, all day long, first to his office, where he answered telephone calls and tried to keep up with his reports, then out into the rooms, where the work on various orders were progressing. He would go from man to man, noting how each ones task was progressing, and if he did not think it was going fast enough would say so. The men who were conscious of the great pressure on him or the desire to have the work done quickly would hurry,—how fast their skill alone would say. Some of them would fairly sweat on a cool day, with their efforts, and they would do this all day long. This foreman Gring, was his name, was a relentless unfeeling creature and he would sometimes smile in a coarse and it seemed to me cruel way, exclaiming the while, "thats the ticket". Sometimes he would pitch in himself, for shows sake largely, and toil and tug himself, only to work the men up to a greater pitch of effort. Then he would go off somewhere and rest while they would work on. (IV:100–102)

In the course of time I managed to get up enough enthusiasm to jest with these people, which releived me some. I used to go out when I had a few minutes to spare and talk with old John, the engineer, or with Fagin, the blacksmith, or with, Ike, his helper. The latter was not much of a companion for me, considering that he imagined the world ended somewhere out west and that you could hunt Buffalos after you got past Pittsburgh, but he had his charms and he was honest. He used to sit on the engineers lockyer whenever he was not working, which was not often, and when I would come out with my shavings would make fun of me.

"Get on to him carryin' shavins", he once remarked when I came in with my basket under my arm and then he leaned back on his box and laughed until you would have thought that I was one of the most humorous sights in the world.

"Him", he would say, "him carryin' shavins"

"Well what about me, Ike?" I onced asked him. "Do I look so out of place."

"You look like you ought to up stairs and let that other big red headed lout come down here and do somethin'".

"Sh, Ikey", old John put in, "not so loud my boy. You'll get yourself in trouble".

"Dats right," he exclaimed. "Dats what he ought.

Just then the smith in the adjoining room rang on the anvil with his hammer end. Ikey went to his task—a signal which he always responded to. Old John got up and looked cautiously about, and through the doors.

"That d—n little fool talks too much. He be out of a job if he dont look out"

Still I could see that old John thought there was some truth in what he was

The latter also was a charming character. He loved to sit and read his daily World or to stand in the door, his big fat arm, reaching up to the transom, and his face running with sweat or out at the side gate, where the tide of the Harlem rose and fell, looking at the water and the boats. He loved to watch the latter, as he had no other amusement and he was never weary of discussing the character of the yachts that passed and that sometimes anchored in the roadsted of the Hudson opposite Spuyten Duyvil.

"Thats Morgans yacht", he used to say of a great handsome black boat that swept by here and of another "that there's the Waterfowl". "Woodenja think them fellers ud feel cumfortable now a sittin' back there on the poop and smokin dollar cigars on a day like this", he once said to me, as he gazed out on the blue water, sparkling in blistering noon heat.

"I fancy they might be" I replied cheerfully.

"Awe Haw, thems the boys as knows how to live. I wouldn' like nothin better on a day like this than sit out there and do up about a pound of tobacco. Come now wouldn' that be the ideal life for your uncle Dudley."

"It certainly would," I replied. "Only I think my Uncle Dudley does fairly well under the circumstances. I notice that he doesnt lose any flesh."

"Well I know," he continued with a jolly smile, "but them conditions er more congenial like. I aint as active as I use to be. A nice yacht and some good old fifty cent cigars ud just about do for me".

"Your too modest, John," I replied "you want too little. You ought to Ask for something more suited to your Lucullian instincts" What you need is a house on Fifth Avenue, and a country place at Newport, and the friendship of a few Dukes and Herls."

"Well I'm not backward," he said heartily. "If them things should come my way I think I could live up to 'em. Awe! Haw! I'm the boy for comfort"

I had to laugh at his genial acceptance of condition and his readiness to change, and we soon were on the best of terms. Between us we got up a little fiction about the shop being a boat, and the engine room the Captains cabin, and then I called him Captain and he called me Mate, and together we went sailing over a fictional main with as reckless a crew as ever hoisted a Jolly Roger. We made the Smith the bosun and Ike, his helper, the bosun's-mate, and we induced Joe, of the front room to take the position of day watch, seeing that he commanded the view from what we considered the prow of necessity. There was all sorts of foolishness about "heaving ho", and "blasting our top-lights", and shivering our timbers, and finally we fell to disputing as to who was the true orginator and what the rights of the mate and captain really were. I think there was a mere touch of feeling in this matter on Johns part, for the honor of being a captain even of a fictional ship was something and he was hurt when I suppressed him and called him Stoker. Finally we agreed to scuttle the old Idlewild as we named it and start a new boat which we called the Harmony, and to the day that I departed we were still sailing that goodly craft and John was Captain and I was Mate.

The Smith furnished considerable diversion for me in these trying hours. As I have said he was not a man who was wholly humorous, but he had his good points. On days when he was feeling good, and that was fairly often, we were wont to indulge in some of the most lightsome badinage principally concerning the poem of

the Village Smithy which I corrupted to to the "village Smith"
> "Under the spreading chesnut tree
> The Village Smith he stands"

and then I dubbed him "the village Smith".

"The Village smith", I used to say as I passed.

"The Village Smith"—he invariably echoed.

"He stands"

"He stands."

"Far be it from me to impugn the industry of the village smith."

"Far be it."

"Its the road thats losing, nevertheless."

"Heaven help the road."

Finally when with the captains consent I made him "bosun", of the good ship "Idlewild", as we called the shop, and the little blacksmiths helper the "bosuns mate"

Then together, we exchanged endless chaff on this subject. (IV:129–45)

CHAPTER XXVII

This situation did not appeal to me. It was merciless and cruel. I thought there must be some way out of it and I used to say to myself that if I were a foreman, that I would not be so insistent. I would not be so sharp. There was no need of driving men. Still I did not see how it was to be avoided unless the company would hire more men, and I did not see how a foreman could compel them to do that. He might do it, if he were a strong man, but it would require some man in whom the officials had confidence and for whose judgement they had respect. Even so, if his efforts, owing to his humanity proved less profitable than those of some others who

were less so he would not last long. Nevertheless I quickly percieved that this foreman was no good for his place.

He was too insistent. He had no judgement. There were times
when the work only piled up reasonably heavy that he would lose
his head and order and drive the men until it was done away with
and then he would find that he had a large staff of men on his hands
with nothing much to do. Now the one law of the railroad world is,
as I soon learned, that where no work is being done, it matters not,
for how short a period, no money must be paid and this put him to
the task of finding work, or of keeping up the appearence of it when
the was really nothing, or not enough to make a showing with. He
was afraid of the General foreman, a man who had charge of all the
shops and factories on this division of the road, and who might drop
in an examine the condition of the place at any time. He usually
came once or twice a week. Sometimes oftener. He was afraid of
the supervisor, the who had hired me, and who was over the
general foreman. He also came twice a week or oftener. He was
afraid of the other foremen, men who had charge of the electrical
work, the plumbing, the bridge-building and the like, all of whom
had offices and store rooms here and who might take a dislike to
him and "squeal on him", or say things derogatory which would
eventually get to the ears of the supervisor. At the same time he
was afraid of letting any man get a good reputation as a general man
for fear he would be looked upon as a likely successor to himself in a
crisis and for this reason he made freinds with no one. He stood off
by himself, a grim, insistent, quarrelsome and at the same time
cowardly figure, gloating over the possession of his little power and
at the same time scared to death for fear he would lose it.

That such a man could not be popular I knew and yet so close
was the situation and so great the fear of personal injury that no one
ventured to make a complaint against him—not even to one
another. They would stand up and tell you that Gring was a nice
man and that things were allright, and then you would see them
casting sullen glances after him, and obeying his orders in a dogged
and fearful way. I watched one person in particular, the amiable

Joseph, and finally I said to him one day "do mean to tell me Joseph that you like that man. He looked all around cautiously, as if he were afraid of being over heard and finally said gaurded terms, not to believe all I heard.

You'll get on to somethings", he said with that peculiar and continuous ducking of his head, and the affably interopolated ha! ha!. "You aint no spring chicken. Theres an old sayin',—I guess you've heard it allright. It aint all gold that glitters, aint that it, ha! ha! Well you'll find a mighty lot of old junk around here that got a fine three-X shine to it, that aint gold. Yuh just want to watch it. Oh, its gorgeous, it is. Its that regular Fifth Avenue glitter. But dont want to scratch it to much. You might make look like brass— you might, ha! ha!—er rusty old iron. Ha! Ha! You cant ever tell, kin you. Ha! ha!."

"No!" I said, laughingly.

"Well you just keep yer eye pealed. You'll get on to somethin', after while."

Cronin, the subtle Irishman, was also gradually persuaded to believe that I was worthy of some confidence. He was impelled to this I believe by the fact that I was of excellent service to him in the room. Being a mere general helper, without any particular skill I was allowed to work wherever I was useful, and as I was of considerable use here he wanted to keep me. I swept his floor, cleaned his machine, carried in his lumber and did other which he or him and his assistant Joe would have had to do together, and naturally he wished to reserve me to himself. He began by informing me that John and Jack, the two dromios, or the "saw dust brothers" as one of the forman subsequently named them, after I was gone, were a bad lot, and particularly John, the individual with the glass eye.

"Keep your eye on him," he informed me once in a very dramatic stage whisper. Hes no good. He's a spotter. Aintcha on to him."

"What do you mean", I said.

"He a spotter—dontcha know what that means. He squeals to the boss. He rides home with him every night. Jack, his partner is afraid as deat of him."

"Why," I asked.

"For fear he'll lose his job of course. He's a bad one. Look out for him".

"Well this is a fine revelation of shop politics I thought, and went thoughtfully my way. (IV:221–33)

. . . me that I was doing more than my share and that it would come "a heap easier" after I had worked awhile. All morning he sat and read his paper, or looked out of his back door, or went to a little gate that opened out on the Harlem and studied the water. He seemed to be amused and entertained by the boats, the passing of trains, anything, so long as it was outside the commonplace round of the things he was always doing.

The Smith quarters and his work also proved a sort of diversion to me. He had a habit of jesting about his work which took my fancy. He would watch for me each time as I would go by and would seize the occasion to tell me a story or to enlighten me on some point of his work, all of which proved very entertaining. For my part I had some idle humor concerning "the village smith" to offer which seemed to please him greatly. I would recite "Under the spreading chestnut tree" changing "smithy" of the next line to "smith he" and turning the pretty narrative into the vilest doggeral, apropos of the immediate scene. He seemed particularly impressed with the words "The Village Smith", which I would always repeat as I went passed and we finally came to call each other by the names "Shavings" and "The Village Smith."

Despite the jesting and the good natured it was not pleasent and I had a hard task to keep my countenance. I was also exceedingly tired.

At last at five-twenty five I saw the men taking off their overalls and putting away their tools. I was saw tired that I thought I should drop, but I hurried over and put my basket and broom away and went below. Then I took off my overalls and washed my hands.

Cronin loaned me a towel and Joe his soap. Then I stood in the door and waited for my train, due at five-thirty five, and at last the wheels of the shop stopped.

"Do they allow you people to ride on the train for nothing," I asked Cronin.

"Sure," he said. "Haven't youse a pass."

"I haven't been given one yet."

"Come wit me" he said genially. "I'll see you true. I have a five man pass, and he pulled out a soiled sheet of paper bearing the information that E. Cronin, and five men were entitled to ride on that. I thanked him and went to the platform, where all the others were gathered—a half hundred or more silent, dusty, tired-looking men. We stood there until the down train at five thirty arrived and then with some thirty others going in my direction I filed in, keeping close to Cronin. It was one of the company's smoking cars, filled to overflowing as usual with workingmen.

"What a thing to get through," I thought. "What a satisfaction to have done a days work. I have worked hard today. Maybe, sometime, if I keep it up, I will get well. Will I."

Then I relapsed into weary indifference and sat until my station came. At Kingsbridge I got off, and the wretchedness of the laborers condition, for me, for the moment at least, was a thing of the past. (V:316–23)

Joseph also was very kind to me. No one with any love of character could resist Joseph. He was another poor unfortunate who worked here from seven a.m. to 6 P.M. as millwrights assistant, and from 6 P.M. to 7 P.M. as watchman, until the night man arrived, and all day Sunday, year in and year out for 17½ cents an hour. Joseph was very glad to get this as he shortly informed me for he had a widowed sister and his little neice to support, a child that was evidently much on his mind. He was always talking about "the neice" and how he bribed her, by giving her a quarter now and then to look after his clothes and run his errands. Joseph as he clearly explained to me arose every day at five oclock and got home every evening at eight. Then he would have his supper and retire to bed where he would sleep until five again. On Sundays he made a great point of sleeping until six. Although he lived in the heart of the city, in one of those poor stretches of tenements that adorn the neighborhood of 10th Avenue and 78th Street, he had never been to Broadway more than a score of times in many years and he had not been to a theatre in four. He had not had a day off, outside of the regular holidays, when he sometimes secured a substitute, as watchman in six. He was a queer, rambling talkative sort of a person with a world of feeling and a kindly manner.

"Oh I'm a good worker, he used to say to me. "I've got the strength allright. I dont like to waste it that all. Jist want to use it exactly when its necessary and no oftener. I know what it is too waste your strength."

"Did you ever work at anything else Joe", I asked him once.

"Did I," he said. "Dysee them guineas working out on that car there, shovelin' stone. Well I did that onst. I was a track worker. Maybe you think its easy, hey! Ha! Ha! Thats when y'd git fooled. Dont ever let em persuade you to do that kinda work. I had my share of it"

I asked him when and where, and he immediately showed he a huge scar on his breast where he had been struck by a falling tie. He had been trying to throw it from a car with the assistance of another man and as the swing or movement by which they do those things had not been exactly caught by him he had fallen off, and the log on top of him. He had been laid up for three weeks by that and when he returned his place was filled. Still he managed to get hold of another, and from that position had worked up to this. Originally he had recieved thirteen and one half cents an hour. Now he recieved 17½ cents, but had hopes of getting a job somewhere else—not here, as he was afraid of the boss who was down on him.

Another man who took my eye was the John Carder of the car-loading team—the two men with whom I carried logs on the first morning. This man was a peculiar creature, a strange, taciturn self-opinionated clod who went about the shop with an air of sufficiency and mock good nature which you could not like. He did not seem to be on very friendly terms with any of the men and yet baited with a mock hilarity which was anything but agreeable. He had a way slapping some of them on the back, particularly one or two carpenters, and his partner John or Jack Hicks, who took it in a silent unresponsive way. I wondered from the beginner what the source of egoism could be, but it was quite a little while before I came to understand.

And the crowning character was the foreman himself. I did not get to see until Wednesday, but when I did some of my illusions about the place were cleared up. He was a tall man, with a long, lank, ill gaited . . . (V:340a–349)

. . . a most sociable temper and intelligent mind. He occupied the room, fifteen by forty, such back of the millwrights room, where I was gathering shavings and which contained, beside the forge of which he was master, a riveting machine, a pipe threading machine, a drop forge, an emery wheel and a bellows all of which were in operation. The forge stood in the centre of the room facing a large open window which looked out on the cinder strewn yard, and beside it stood the smith a veritable little titan for his size. He was a small man not more than five foot one, with a great expanse of chest and neck and arms like an athlete. He had a thin keen intelligent face, with bright eyes and brown curly hair. On this morning he was stripped to his under shirt and was hammering away away at a great rod of hot iron which he was shaping. He greeted me most cordially with its, "It easier carrying shavings than turn-spikes" and I assured him that it was.

"You dont want to work too hard he said. "Take it easy. Remember your workin' for a railroad. Its allright to do your share but dont overdo it, until you get your hand in.

I smiled at this self-considerate philosophy and went my way. I was sure that the great railway could not get more than a reasonable effort out of these men if it got that.

In the same hour I noticed the smiths helper also—a little lad, dirty, misshapen, strange, with a battered physiognomy which resembled that of a satyr, and teeth that were the color of amber. He had a large head and large ears, and his two hands were all out of proportion to the rest of his body. He wore an old coat that was three, and a pair of trousers that were four times too large for him, and when in repose his countenance was sad. When he was working or talking however it lighted up wonderfully and then he became one of the most genial looking little images imaginable. When I first saw him he was sitting looking out into the cinder strewn yard, with heaven knows what thoughts running through his mind. It was a poor place to look, but he seemed interested. The ground, the empty boxes, the litter of wood and iron were all before him but he was lost in a form of animal-like thought. Little Ike, as I heard someone call him captured my fancy at once. (V:385–90)

V. Thoughts on Labor

. . . of one another. It was all an old story to them—like the proverbial tale that is told

I never knew how dreary such a life could become to a person of my temperament until I had been there awhile. For the first weeks it was interesting enough though inexpressibly wearisome. I was not used to this sort of work. The necessity of standing all day on my feet had never been mine. I did not know how to handle the peices of lumber that I was sometimes compelled to carry and I was too old to learn the trick. Sometimes Joseph, and sometimes Hicks, the partner of the man with the glass eye would attempt to show me, but without much result. I had never acquired the art in my youth, when all these things are learned. My muscle had not in their pliable virgin state been set to the position of it. I never realized quite so clearly how out of it the man of the world is when it comes to toil, or indeed anything that he has not done or learned to do in his youth. I had always imagined that if worst came to worst I could work with my hands. I had even said as much to the secretary of the first railroad official when he had doubted whether I could do the work. Now I learned that there was no gulf like that which separates the layman from the man who toils, and I saw that I was as unfitted to be a hewer of wood as I was to be president of a railroad. These people, the least of them, had served their apprenticeship and knew their business. All I could do was to stand and look on, or to do in a half cringing half blundering way what they did with ease and grace. (IV:11–14)

CHAPTER XXVII

For sometime thereafter I was kept amused and entertained by what I considered the character phases of this life, though it had its grimmer side. These people whom I found working here seemed an ordinary lot. They were for the most part ignorant or uneducated men, who who knew the tricks of their tools, but little else. They were prone, as I could see, to marvel at the appearance of anyone of my character and temperament among them, even as I was marveling that I was daily finding myself among them. They seemed curiously interested in everything I did and I could see them watching me, at first, out of the corners of their eyes when I was (supposedly) not looking. One of them finally accosted me one day with, "What do you be doin' here anyhow? if I may ask ye. Yere not the kind of lookin man I'd expect to find doin' this sort of work."

"Well now what kind of a man would you take me to be," I smilingly inquired.

"Well, I don know," he replied. "Yere not the kind of a man that 'ud be doin' labor. I sh'd think ye'd be in a store or office now."

"Well I'm not used to the work," I replied. "I have been a writer, before this I have to work this way to gain my health again before I can do anything else. I hope I'm not utterly unfitted to be a working man, however!"

"Oh, no," he replied quickly and with good nature. "I don't say that now. You do yer work very well as far as I can see. Better then some thats been at it longer. I couldn't help wonderin' seein' that you didn't look like a workin' man."

I pondered over this for sometime for it set me thinking about the innate difference that exists between the mental and the physical types. These men given to facing the world with their physical skill only could detect at once the mental interloper. I was seen to be unused to this world—not to belong to it. My old clothes, with their outer covering of overalls and jumper, and my earnest desire to be a workingman in the true sense while I was thus situated did not avail me. I was an interloper, and everyone knew it. (IV:16–21)

. . . that is to act as simply and as naturally as I could.

Fagin the Blacksmith too, was very kind. I had not been there an hour this morning before he began to tell me of the condition the shop, the nature of the work and so, which was very interesting. He explained to me how steel is tempered—a thing I never knew before, and I had some pleasure out of watching the hot iron as he held it up to cool to a certain color before "fixing it by immersion. As I learned then, to let steel cool from its natural glow makes it softest of all, and diping it in cold water at a peacock blue shade of heat makes it the toughest. Immersion at a white heat merely makes it brittle.

The thing that interested me was the variety of character displayed here. These men at first glance appeared to be average people—a little bit the worse for training and labor, but average men. One old man I noticed was a cripple with the kindliest most contented face I had nearly ever seen—he was a carpenter. Another was a pale, anaemic creature an Austrian I judged, who worked so silently and energetically at his bench that I could not help but notice him—he breathed an atmosphere of melancholy like a perfume. Still another was a long, lank, free-handed American who loved to talk, a nosy, windy person who greeted me with some perfunctory advice about not sweeping away his tools. "As the old story goes" was his favorite expression, usually followed by some inappropriate yarn that had neither wit nor humor in it. He himself however was comic to look at and listen to.

I went about this day wondering at these people, trying to get an inkling as to their feelings and asking myself how they stood it. I knew of course or fancied that I did that there was some placid acceptance of their conditions in most of them or they would not be where they were. I wondered if they had in any troublesome desires about a better life; whether they yearned with the same urgent sensations for something better or whether they were largely satisfied. I went about exchanging nods and smiles and eyeing them keenly, and all the while I was saying to myself what a life, what a life?

The village of Kingsbridge and the neighborhood of Spuyten Duyvil were a soothing thing to me in this situation for I found myself turning with an infinite delight and affection and tenderness for the great beautiful features of the earth as they were here set forth. This magnificent river that flowed about the shop yard, the scurrying tide of the Harlem, running in fine rough waves over rocks thirty five feet below; the green breasts of the two hills so close at hand, and one vista between, where upon the green sward of a field that rose gently upward, a drove of cattle were gazing touch me infinitely. Why might not a person be happy here? I asked myself.

If I were fitted for this work, how pleasent it would be to stand at one of these benches where the river could be seen and work my days peacefully away. To have my hands full, to have something to do. How delightful.

And to tell the truth the first days I did find some gratification in this idea. There was a comfort in carrying my basket of shavings to and fro, to and fro, without anything more to think about. It was something to stoop and bend, when the mind was wearied with much thinking; to know that I had this one thing to do, ill or well. I have the cure for neuresthenia, I said to myself. I have the thing that will make me forget, and I went earnestly on carrying my basket, filling and emptying it until my arms were so sore and my back so tired that I thought I should . . . (IV:79–87)

CHAPTER XXIV

THE passing of the morning was one of the dreariest things imaginable to me. I had always fancied that labor of any kind especially in my present condition, and when I was struggling for health would prove agreeable to me, but now that I was in it, and doomed for a time to remain in it, I felt quite differently about it. One of the things that made it so of course was my own mental sickness but still outside of that I fancied I saw a grind here. There was an atmosphere of oppression and necessity which weighed on me. Instinctively, and with a true touch of individuality and a long cherished love of freedom I suspected tyranny and wondered, as I walked to and fro, how it would affect me. Also I brooded over my own falling state, foreseeing only a long seige of labor and great difficulty in maintaining my self. Fifteen cents an hour was not much. It summed up nine, forty five all told and out of that I had six dollars rent to pay. I was in need of medicine I thought—my beloved prescriptions and I was in debt. How I should ever get on my feet again I could not see. I worked on in a dogged gloom, gazing at the dark walls of the shop and the cinders of the yard and saying to myself that I could only try. What harm could come of it. It might do me good and I could no more than die. Still the gloom of it—the remembrance of my lost state weighed heavily upon me and I looked about me with a melancholy eye. (IV:111–14)

. . . I could take him. Work was the only solution—to do my work well and avoid any comment whatsoever

For sometime thereafter things went satisfactorily enough except as I say that I began to learned that the working world was no improvement on any other of existence if anywhere near so good. It had always been my fancy that the workingman, the man with the trade, was after all the happy man. He did not have to think, very much, he did not have to worry. He work was a pleasure to him, the making of something and when it was done his joy was assured. What more could one desire than to have a trade, a place to exercise it and your place, because of your merit, assured.

Here I found that there was no such ideal in existence. These men—most of them—had their trades, but they were not free from the dreads of competition. The company as I soon learned from various sources was constant threatening to lay off men, and men out of employment were applying for positions every day. There was the secret fear, constantly hanging over all of them that they were slated for dismissal. Only the most urgent work the most satisfactory results were deemed sufficient excuse for retaining a man and he was retained on that basis solely. There was no one there, as I readily observed who could not be immediately dispensed with and who would be except that he made himself useful enough and uncomplaining enough to avoid opposition or even notice. (IV:115–18)

In fact he was deferred to in a way and in places that made me think that not malice alone had prompted what Cronin had said, but that there was nevertheless some truth in it.

Days passed and in that time I learned what it means to work. This shop was no idlers paradise. Indeed it seemed to me at times as if it were one of the gloomiest places in the world. The regularity and sameness of it. The persistence with which the work of the world poured in, the monotonous way in which it was dealt with all had a wearying I may almost say maddening effect on the thinking mind. There was no art in it, no change, no variety, no initiative. Once you learned the simple details of the thing you had to do, it was a matter of doing it over and over and over and over. How

many times have I have filled a basket with shavings in ten movements! How many times carried it to the bin and returned in a
given space of time, how many times swept the floor, filled the bin
of the floor above with its shaving and emptied it, how many times
gone to the yard and carried board after board, board after board, in
sun and rain, in bright weather and dark weather, when I was weary
and when I was strong, when I was happy and when I was sad.
Every morning the wheels started at the same hours, every night
they stopped at the same hour. There was the regular intermission
at noon when I ate my lunch. There was the time at eleven, when I
put my coffee on the boiler to get hot, at three when I went with
most of the others to get a drink of water. During that time how
many times have I straightened and bent, walk to fro turned to the
door and back, all in some routine way that meant I would do it
that way again and again.

During this time I managed to get some solace out of the fact
that I was getting well or rather that I was working in the direction
of something that would make me well. This constant walking to
and fro, this carrying one thing, and then another, and then
another would serve to relieve of the thoughts that were as frightful
as anything could be to me—While I was bending over my basket
or crawling under the machines, I was not, at that particular
moment thinking of death, and the reason for the existence of
anything, and the dread of subsequent annihalation, was for the
time being far away. Sometimes however even here the mystery of
life would slip in between me and what I was doing and the mass of
chips or dirt before me would resolve itself into the the old dread
problem. Where did it come from? Why was it here. Yesterday a
tree, green and growing; today, a dry block, or ground dust; tomorrow, fire and heat and smoke. The next elemental force blowing
about—where, to what end. Did it think. Did it feel. Was all the
glory of life known to it, or was there only indifference and noth-
ingness there. And I was I anything more.

These thoughts used to have a sad effect on me. I could not
get away from them. They haunted me when I looked out the
windows and the running water; the swept before me when I stared

at the sky. The ground, the trees, the clouds, the lumber, this shop, me, all these men—they were merely a strange sweep and sway of something that was not wise, that was not kind that did not know it.

"Oh God," I used to say to myself. "If I could get back into life. If I could forget this thing. I do not want to be lost in the elements. I do not want to be submerged in this thing. I want love, I want health, I want individuality. Give me individuality my old belief in the reality of things and I will be happy again. I will be at peace"

It was not to be however—not yet. I went on with my work, stooping and gathering, and crawling under machines, as if by so doing I could get away from this vastness and indifference, and it was always there. I looked and the doors and the corners and they were still out of angle. (IV:119–28)

During this time ability to do this came as a wonderful solace to me in my nervous state. I had been so long suffering from those inexplicable dreads that so suddenly attack the neuresthenic that I felt this to be true relief. Here was something at last, not too hard and which I could do, which would occupy my mind and let me escape from the thought of those dread abysses of life which were then haunting me—time, space, the vast subtlety of force, the inexplicable shift and change of everything about me that seemed now more like a horrible nightmare than anything else.

In the course of the afternoon I managed to get this room clean. It was rather dreary work and in a way humiliating I thought. To have to crawl under machines and about the legs of men picking up blocks and sticks and carrying them like a scullion to the pile in the back of the room, and then when I had enough to warrent it, down to the engine room, was poor work for a man of my age and bearing. I tried to look indifferent and as if I thought nothing about it, but these men would not let me conceal my true appearence from myself. They watched me and did so closely and I had to repeat to myself, over and over the thought that I was doing it for myself—that I needed the exercise for health. Too, I looked of the window at that vast beautiful indifferent world. "It will not care" I thought. "My pains and my pleasures will all be over after a time. When the waters engulf me, when these hands and this body or dust and ashes what difference will it make. None at all, none at all. I am larger than a shop condition; I am larger than opinion. I am conscious of this vastness and power, in which I rest and too which I belong. Wherefore need I to be ashamed."

Nevertheless for all my philosophy . . . (IV:215–19)

In the course of time these shop politics began to develop. I had not been there a week before a three cornered fight began for my services a thing which I first took as a complement but which I subsequently learned was a mere outcropping of selfishness and human desire to shove the labor of everything on the back of the other man. Being a new man, without any particular skill and assigned to no particular department each of three groups sought to retain me for themselves. One of these groups was the crowd of carpenters on the second floor, who found in my industrious broom and shovel a great source of relief. Hitherto the room had only been cleaned twice a week by the two dromios—"the sawdust brothers" as one of the outside foreman had nicknamed them, but now since I had come I had been cleaning it every day, and keeping it clean. The blocks that fell I gathered up in baskets and carried down to the engineer. The sawdust and shavings I swept in piles and transferred to the bin. The long peices of lumber and half used sticks I gathered in orderly heap from under the tables and either carried them to the engineer or transferred them to the yard. I also dusted the machines, and kept the room as clean as a parlor.

This pleased the men and they wanted to keep me. One of them, who had first objected to my gathering up the shavings on the ground that it made them look as if they were doing nothing, now sided in with me, and asked me openly why I did not stay upstairs. "Theres plenty to for you right here", he said. "You can go down and bring us up our lumber, when you haint got nothin else to do".

I did not relish this latter idea as much as he thought, for I remembered from my first morning the trouble I had had in bringing up the posts. If there was anything more like that I did not want it, and I could readily see from the floor that there was.

On the other hand, the two dromios who were now confined exclusively to the yard, where they loaded an unloaded cars with special orders of manufactured stuff—material to good for the alien hands of Italians or "Guineas" as they always called them—wanted me for their man. They had had some experience of me as a man to pile stuff in cars, and as they could not agree on which should have the honor of standing in the car and placing, while the other carried the one always shoving the heavy carrying end off on the other, if he could, they hit on me as an easy way out of the matter. I could get in the car and pile and they would both carry.

Then there was the head of the milling room, Cronin, who wished me for his especial man, since I swept his room, carried out his shavings, carried in his lumber and cleaned his machines or did so much of it as I had time for. If I had had more time I would have done more work and I proposed to see that I got more time.

"You stay here", he said to me one day, when one of the men from upstairs came by and wanted to know if I was going to clean up, up there. "Theres enough to do for you right here. If you run after them fellys they'll be wantin' ye to carry up more posts again. Stay down here and you'll never have more than you can comfortably do."

At the same time the leader of the two dromios, John Carder, he of the glass eye was after me to go with him. He was quite friendly in his attitude now, though very authoritative, and said I could come "if I wanted to". As I had hoped to be out in the fresh air in the first place, this suited me best and I went a few times with him.

This angered Cronin, though I did not know it, and he told

me one morning in a sullen Irish way that I had orders to stay inside with him. "Let them load their own cars", he said. "You dont want to be doin' that. Its too hard for you. There big enough to do there own lodin'."

As it turned it out he had no orders to keep me in, but I did not know this, and when Carder sent his associate Hicks to get me refused to go, telling him, I had been ordered to stay. This angered Carder who as I subsequently learned to my cost had influence with the foreman and he went to the latter and explained that he needed me. The next thing I knew he came lurching by declaring

"Your to come with me, Theodore. The boss says so.

I looked at Cronin, who merely turned a sullen face on his adversary.

"Allright," he said.

From that time on the politics of the shop began to develop. I was not always busy on the cars, and when I was through I would sometimes come in and help carry shavings or supply lumber to the machines. On these occasions both Cronin and Joe would invariably inquire of me how I liked it outside, and one day Cronin called me over and amid the roar of the machines said "Howya like your new boss?"

"Whom do you mean," I inquired.

"Why Hawkeye, of course"!

"Whose Hawkeye?" I asked

"Why Carder, of course. D' felly your workin' wit. D' felly wit d' glass eye. Aintcha on to him yet. Your a good one"

"No, I said. Whats the matter with him. What about him.

"Look out for him. He's a spotter. He rides home wit the boss every night up in the front car. You watch him. You'll see him do it." His partner John is as fraid as deat' of him. You see, if you look out. You watch him.

"How do you know he's a spotter," I inquired.

"He's been caught in it," he whispered. "He runs wit everything he hears to Gring. Dont let on I told you, only you watch him"

"I thought you said Gring was such a nice fellow", I said.

He opened his eyes owl fashion, and smiled a wide cat like smile, without opening his lips. "Dats for beginners he . . . (IV:237–51)

This revelation was rather a schock to me. Although I did not care for myself particularly—these shop difficulties were a thing apart from my life, or I tried to think they were, I was nevertheless sorry that anyone should be looked on as a spotter. I began to watch this man more closely and to think that I saw signs which proved it to be true. For one thing he was constantly running to the boss for instructions and for another he assumed such a cavalier air. Clodhopper though he was he had a patronizing air, which extended not only to his partner Hicks and myself, and to all the Italians as a matter of course, but to the carpenters and tinsmiths, and the other dignitaries of the ordered hierarchy of trade who by all rights and priviliges of their condition should have been above him. He did not disturb me at first, as I felt that I was a mere spectator in all this but the attitude he took to some of the older men grated on me. I saw him slap an old carpenter on the back one day, a man fifteen years his senior and greet him with a familiar, "hello Tom". He had another habit of calling a very clever worker in in inlay "little man", and would walk up alongside of him when he was coming in mornings or going out evenings and say "hello little man". It was queer I thought that a man with so little education—none at all in fact—and no trade, a mere hewer of wood and drawer of water should be allowed to take such priviliges and yet no one seemed to object. In fact he was deferred to in a way and in place that made me think that it was not malice alone which prompted what Cronin had said. There was some foundation of truth beneath it.

Day passed and I watched the progress of this thing with an interested eye. For one thing I saw that Carder was openly exulting over Cronin for he walked through his shop with the air of a lord, and would frequently come up when I stopping to exchange a friendly word with the lather and say "come on Theodore". As I saw Cronin look at him on the sly I realized that there was no love lost here. If chance had offered I think Cronin would have done some evil to him, though I did not see how he could very well. (IV:252–56)

The work of that day had an amazing effect on me. I use to think out at Muldoons, that his light exercise was work, but here and now I learned what it was to be tired. It was stiff and almost lame. As I walked up the lovely hill on this June evening the sense of buoyancy and joy of life which the scene represented and which was now in a way a thing apart from me, touched me to quick. I felt weak and degraded, a thing of the underworld, and yet the equal of that underworlds rulers, one who for want of a little money, and of health lacked recognition. What did I care for those who with their cheap systems, by mere drill work and process of hanging on had come into the possession of wealth and authority. Was not my mind as good as theirs, or better. Did I not sweep with my bredth of imagination realms of which they did not dream. What did they know of this underworld which they ruled; what did they know of themselves. Blind leaders of the blind, strutting about the world and thinking themselves somewhat, and ignoring true emissaries of thought.

And yet what did they care for me. Here they were speeding along this country road in their automobiles, and driving by in their carriages. I was nothing to them. They did not see me. Rail as I would the differences of life were largely based on materials, and though who had them could afford to let the beggars dream. I might know all or nothing, but I could not buy my way with money nor command attention with show. Hence I must creep only this village road weary and practically forgotten. (V:259–63)

CHAPTER XXV

THE days that followed made no marked change in my original impressions. Although I found it somewhat less grim than I had originally imagined it to be, I also found it to be more monotonous. The constant walking to and fro in the same given area the stooping and lifting over details that required no thought—only strength, the constant rattle of the wheels, and the sight of the dismal objects—dismal to me, in that they had no pleasing forms or colors was distressing. I did not like it and I did not see how I could make myself like it. The only thing that was really beautiful to me was the location of the shop and that was a matter outside my present enjoyment. Half the time or more I could not see it because I was not on the second floor, from whence the waters and the hills of the two rivers were visible

Another thing that irritated me was the fact that I did not like many of the men that were working here. I will admit that I am a crank and that human beings deserve to be much more tenderly judged than they are, considering that we are all so wretched, but nevertheless in my present state I was in no mood to judge kindly. They struck me in the main as a barren lot, narrow in ideas, small in mental calibre, well fitted to bother with the infinitely common things with which they were laboring. The only people I saw there whom I really truly liked, were the Smith and his helper little Ike, old John the Engineer, Henry the night watchman, Joseph the assistant to the millwright in whose room I was working, and old John Caffy the carpenter. There may have been others who were nice but I did not come in contact with them. The bosses, and there were a dozen or more of them moving in and out here were a vain silly lot—the majority of them. There were some who had more general information than the men but the principal difference between them seemed to me to lie in the fact that they were colder, crueler, more insistant. Perhaps this sprang from the necessities of their position. I will not say. It is only my impressions as this particular time that I am recording.

And yet the place was not without its phases of interest. Thus on Tuesday when I returned after my first nights rest, and by the way I did rest for the first time in many months, I found the men, those nearest to me to be exceptionally considerate. Old John, the engineer whom I had come to like very much was most anxious to know how I had made out and predicted great things for me. "It'll be hard, first off", he repeated, "but you'll get use to it. Take your time. Sit out here if your tired. The boss aint goin' to see you. He aint here today nohow. You done enough yesterday to warrent your taking it easy today. (V:324–30)

CHAPTER XXVI

THE progress of my life in this workaday world was an interesting, if to begin with it was a wearisome thing. It was involved with my discoveries and observations entirely new to me. I found, for instance that I was dealing with any ordinary set of human natures, selfish, greedy, or gentle and kind as the occasion warrented or the temperament of each permitted. There were good men and bad among them, warm hearted and cold hearted; taciturn and genial only they were all more or less ignorant of what we consider the wisdom of life, and they had a trade. Some of them were satisfied, some dissatisfied. I was never weary of watching the way in which they accepted this condition of which they were a part and of which few, if any of them had ever any hopes of leaving.

The thing that interested me in this connection was that there was no open grumbling or if there was I did not percieve it. All of the men went about there work in a silent uncommunicative way which bespoke conclusions and opinions of their own. Some of them talked but it was largely because I made them for they were unused to me and interested in what I had to say or to learn for what reason I was here. As for their companions they were used to one another, and as I sometimes fancied exceedingly weary of them. For the most part they stood at their benches and looked only at their work—a thing which made me comment unfavorably upon their lack of poetic feeling. For here, stretched before their gaze was one of the most beautiful scenes imaginable. You could not look out of any window of this building from the second floor without the eye taking in the poetic scenes, here a group of oyster boats, right outside the shop door, where oysterman came to dredge and plant seed oysters; yonder a smooth round green hill, rising three hundred feet above the river perhaps and covered with a luxurious growth of green trees, to the west the wide roadstead of the Hudson, paraded by large craft of all kinds and set with handsome steam yachts, like toys, and over the way and northward, the green line of the palisades stretching in a solid wall until the eye could follow no longer. Gulls were here, and flocks of pigeons, and the sight of the sky, dotted by them was a lovely thing to contemplate. However it was nothing which these men could ordinarily see, or if could, would have been interested in. The work, as I found, was largely too exacting, and the labor of tending to it too conducive of weariness to permit of much thought.

My first days were spent in speculating on this life and the nature of the man under whom I was to work. As I have indicated he was away at the time when I came there and had not yet returned on the second day. On the third however he put in an appearence and then I beheld a tall, lank, raw-boned man, with a . . . (V:350–57)

The water ran in dark swirls among the branches of the trees. Over the river a collection of Hungarian cottages collected at the base of a hill, revealed a twinkling collection of lights. The water danced with yellow and red splotches, and ever and anon a train thundered by, its windows glowing.

So runs the world away, I thought. Here I am, sidetracked for an indefinite period, in a strange place, with nothing but the water and the trees and the ground eternally familiar.—Strange? Who is strange? And what?

Whereat the old thought of life and death, of the wherefrom and the whereunto, the fact that I was water and earth and activity myself came back and I felt more desolate then ever. I felt the dread of death and dissolution coming back on me and to avoid got up and went to my room where I laid out my things for the next day.

Then being infinitely weary I laid down and to my surprise the next morning fell immediately asleep. The noise of the trains, which I feared might disturb me, did not have any effect on me at all. I was still dozing when a knock came at my door, and an unwelcome voice called half past five. I got up, stiff and weary and with groan faced another day. It was indeed 5:30 and I had had the first nights rest that I had had in years. I could scarcely believe it. (V:371–74)

The progress of my life in this workaday world comprised a series of routine days which now as I look back on it, and then as I was in it, fill and filled me with the saddest, most melancholy, and yet sweet and lovely thoughts and emotions. It was a commonplace world in the main filled with commonplace, ordinary human beings, and yet hemmed about and colored by such contrasts of poverty and luxury, such a world of beauty and of indifference that even now, as I write it, my eyes all but filled and I am filled with emotions to deep for words.

The workaday world. Do you comprehend it, oh my brother. Do you know what it means to rise with the sun and earlier, to hasten away with your little basket or bucket and to enter a dull shop, whether nothing is in evidence save the implements of labor—machines, tools and darksome oil stained walls and floors, and work, work, work, the live-long day, week after week, month after month, year after year. Do you know what it means to witness the best of your strength, the keenness of your intelligence going into the manufacture of something, the use of which you never have; the display of which you never see; the comfort of which you never feel. Sometimes as I look back on it now, those common-place walls seem to contain nothing but that which is obnoxious and disagreeable to me, and yet I know that men labor there with contentment, or if I cannot say that at least with indifference. Horses they seemed to me, or machines, in the main, blind, unseeing animals, given to understand a little of the meaning of life and harnessed in their youth by circumstances, before they could choose, before nature had provided them with intelligence and made to work.

Work. Ah the meaning of that word. To rise with the sun. To keep going back and forth in a routine path all the day long. To lift and to bend. To move and to stop. To wind and unwind. Always and always to do. And for what.

In my youth I fancied that . . . (IV:421–27)

Explanatory Notes

3.8   **three years**
Judging from the prescriptions accompanying the Philadelphia diary, Dreiser took medication for a nervous condition from early January 1899 until at least April 1904; however, the debilitating symptoms did not set in until after publication of *Sister Carrie*.

3.15   **seemed absolutely alone**
Dreiser's wife returned to her parents' home in March 1902 during his walking tour through the Southeastern states, then rejoined him in Philadelphia in July. On 26 January 1903 she returned to Missouri, staying this time until September.

4.13   **slight physical indisposition**
Periodically in the Philadelphia diary Dreiser attributed his fatigue to excessive sexual indulgence.

4.18   **went to Philadelphia where I lingered for six months**
Dreiser arrived in Philadelphia in mid-July 1902 and left in mid-February 1903. He returned to New York between 17 February, when the Philadelphia diary breaks off in mid-sentence, and 21 February, when he was treated by Dr. Franklin Deuel Skell, an ophthalmic surgeon at the New York Eye Infirmary.

4.23   **just ten years before**
Dreiser had first visited New York City during the summer of 1894 and then moved there permanently the following November.

4.26   **native village**
Presumably Dreiser means Terre Haute, Indiana, where he was born and lived until 1879. Terre Haute's population during this period was approximately 25,000. He also lived briefly in Vincennes, Evansville, Sullivan, and Warsaw before leaving Indiana for Chicago in 1887.

5.8   **was it not as the preacher had long ago written, a vanity and a travail of the flesh**
An apparent merging of Ecclesiastes 1:14 and 12:12.

5.25   **learned specialists whom I sought**
Dreiser identified three physicians he consulted during this period: Dr. Milton H. Fussell, instructor at the University of Pennsylvania and practicing physician at 189 Green Lane in Philadelphia; Dr. Louis Adolphus Duhring, professor of dermatology at the University of Pennsylvania and consulting physician at the Dispensary for Skin Diseases in Philadelphia; and Dr. Charles Loomis Dana, professor of nervous diseases at Dartmouth Medical College and Cornell University and physician at Bellevue Hospital. Fussell and Duhring are identified in the Philadelphia diary, and Dana is identified in the typescript, "Down Hill and Up."

6.31   **The opening fee in this case was ten dollars.**
The details of this diagnosis and proposed treatment suggest that Dreiser was recalling his first visit to Duhring, who was known for his unorthodox use of medication. The first visit took place on 22 October 1902; the consultation fee, however, was only five dollars (see *American Diaries*, p. 55). For a fuller discussion of Dreiser's involvement with Duhring, see Herman Beerman, M.D. and Emma S. Beerman, M.A., "A Meeting of Two Famous Benefactors of the Library of the University of Pennsylvania—Louis Adolphus Duhring and Theodore Dreiser," *Transactions and Studies of the College of Physicians of Philadelphia*, 42 (July 1974):43–48.

7.15   **I was comparatively young**
Dreiser was thirty-one.

7.22   **I had but thirty-two dollars in my pocket**
On 17 February, Dreiser had received a check from Joseph H.

Coates, editor of *Era,* for what he expected to be thirty-five or forty dollars. This is presumably the sum with which he returned to New York. See *American Diaries,* pp. 98, 112–13.

8.18 **The room which I was able to engage in this neighborhood**
Dreiser's Brooklyn address was 113 Ross Street.

11.9 **It had not been quite two years since I had left New York**
Actually, Dreiser had been gone from New York approximately fifteen months.

11.11 **I had successfully finished one novel and had begun another**
Sister Carrie was published in November 1900, and *Jennie Gerhardt* was in progress and under contract to J. F. Taylor and Company, though Dreiser had abandoned work on *Jennie* in mid-December 1902.

11.18 **The period of my trying covered just fifty-six days in all.**
Presumably Dreiser moved to Brooklyn on 21 February.

14.21 **different editors**
One of these editors was Rutger B. Jewett of the J. F. Taylor Company, whom Dreiser had written on 12 February to announce his return to New York (*American Diaries,* p. 105). Another was Ripley Hitchcock, who had written Dreiser expressing interest in the *Jennie Gerhardt* manuscript (Hitchcock to Dreiser, 24 February 1903, *Letters,* p. 70).

14.25 **editors of the *Evening Sun* ... Brooklyn *Eagle***
Editor of the *Evening Sun:* Paul Dana; City Editor of the *World:* Pomeroy Benton; Editor of the *Union-Standard:* William Berri; Editor of the Brooklyn *Eagle:* St. Clair McKelway.

15.5 **A brother of mine was a publisher in New York**
Paul Dresser was a partner with Pat Howley and Fred Haviland in Howley, Haviland & Company, a music publishing firm for which Dreiser edited the magazine *Ev'ry Month* from October 1895 until September 1897.

15.6   **Another was an actor**
Edward Dreiser, using the stage name "Edward Dresser," had recently appeared in New York in Richard Harding Davis' "Soldiers of Fortune" (Vera Dreiser to Richard Dowell, 15 February 1977).

15.6   **I had a sister who had a comfortable home in Washington Square**
Mrs. Austin Brennan ("Mame") lived at 39½ Washington Square.

15.8   **another who had a pretty flat in Brooklyn**
Emma lived for a time in Brooklyn (Vera Dreiser to Richard Dowell, 27 November 1976).

15.16   **I had never needed to borrow ... obtaining advance royalties or payment for work that I should do when I regained my health**
In reality, Dreiser had lived on a $100-a-month advance payment on *Jennie Gerhardt* from J. F. Taylor & Company from November 1901 until June 1902.

28.3   **the remembrance of a man who owed me ten dollars**
While in Philadelphia, Dreiser was expecting payment of a small debt from Charles N. Gray, an "enduring and true friend" who worked at the Jewelers Association and Board of Trade in New York. When Dreiser left Philadelphia, the payment had not yet been made (*American Diaries*, pp. 94, 198).

32.14   **Mr. B——**
Austin Brennan.

33.2   **Panopepton**
Dreiser would have been familiar with this medication, since it had been prescribed by his physician, Dr. W. Seman Bainbridge, in January 1897.

39.30   **We had quarreled over little or nothing a few years before**
While editor of *Ev'ry Month*, Dreiser became increasingly disenchanted by the journal's utilitarian role and pedestrian

tone and sought more editorial freedom to improve the literary level. Arguments over the magazine's function developed, and ultimately Dreiser left the firm, particularly annoyed by Paul.

40.6   **my brother-in-law, a young lieutenant in the Navy**
Dreiser's wife's brother, Dick White. Over the Thanksgiving holidays of 1902, Lt. White and his new bride, Carlotta, had visited the Dreisers in Philadelphia (*American Diaries*, pp. 68–69). Ultimately White rose to the rank of Commander in the U.S. Navy.

41.8   **the battleship**
Lt. White was stationed aboard the U.S.S. *Indiana*.

42.25   **main Metropolitan station in New York**
The Metropolitan Street Railway Company, with main offices at 621 Broadway.

45.32   **stood at the corner where the charity building stands**
The United Charities Building, which housed many charity organizations including the Charity Organization Society, was located at the corner of 22nd Street and Fourth Avenue.

46.13   **the General Passenger Agent**
George Henry Daniels was the General Passenger Agent for the New York Central from 1889 until 1907. His office was in Grand Central Station, located at 42nd Street and Vanderbilt Avenue.

47.13   **Mr. F——, the Chief Engineer**
Henning Fernstrom was then Chief Engineer for the New York Central.

47.18   **Mr. D——**
Probably a reference to Daniels; however, in later retellings of this episode Dreiser insisted that the New York Central president, Chauncy DePew, had been the reason for his choosing that railway.

48.17   **the Engineer of Maintenance of Way**
A. T. Hardin was then the Engineer for Maintenance of Way for the New York Central.

49.5   **the Whitely Exerciser**
An apparatus constructed of three pulleys and an elastic cord with handles at each end. The exerciser was typically mounted on a door frame and used to strengthen the arm and back muscles.

50.9   **Provident Loan Association**
This institution was also housed in the United Charities Building.

50.24   **handed in my watch**
In retelling this incident for "Down Hill and Up," Dreiser recalled that he had attempted to pawn his coat rather than this watch (p. 29).

51.9   **the Mills Hotel**
Located at 164 Bleecker Street, the Mills Hotel was erected in 1896 by millionaire banker, financier, and philanthropist Darius O. Mills to provide inexpensive food and shelter for New York's transient and unemployed male population.

52.18   **Imperial Hotel**
One of Paul Dresser's favorite hotels, located at 1254 Broadway.

52.20   **a small, dark little hunchback**
Paul's publishing partner, Pat Howley.

55.17   **a very eminent nerve specialist in Philadelphia**
Dr. Louis Adolphus Duhring.

57.17   **there were fifteen hundred in all**
The Mills Hotel had 1560 single rooms.

58.8   **Fort Lee**
A small village on the New Jersey side of the Hudson River, approximately five miles southeast of Hackensack. Located about three hundred feet above the river, Fort Lee's rugged terrain and scenic beauty served as the setting for many motion pictures in the early 1900s.

61.4   **Muldoon's**
William Muldoon, world champion professional wrestler and

trainer of prize fighters, including John L. Sullivan, retired in 1900 to establish the Olympia, a health sanitarium in Westchester County, three miles northeast of White Plains, New York.

64.4   **The next day**
Dreiser began his stay at Muldoon's on April 21 and remained until June 2.

64.8   **one of my brothers**
This reference is to Alphonse Joachim Dreiser, fourth youngest of the ten surviving children. Al was four years older than Theodore.

65.7   **that I was the missing sheep in the ninety-and-nine legend**
Matthew 18:12–14.

65.31   **our country home out in Indiana**
During the Dreiser family's residence in Sullivan, Indiana (1879–82), the children periodically stayed at the farm of Jesse Rector. Paul had lived with the Rector family for several months during his boyhood after an argument with his father. Both Paul and Claire Dreiser corresponded with the Rectors throughout their lives. Theodore maintained a brief correspondence with Emma Rector during 1893–94. The Dreiser-Rector correspondence is available at the Lilly Library, Indiana University.

65.33   **a well-known actor**
Probably a reference to Robert Edeson, who starred in "Soldiers of Fortune." This play, however, had left New York in October 1902.

65.34   **Rome, alas poor Rome**
Marcus Romanus (Rome) Dreiser, the nomadic brother who Dreiser thought for a time had died of delirium tremens in St. Louis. See *A Hoosier Holiday* (New York: John Lane Company, 1916), p. 393.

66.2   **a decided success**
Paul's most popular song of this period was "Mr. Volunteer" (1901). Other "latest songs" were "In Dear Old Illinois"

(1902), "The Voice of the Hudson" (1903), "Where Are the Friends of Other Days?" (1903), "Lincoln, Grant and Lee" (1903), and "The Boys Are Coming Home To-Day" (1903).

66.3 **we would go back to our old home and surprise the natives**
When visiting the Chicago branch of Howley, Haviland and Company, Paul would often make time to visit Terre Haute, where he was a great favorite. Dreiser did not return to Terre Haute until 1915, nine years after Paul's death.

67.10 **Two years before a brother-in-law of mine—Mr. B——, had been here and a year before my brother's partner**
These references are to Austin Brennan and Pat Howley (Vera Dreiser to Richard Dowell, 27 November 1976).

68.28 **Kennedy**
Except for celebrities like Paul and Muldoon, surnames used in this manuscript were typically fictitious.

72.25 **retch**
Dreiser is using the Old English form of "stretch."

75.8 **the family, who owned a very well-known theatre in New York**
The Vanderbilt family were major stockholders in the Metropolitan Opera House.

76.28 **"At fifty a week," I thought.**
Muldoon charged Dreiser $35 a week. See Muldoon's statement, reproduced on p. 196 of this edition. Dreiser's total bill for his six weeks stay was $256.75, which Paul paid in two installments, 30 May and 13 June.

87.4 **"me," as Walt Whitman would say, "the coldest, most selfish and meanest of them all."**
Not an exact quotation from Whitman, rather a Whitman-like statement inspired by such lines as "What is commonest, cheapest, nearest, easiest, is Me" ("Song of Myself," 14:15).

92.29 **Authorship was a long way off from me then**
Something of an exaggeration, for during his first three weeks

at Muldoon's Dreiser wrote and submitted "Scared Back to Nature," which appeared in *Harper's Weekly*, 47 (16 May 1903):816.

93.32 **then to my brother**
Actually, Dreiser had consulted Paul before writing A. T. Hardin. On 25 May, Paul responded, enclosing Hardin's address "as per your request."

96.27 **It was so that I burned my bridges in that direction.**
As the correspondence indicates, Dreiser did continue to accept money and other favors from Paul during his months as an "amateur laborer." See, for example, Paul to Dreiser, 2 September 1903, Dreiser Papers, University of Pennsylvania Library.

96.28 **a friend in Newark**
Peter McCord, who at this time was working on the Newark *News*. See "Peter," *Twelve Men* (New York: Boni and Liveright, 1919), pp. 1-52.

97.26 **Supervisor of Buildings**
R. P. Mills.

99.23 **Spike**
Railroad slang for Spuyten Duyvil, a village on the outskirts of New York City at the juncture of the Hudson and Harlem Rivers.

100.4 **R.P. Mills**
In recreating this letter, Dreiser retained the actual names of both parties.

103.3 **Wollestencrafts**
A fictitious name for the Hardenbrooks family, Terrace View Avenue, where Dreiser first stayed in Kingsbridge.

103.9 **Wesley**
John Wesley (1703-1791), British founder of Methodism.

112.11 **dromios**
The two Dromios, twin servants to the twin brothers, Anti-

pholus of Ephesus and Antipholus of Syracuse, in Shakespeare's *Comedy of Errors*.

113.25 **one-fifty a day**
Dreiser began at fifteen cents an hour and on 22 June was raised to seventeen and a half cents. See Mills to Dreiser, 22 June 1903, Dreiser Papers, University of Pennsylvania Library.

127.3 **a novel**
Sister Carrie.

127.13 **Blackwells Island**
A long, narrow island of approximately 120 acres, located in the East River and extending from East 50th Street to East 84th Street. It was the site of New York's Charity Hospital, Penitentiary, Alms-House, Hospital for Incurables, Work-House, Asylum for the Insane, and other public institutions.

128.7 **a celebrated nerve specialist**
Dr. Louis Adolphus Duhring.

142.2 **He seemed pleased**
The blacksmith, identified elsewhere as Fagin.

143.9 **a carpenter by trade**
Identified elsewhere as John Caffey.

143.22 **an old German**
This character is not more specifically identified. It is apparently not Henry, the German night watchman.

144.12 **the long nosed Yankee of literature**
Ichabod Crane of Washington Irving's "Legend of Sleepy Hollow."

148.9 **the foreman of the Italians**
Identified elsewhere as Burnham.

149.9 **This foreman Gring**
The fictitious name given to F. A. Strang.

151.13   **a little fiction about the shop being a boat**
The source of "The Cruise of the *Idlewild*," published in *Bohemian Magazine*, October 1909, and in *Free and Other Stories* (New York: Boni and Liveright, 1918).

152.2   **"Under the spreading chesnut tree**
"The Village Blacksmith" by Henry W. Longfellow.

Illustrations

Reading room of the Mills Hotel, 160 Bleecker Street, New York City, courtesy of the Museum of the City of New York.

Paul Dresser, Theodore Dreiser's brother.

William Muldoon at the time that Dreiser knew him at the Olympia Sanitarium in 1903, from Edward Van Every, *Muldoon, The Solid Man of Sport* (New York: Stokes, 1919).

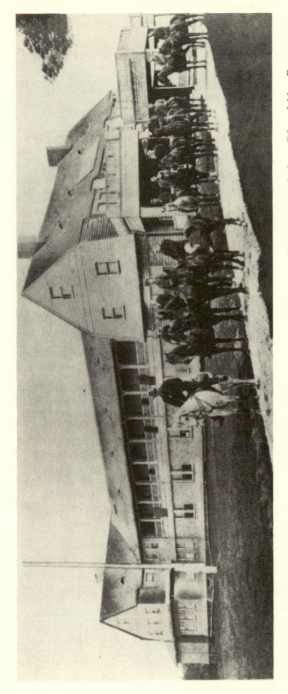

Olympia, the Muldoon Hygienic Institute at Purchase, N.Y., where many famous people were trained, from Edward Van Every, *Muldoon, The Solid Man of Sport* (New York: Stokes, 1919).

Muldoon's bill for Dreiser's stay at the sanitarium, 21 April to
2 June 1903.

"The Mighty Burke," an illustration from an article by Dreiser, published in 1911 in *McClure's*.

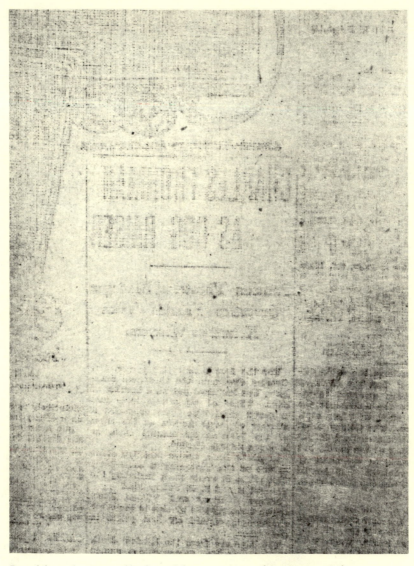

Detail from the verso of leaf 31 of the manuscript of *An Amateur Laborer*.

CHARLES FROHMAN AS DOG RAISER

Famous Theatrical Manager Surprises Friends With Kennel of Winners.

For the first time in his career, Mr Charles Frohman, the theatrical magnate, has launched out as a breeder of dogs. Three of his entries have just captured eight first prize cups and a number of lesser honors at the show of the Westminster Kennel Club, in Madison Square Garden.

Bouncing Lass, shown standing alone in one of the photographs, carried off first prizes in every class, including the Vanderbilt and S. P. Peters cups.

Hidden Mystery and Village Lass, shown standing side by side in the other photograph, carried off first prizes in their class.

The dogs are from the Hidden Brook Kennels, as Mr Frohman has named his place.

This fad is a somewhat startling innovation for the great American manager who was supposed to be devoted

Detail from p. 3 of the 13 February 1904 issue of the New York *Daily News*.

Apparatus

Selected Emendations

The table below records all substantive and all significant accidental emendations made in the manuscript of *An Amateur Laborer* to produce the text of this edition. The page-line reference in each entry is followed by the reading printed in this volume. The left-pointing bracket stands for "emended from." The reading which follows is the rejected reading from the manuscript. Below is a sample entry:

7.11   York as an author] York

The entry indicates that at page 6, line 9, of this edition the words "as an author" have been added to the text immediately after "York". An asterisk beside a page-line citation indicates that a textual note has been written to explain or defend the emendation. These textual notes, grouped together at the end of the table, are keyed to the entries by page-line numbers.

5.1	I asked] asked		12.15	I would begin to] would begin
5.3	the long] long the			
5.13	the verge] verge		12.26	my efforts] efforts
6.30	should have] have		12.34	accordingly] according
7.11	York as an author] York		13.15	or] nor
7.18	the chill] chill		13.31	intelligence think] intelligence
9.2	at it] at			
11.21	lay] laid		15.10	knowing] who knowing
11.27	heaven] heavens		15.11	doors] door
12.2	I should] should I		16.14	down to] down
12.5	trouble about] trouble		17.31	lead is] led was

18.12	way] work
18.34	could do] could
18.36	bear] bear that
19.3	who] whom
19.25	him] me
20.4	had looked] looked
20.31	again,] again
21.24	seemed] seem
21.34	name,] name
22.15	a dingy] dingy
22.19	She was] She
23.16	friendlessness] friendliness
23.19	touched] ever touched
24.28	wonder] wondered
24.34	not sleep] not
24.34	could do] could
25.3	soon] soon that
25.9	to become] become
25.33	hand—would] hand would
26.17	could not] could
26.25	feeling an] feeling
26.29	servitor—must] servitor must
26.33	line of] line
27.17	I tossed] he tossed
28.33	was] were
28.36	take me in—a] take in me in a
29.1	period] periods
29.28	had told] told
30.1	try] tried
30.11	go to] to go to
30.29	could find] could
30.35	appeared] appealed
31.1	to come] come
31.14	that,] that
31.28	good] well
31.28	my shoes] shoes
32.13	luxury] luxury,
32.34	overwhelmed with] overwhelmed

33.29	of milk] milk
34.22	night,] night;
34.24	apprehension] apprehensive
34.24	facing] face
35.4	subway, there building,] subway there building
35.28	watchman,] watchman
37.16	good] well
38.10	house—113—and] house 113 and
38.15	miles] mile
39.26	and the letter] and
40.20	do and] do but
40.28	with so] so
40.30	greatly in] greatly
40.32	us protest] protest
41.8	looked at] looked
41.13	had been] been
41.15	from which] which
41.22	to do] do
41.23	did] had
41.32	difference—and] difference and
43.34	and in] and during
44.6	overcoats . . . days] overcoat . . . day
45.25	provide me] provide
45.35	this being] being
46.13	worse] worst
47.20	known:] known
47.28	he could] I could
50.3	at it] at
50.17	it in] it
51.11	tomorrow . . . Palisades] tomorrow, . . . Palisades,
*51.—	[untitled chapter]] The Good Brother.
52.16	what] whats
53.7	kind of] kind a
53.9	he go] go

53.11	to offer] to
53.36	he said] said
54.8	push it] push
54.17	that it] that
54.19	brother,] brother
54.20	publicity] publicly
55.6	the hat] hat
56.9	room] rooms
56.12	looked] look
56.14	newspapers] a newspaper
56.26	poor—] poor,
57.16	weary of] weary
57.17	there were] there
58.19	was a] was
59.9	the way] way
*59.26	about.] about. (Groceries being carried in.)
60.9	should have] should
60.24	physically,] physically
61.3	to the] to
62.33	away from] away
63.17	were] was
63.29	If it] If
63.31	had rescued] has rescued
64.7	"retired"] retired
64.8	boyhood idol of one of my brothers and] idol of one of my my brothers (Als) boyhood and
65.27	well, I thought,] well I thought
65.33	with a] with
66.17	we were] we
66.35	dining room] dining
66.36	partition] pairtion
67.16	walking or] walking
67.20	characterized] characterized of
67.25	the general] its general
67.27	order of] order
67.27	considers] consider
68.30	who was] who
69.2	actress—] actress
69.7	for they] and they
69.36	every] ever
71.28	He has] He's has
72.5	as a] as
72.18	of two] to two
72.19	room,] room
74.12	shower] shoe
74.19	(the . . . before),] the . . . before
74.35	feet,] feet;
74.36	became] began
76.10	drunk] drank
76.13	me just] him just
77.5	Muldoon like] Muldoon—like
77.12	weakness—] weakness,
77.26	balls—one] balls one,
78.17	were more] were
79.19	much more] much
80.1	the world] world
80.5	while] which
80.15	you mean] mean
80.15	has a] has any
80.23	a few] few
80.28	me through] me
80.29	very] a very
82.13	along. "He] along and said "he
82.21	long-legged] long and legged
83.27	I will] I
84.4	shouting] shouted
84.17	ate] eat
85.1	here (for . . . times)] here, for . . . times,
86.1	how he . . . if his health held out.] how if his health held out he . . . if his health held out.
86.13	"society"] society
86.14	were] was

86.17	and the] and
86.18	beasts"—] beasts,"
86.30	whose] who
87.3	he himself] they
87.7	days] day
87.12	positions] position
87.19	the others] them
87.23	some, I know,] some I know
88.16	or a way] or
*89.—	Chapter XVII] Chapter XVIII
89.29	there] here
90.14	of the] of his
91.12	at it] at
91.20	when he] when
91.22	these] the
91.27	most opulent] most
92.7	life—variety—] life, variety,
92.—	Chapter XVIII] Chapter XIX
93.3	was thinking] thought
93.11	and I slept somewhat better] though I slept some better
93.14	his] him
*93.18	particular, which] particular, a [blank space] which
93.33	not know] not
94.6	offered] offered more
94.16	that it] that
94.33	who took his place] who
95.7	some one or other] some of other
95.8	he did] I did
95.29	Avenue, the hot asphalt-paved] Ave. the hot asphalted paveed
95.33	gain] gained
96.25	I'll] I
96.29	as suave] suave
97.—	Chapter XIX] Chapter XX
98.9	This clerk] He
98.17	(I . . . this)] I . . . that
98.18	an adventure] adventure
98.27	have me] have
99.12	he finally] finally
100.15	to be] be
100.22	work,] work that
100.32	man who] who
101.4	green, shaded] green shaded
101.22	do not] do now
101.34	eye—] eye,
101.35	were] was
101.36	the] its
102.4	my being] me being
102.6	I could be] that I could
102.7	word; but] word, though
102.—	Chapter XX] Chapter XXI
102.17	on one] one
102.20	references] reference
103.9	Wesley (he . . . time)] Wesley, he . . . time,
103.11	Wollestencrafts] latter
104.26	machines—] machines,
*104.27	moulding machine, and] moulding machine, a [blank space] machine, and
105.14	was wondering] wondering
105.29	he opened] opened
105.31	cynical—] cynical
105.34	not to] not
105.36	my] might

106.— Chapter XXI] Chapter XXII

106.5 were] was

106.27 see] seem

106.28 arrived] arrival

107.14 was cold] cold

107.33 me," she said. I] me." I

108.3 anywhere,] anywhere

108.6 I saw] saw

108.21 mood,] mood

109.2 I must] must

109.13 call at five forty-five, though I had been wide . . . sleep for two hours.] call, though I was wide . . . sleep two hours before at 5.45.

109.30 the idea] idea

110.1 passing, I] passing Then I

110.4 minutes early] minutes

110.8 I sat] sat

110.— Chapter XXII] Chapter XXIII

112.11 two other posts] another

112.21 the message] message

112.21 They] Then

112.22 and then] when

112.34 them in] it in

113.6 this sort] sort

114.2 be seen] been

114.6 red-headed] red head

114.7 me,] me

114.16 hold of] hold

115.8 consisted of] consisted

116.— Chapter XXIII] [unnumbered chapter]

117.28 was] was

117.34 floor,] floor

118.5 day] days

119.— Chapter XXIV] [unnumbered chapter]

119.23 work, and . . . foreman] work and . . . foreman,

119.24 attend to] attend

120.10 world is . . . one is . . . there is] world was . . . one was . . . there was

120.15 and bemoaned] bemoaned

120.17 which I] which

120.19 had] all had

120.24 hill,] hill

120.26 stores] store

121.21 and surprised] which surprised

121.23 their noise] their

121.28 that they] that which they

122.15 and hope] and

122.23 and was] and

122.33 Carder] Horton

123.23 atmosphere of] atmosphere for

*123.24 taciturn.] taciturn. ¶For some time thereafter I was

124.1 as I] I

124.24 jewel-studded] jeweled studded

TEXTUAL NOTES

51.— **[*untitled chapter*]**

At some point during the composition of the MS, Dreiser may have contemplated titling his chapters, but this is the only titled chapter that survives. This single chapter title has therefore been omitted for consistency.

59.26 **about.**

The note within parentheses was interlined by Dreiser after the initial inscription of the leaf. The note was apparently meant to remind him to add details here about the houses of the wealthy. Perhaps he was to see groceries being carried in by servants. Dreiser never added the details to the MS; the parenthetical note is omitted.

89.— **Chapter XVII**

In revising, Dreiser apparently merged original Chapters XVI and XVII into the present single Chapter XVI. That would explain the misnumbering, or failure to number, the chapters following XVI in the MS. Dreiser did have his MS chapters arranged in the correct order, however. He probably meant to return to the MS and rectify the chapter numbering in a final stage of polishing, but he never did so. The correct chapter numbers are supplied in this edition; see the emendations for pp. 92, 97, 102, 106, 110, 116, and 119.

93.18 **particular, which**

Dreiser could not bring to mind the bird's name and so left a blank space in the MS. An ornithologist has suggested that Dreiser was probably thinking of some species of thrush, but one cannot know exactly what he had in mind. The reference is omitted.

104.27 **moulding machine, and**

Dreiser could not recall the name of one of the machines he was describing. He left a blank space in the MS but never returned to fill it. One cannot know what machine he had in mind; the reference is omitted.

123.24 **taciturn.**

Dreiser left the words "For some time thereafter I was . . ." at the conclusion of this chapter. He probably meant to return and add more material but never did so. The words are deleted from this edition.

WORD DIVISION

Dreiser rarely hyphenated compound words at the ends of lines in his MSS. Those few instances in which he did so in the MS of the *Laborer* have been resolved by reference to his usage in other parts of the MS, or in other MSS of this approximate period. Numerous hyphenated compounds (and possible hyphenated compounds) are divided at the ends of lines in this edition, however, and the scholar using this text must know how to render these words when quoting for publication. The words listed below are all divided at the ends of lines in this edition of the *Laborer*. In quoting these words, one should preserve Dreiser's hyphenation. All other compounds divided at the ends of lines in this edition should be quoted as one word.

8.25	wall-paper
36.10	empty-handed
54.17	warm-hearted
64.18	green-covered
65.1	night-revelling
68.6	ill-concealed
68.22	kindly-faced
82.21	long-legged
91.14	society-man
97.22	zealous-looking
102.5	high-flown
104.6	half-dozen
114.6	red-headed
114.13	sixteen-foot
114.31	two-inch
140.35	close-fitting
141.7	self-conscious
148.13	self-sufficient
171.11	Clod-hopper